PLURINATIONAL DEMOCRACY

Plurinational Democracy

*Stateless Nations in a
Post-Sovereignty Era*

Michael Keating

OXFORD
UNIVERSITY PRESS

OXFORD
UNIVERSITY PRESS

Great Clarendon Street, Oxford OX2 6DP

Oxford University Press is a department of the University of Oxford.
It furthers the University's objective of excellence in research, scholarship,
and education by publishing worldwide in

Oxford New York

Auckland Bangkok Buenos Aires Cape Town Chennai
Dar es Salaam Delhi Hong Kong Istanbul Karachi Kolkata
Kuala Lumpur Madrid Melbourne Mexico City Mumbai Nairobi
São Paulo Shanghai Taipei Tokyo Toronto

Oxford is a registered trade mark of Oxford University Press
in the UK and in certain other countries

Published in the United States
by Oxford University Press Inc., New York

British Library Cataloguing in Publication Data

Data available

Library of Congress Cataloging in Publication Data
Keating, Michael, 1950–
Plurinational democracy : stateless nations in a post-sovereignty era / Michael Keating.
p. cm.
Includes bibliographical references and index.
1. Sovereignty. 2. National state. 3. Statelessness. 4. Nationalism. 5. Democracy.
I. Title.
JC327.K36 2002 320.1'5—dc21 2001036732
ISBN 0-19-924076-0

3 5 7 9 10 8 6 4 2

Typeset in 10/12 pt Times NR
by Kolam Information Services Pvt. Ltd., Pondicherry, India
Printed in Great Britain by
Biddles Ltd., Guildford and King's Lynn

ACKNOWLEDGEMENTS

Many people have helped with the research, including political leaders in all the nations concerned. Research assistance was provided by Matthijs Bogaards, Sara Davidson, Kristine Holder, Raffaele Jacovino, Amaia Lamkiz and Silvia Otero. Kate Taylor read the proofs and compiled the index. Public opinion data are used by permission of the owners. Some data on Canada were made available by Queen's University, Kingston, Ontario. Neither the original source or collectors of the data nor Queen's University bear any responsibility for the analyses or interpretations presented here. Richard Bellamy, Tony Hepburn, David McCrone, John McGarry, and Neil Walker read and commented on parts of the draft. Bart Kerremans, Jaak Billiet and Lieven de Winter helped with finding data on Belgium. The research was made possible with the financial assistance of the Social Sciences and Humanities Research Council of Canada and the European University Institute. I am also grateful to the government of the Basque Country, which hosted a research visit during which I was given access to political leaders of all persuasions.

MK

Florence, April 2001

PREFACE

This book is in some ways a completion of earlier work exploring the new nationalism of Quebec, Catalonia, and Scotland (Keating 1996a, 2001a). These are, of course, old nations and their nationalist movements go back at least to the nineteenth century. Yet they had re-emerged in strength in the late twentieth century, with some new features. They tended, with some exceptions, to be inclusive rather than ethnically exclusive, committed to a civic nationalism based on common values and culture, and open to newcomers. They had fully embraced free trade and transnational integration through the North American Free Trade Agreement and the European Union; and they were committed to forms of self-determination different from statehood in its classic sense. In these respects they could be seen, not as remnants of the past or a reversion to 'tribalism', but as harbingers of a new form of politics. That book focused on the genesis of these new nationalisms, on their support base, and on stateless nation-building. This book takes the analysis a stage further, asking whether these new movements can be accommodated within the political order, by means short of independent statehood, while respecting the principles of liberal democracy. The conclusion is a cautious 'yes, but'. Nations do not have to become states to achieve self-government. They can be accommodated in principle and are being accommodated to varying degrees in practice in the emerging state and transnational order, but we are far from a new order in which institutions and practices take full account of nationality questions.

The empirical focus of the work is on political practice in the nations of the United Kingdom, Spain, Canada, and Belgium and, in the later part of the book, the emerging European order. The United Kingdom is a complex state with four nations, each of which has a different relationship with the centre. In Northern Ireland it has a divided society, in which the two communities tend to look to the two neighouring states. Scotland is a historic nation which has largely overcome internal divisions but whose relationship to the United Kingdom has become increasingly problematic. Spain is also an old state, containing three 'historic nationalities' and a Spanish nationality which seeks to encompass these as well as the rest of the state. The nationalities problem has been a main preoccupation since the late nineteenth century but takes different forms in different parts of the state. The Basque Country has a separatist tradition, as well as a more moderate 'home rule' one and, like Northern Ireland, has been the site of violent conflict. Catalan nationalism has historically been more moderate and generally disavows separatism, seeking to project Catalonia as a nation within a reconfigured state. Nationalism in Galicia has been weaker but has been rising in importance in recent years.

Belgium is a more recent state, created in 1830 after a short union with the Netherlands. It has long been marked by linguistic conflict between Flemish and French speakers, overlaid with territorial conflicts rooted in uneven development. Unlike Spain and the United Kingdom, Belgium has no 'centre' but is divided between two linguistic communities, each of which has developed its own form of national identity and demands. Canada is also a creation of the nineteenth century marked from the start by a division between English and French speakers. In the course of the twentieth century, French Canadian identity evolved into a territorial-linguistic identity based on the province of Quebec and a search for recognition as a distinct nation. Like Spain, Canada is asymmetrical in that the majority has no distinct national identity apart from that of the state. All four states have experienced substantial internal constitutional change in recent years, and all are deeply affected by transnational integration, but show very different forms of adaptation to the challenge.

These are not the most difficult cases of nationality conflict and I am not claiming that they provide a blueprint for resolving nationality questions elsewhere. They are chosen because they are the most advanced cases of stateless nation-building in industrial democracies, while Europe represents the most advanced case of a transnational economic, political, and institutional order. They also contain a variety of nationality conflicts of greater or lesser tractability, and illustrate a range of mechanisms for adapting to the plurinational challenge. This provides something of a laboratory for demonstrating what can be done, especially as the state is transformed and authority is shifted. I am not claiming that we have arrived at the definitive post-sovereign order in which states have faded away, still less that we have resolved the nationality question, merely we are heading into a new era in which these issues are being reframed, opening up new possibilities. The argument thus has many loose ends and unresolved issues.

If the book appears untidy in places, this is because I am drawing together elements of an incohate order, seeking a path for nations which aspire to be something other than states but more than mere regions. This takes me into abstract arguments about the doctrine of sovereignty; to the fate of the Habsburg Empire; to the contested histories of multinational states; through analyses of public opinion data; into doctrines of legal pluralism; and to the construction of the European Union. There is some order in all this, for the book relies on a series of analytical propositions; a set of normative arguments; and a range of empirical findings. The analytical propositions are the following:

- We need to separate the concepts of nation, state and sovereignty, so often conflated in political analysis.
- The nation is a sociological concept, based upon a community which, while constructed, represents a reality based in social institutions and practices. It also a normative concept, carrying with it claims for self-determination.

- Nationality, however, is not always singular or non-negotiable but can represent a form of 'normal politics' susceptible to negotiation and compromise. People can well have multiple national identities.
- Nationality claims are more than pleas for cultural recognition but entail a demand for power normally based on the control of territory. This does not, however, need to take the form of a state.
- Sovereignty is not an absolute concept, or vested exclusively in states. Rather there can be multiple sites of sovereignty or 'normative order' below and above the state.

The normative arguments are the following.

- Nations can be deliberative and decision-making spaces, sustaining democratic practice and community in the face of a weakened state and public sphere. This is not exclusively true of nation-states but can be true also of stateless nations and indeed of other communities—stateless nations are not necessarily less liberal, democratic and progressive than states.
- Democracy requires the constitution of decision-making spaces at the level of these communities.
- If national communities are asymmetrical, then asymmetrical constitutions can be defended on liberal and democratic grounds.

The empirical findings are these.

- There are alternative traditions of sovereignty and order in the history of the four states, based on pactism and shared authority.
- Stateless national movements in the four countries are increasingly embracing post-sovereigntist doctrines which look back to these traditions and forward to the emerging transnational order.
- Public opinion in the stateless nations is not an obstacle to this. Citizens are generally able to embrace multiple identities and, while supportive of self-government, do not make rigid distinctions between sovereign independence and other forms of home rule.
- States already provide a variety of forms of recognition of plurinationality and, while these differ considerably from one to another, they show what can be done.
- The emerging transnational and, especially European orders, provide new opportunities for nations to project themselves without becoming states. This does not amount to a complete new regime, but to a complex opportunity structure, to which stateless nations have responded in different ways. The open-ended nature of the European project itself defuses nationality conflicts and encourages gradualist strategies of nation-building.

There is a wider context for this discussion in the general intellectual appreciation of social and political diversity; in the current scepticism about grand narratives; in the acceptance of the need to live with conflicting moral imperatives; and in the demystification of the state as the organizing frame for social and political life. This book touches on these issues but does not attempt to cover them all. It is not about 'identity', a term stretched so far in recent years as to cover just about any political manifestation. It is not about multiculturalism and it is not about ethnicity. Still less is it a postmodernist plea to abandon the universal in favour of the particular. It is about a very specific question, the ways in which nationality underpins political order, and the fact that nationality is plural, contested, and shifting. The argument is that we cannot resolve nationality issues by giving each nation its own state, but neither can, nor should we seek to eliminate nationality as a basis for political order. Rather we need to embrace the concept of plural nationalities and shape political practices and institutions accordingly.

The book starts with a review of the question of nationality, arguing that it is to be distinguished from other forms of collective identity above all by its normative implications, above all by the claim to self-determination. This does not, however, necessarily entail sovereign statehood, and in any case the concept of sovereignty is a difficult one. A central argument of the book is that we are moving from a world of sovereign nation-states (although this was never more than an ideal-type) to a postsovereign order, in which states must share their prerogatives with supra-state, sub-state and trans-state systems. The case of the Austro-Hungarian Empire is used to show that the principle of nationality does not necessarily lead to the break-up of complex multinational systems, but that this was the result of historical contingencies in the late nineteenth and early twentieth centuries, and especially of the First World War.

The remainder of the book explores the possibilities for a 'plurinational' and 'post-sovereignty' political order in which nationality in all its complexity is recognized and in which sovereignty is shared. This involves looking to the past, to the present and to the future. Chapter 2 takes an unusual turn for a work in political science, searching for alternative understandings of the state in the competing historiographies of the four countries under examination. The aim of this chapter is not to reveal a 'true' past as opposed to the inventions of partisan historians, but to criticize the teleology of much state-focused history. Traditions of plurinational accommodation and dispersed authority are, I argue, not a mere remnant of the past, but can provide new ways of coping with the present, post-sovereign order. Chapter 3 focuses on the present and is a review of the demands and programmes of stateless national movements in the four countries. While some of these are attached to traditional ideas of sovereign independence, others are moving to a post-sovereignty stance, in recognition of the transformation of the nation-state. Public opinion, far from insisting on unitary nationality and traditional statehood, appears very open to the new thinking. Individuals within the stateless nations are able to operate with more than one national identity and they do not seem to make sharp distinctions between sovereign statehood and advanced forms of decentralization. There is thus, a political market for plurinational democracy, if political elites and institutions could be brought to accept it. Chapter 4 looks at the practice and the possibilities for accommodating nationality claims in a new form of asymmetrical state, which could allow them both symbolic and substantive expression. Chapter 5 is more forward-looking, examining the possibilities for plurinational accommodation in the evolving European order characterized by the detachment of key functions from the state, by legal pluralism and by complex, overlapping transnational regimes. It shows how stateless nations are using the new European dispensation to share their own strategies for self-affirmation and political action. The final chapter considers the possibilities for a plurinational post-sovereign democracy.

Scholarly work in this field is bedevilled by terminological argument, of which more below (Chapter 1), but the problem starts with the book's very title. 'Plurinational' is a term I have adopted in place of the more common 'multinational' in order to express the plurality not merely of nations, but of conceptions of nationality itself. In particular there is a nationality pertaining to the whole state and one pertaining to some, but not usually all, of its parts individually. The term 'stateless nation' is used of the component parts of the four states in question as the least prejudicial term available, while the term 'minority nation' is used only when the smaller components are being treated in relation to the state majority. A 'national minority' in my vocabulary is another matter, involving people within a state whose primary reference point is a nation situated elsewhere.

Finally, I have had endless problems with the terminology of sovereignty. Since the term is used so frequently in the political and academic debate on nationality and transnational integration, it would seem like mere evasion to abandon it in favour of some unfamiliar neologism. Yet sovereignty is a much contested term, and its meaning is changing in the modern world as we move from one paradigm, the 'sovereign nation-state' without finding a new one. Social scientists are given to resolving this type of terminological conundrum by resorting to the prefixes 'neo' and 'post', not abandoning the old terms but incorporating them in the new. So the term post-industrial society does not denote the abandonment of industry but a move to an era in which it is no longer the defining feature of social order. Post-modern, according to the Cambridge English Dictionary, 'includes features from several different periods in the past or from the present and past.' Unable to find a better alternative, I use the term 'post-sovereignty' to denote an era in which sovereignty has not disappeared but rather has been transmuted into other forms and is shared, divided, and contested. Sovereignty discourse persists but is detached from its previous state referent. Just to complicate matters, I also argue that we can link present debates to pre-sovereignty era, in which sites and claims of authority coexisted as they do now. If some terminological confusion persists, it is perhaps the price we must pay for abandoning outmoded certainties.

CONTENTS

FIGURES

TABLES

ABBREVIATIONS

BNG	Bloque Nacionalista Galego
CiU	Convergència i Unió
EC	European Community
ECHR	European Convention for the Protection of Human Rights
EEC	European Economic Community
ERC	Esquerra Republicana de Catalunya
EU	European Union
HB	Herri Batasuna
LOAPA	*Ley de armonización del proceso autonómico*
NAFTA	North American Free Trade Agreement
NATO	North Atlantic Treaty Organization
OSCE	Organization for Security and Cooperation in Europe
PNV	Partido Nacionalista Vasco (Basque Nationalist Party)
PP	Partido Popular
PQ	Parti Québécois
RoC	Rest of Canada
SDLP	Social Democratic and Labour Party
SNP	Scottish National Party
VB	Vlaams Blok
VU	Volksunie
WEU	Western European Union

1

Nations and Sovereignty

Nations and Nationalities

The 'nationalities question' is both an old question and a new one. It was a main preoccupation of the politics of nineteenth-century Europe as submerged peoples, especially in the large empires, asserted their nationhood and the right of self-determination. This phase culminated in the peace settlements of 1918–22, perhaps the most comprehensive effort to date to resolve the issue by aligning the boundaries of nations with those of states. The failure of this solution was soon apparent as successor states struggled with the impossibility of drawing lines on maps to separate discrete national groups. After a generation in which nationality claims were subordinated to the geopolitical imperatives of the cold war and to a new system of imperial domination, the issue has re-emerged not only in the new democracies but in the old states of the west.

Like earlier waves of nationalism, the current one has thrown into question the political order within and among states; it has also confounded a generation of modernization theorists who saw the consolidated nation-state as the end point of political development. For some, this resurgence of stateless nationalism stands in contradiction to the predominant modern trends of globalization and transnational integration, which might have heralded the end of the nation-state, or even of nationalism itself (Hobsbawm 1990). In Europe, it seems curiously at odds with the construction of a new and wider political order, often referred to as supranationalism, which is seen as the culmination of the very trend to functional integration that is credited with producing the nation-state. More recent appreciations, however, see the two trends as consistent, undermining the nation-state system from above and below, and encouraging minorities to explore new possibilities for autonomy within the emerging global order (Keating and McGarry 2001).

Normative evaluations of the new nationalism also differ. Modernists like Dahrendorf (1995, 2000) see the large, consolidated nation-state as the essential framework of democracy, liberalism, and social solidarity and deplore any reversion to 'tribalism' (Walzer 1999). Some postmodernists, on the other hand, celebrate the revival of particularism and the end of a constraining and false universalism, which merely served as a mask for domination. Neo-traditionalists similarly seek more 'authentic' forms of identity and community stripped of the 'false' uniformity of the state. A growing school of thought, however, sees nationality as an enduring form of political order and accepts that there may be multiple ways of accessing the universal values of liberalism, democracy, and solidarity (Kymlicka 1995; Tully 1995). The nation-state as we have known it since the nineteenth century is merely one way of organizing the polity, and changes in the relationship among territory, identity, political institutions, and function may open up new possibilities for the future (Keating 1998a, 2000a). Nationality as a form of collective identity is neither more nor less 'natural' than others, and is constantly made and remade in the course of political experience. The central question of this book is how to accommodate nationality claims within the emerging political order, while respecting the universal principles of liberalism and democracy. This is not an attempt at a universal account of how to reconcile all forms of collective, cultural, or identity-based claims. On the contrary, I argue that nationality claims are a particular type of demand, requiring specific forms of recognition and accommodation.

Academic analyses have followed two principal approaches to the issue of nationality claims. One is grounded in a 'Platonic' form of universal reasoning, which seeks to identify general principles for recognizing claims to nationality and self-determination. The other is more pragmatic and empirical, and concentrates on conflict resolution and problem-solving. The former is given to general theories, the latter more to case studies and specificities. Neither provides an entirely satisfactory analysis. Purely deductive and universalizing approaches never seem to fit all the cases, are abstracted from their historical, cultural, and empirical contexts (Requejo 1998), and do not easily lend themselves to problem-solving where nationality claims are in conflict. Nor is it always easy to see how some of these universalist arguments could be deployed in political debate. Most political arguments are addressed to the citizens of a polity and concern ways in which it might organize its common affairs. When the boundaries of the polity itself are in question, it is difficult to see to whom these arguments are addressed, unless we imagine some nationless jury charged with arbitrating claims and assessing arguments. It is striking how many theoretical works on self-determination invoke the 'international community' as arbiter, as though this were a less problematic concept than nationhood itself. Frequently the status quo is taken as a morally neutral starting point with the minorities portrayed as the exceptionalists or violators of universal order. Yet any status quo embodies a power structure, which allocates influence and resources in more or less unequal ways, and to subject the minorities to the test of universal norms while exempting the majority is itself a violation of universal values. On the other hand, purely ad hoc, pragmatic approaches to the nationalities question have their problems too. There is a large literature on managing or accommodating nationality claims not on the basis of abstract ideals but on sociological realities. The problem here is that often ethical or universal principles disappear altogether in favour of solutions that 'work'. Consociationalism, for example, has often been criticized for stifling democratic participation, freezing ethnic boundaries, and placing excessive power in the hands of group leaders.

A third approach combines the 'realist' one, accepting the fact and diversity of nationalism, with the 'idealist' one and is guided by normative criteria in addressing it (Miller 2000). This involves taking nationalist claims seriously, to the extent of penetrating their own logic and moral reasoning, in order subsequently to assess their compatibility with other normative orders (Tully 1995). It further requires that the analyst not so much position him or herself above the world so as to make supposedly context-free judgements, but rather 'stand in the shoes of the other' (Laforest 1998) for a while as the start of intersubjective dialogue.

This book follows such an approach, combining normative theorizing and empirical analysis. It presents nationality conflicts as a form of politics to be negotiated continually, rather than as a problem to be resolved once and for all, after which 'normal' politics can resume. Nationality claims are a form of identity politics and have much in common with other manifestations of the politics of difference, like multiculturalism or feminism. Yet there is an important difference. This is not because the nation can be objectively distinguished as a sociological category; despite the millions of words expended on this task, it has proved impossible. Rather it is because nationality claims have a special status, carrying with them a more or less explicit assertion of the right to self-determination. These claims have been based on three grounds. For some, the nation is a self-evident sociological category[1] or an immanent community of fate. This kind of argument, common among romantic nationalists, has tended to fade in importance as we now know too much about how nations are constructed. Nationalists themselves have had to face up to social and demographic change, which constantly reshapes the contours of the nation. The primordial view is, moreover, profoundly undemocratic in its implications since it has given sanction to press the 'interests of the nation' against the wishes of its people. In any case, there is a missing link in the connection between a sociological category and the moral right to self-determination (Norman 1998).

The two other claims, however, have survived and are explored in the following chapters. These are that the nation is historically constituted as a self-governing community; and that its people see themselves as a nation and wish to determine their future as a collectivity.[2] The argument that we

---

[1] Claims that it is a biological or 'racial' category have long since been discredited.

[2] This approach, recognizing the normative content of the term, gets away from attempts such as Kymlicka's (1995), to distinguish between multination and polyethnic states on the basis of the way in which people's ancestors arrived, as though we could ever arrive at a scientific, let alone a political, consensus on that issue.

cannot derive a right of self-determination from the facts of nationality (Norman 1998) is thus beside the point since self-determination is part of the normative content of nationality itself.[3] It is not that all claims to self-determination are clothed in the vocabulary of nationality. The Swiss cantons claim original rights underpinned by strong identities, but without resorting to the language of nationhood.[4] Since the late nineteenth century, however, the nationality principle has carried such force that claims to self-determination have usually invoked it. In the late nineteenth and early twentieth centuries, for example, the Catalan movement moved rapidly from regionalism to nationalism, while the Basque movement developed from a claim to provincial foral rights to a full nationality claim (Hernández and Mercadé 1981; Colomer 1986; de la Granja 1995; Gurrutxaga 1996; Beriain 1999). Acceptance of the nation as a historically constituted community does not commit us to a form of primordialism, as some critics of nationalism have assumed, dismissing nationalist movements as 'inventions' of the nineteenth or twentieth century. Nor do we have to get into futile and endless arguments about exactly when a nation became such, since nations are constantly being invented and reinvented. Linking nationality to the self-determination claim also frees nationalities from having to demonstrate that to exist, let alone self-determine, they must somehow be 'different', where normality is defined by reference to the encompassing state. Such arguments have been used to catch nationalities in a logical trap—they cannot claim self-determination without proving that they are 'different', yet if they are different they are condemned as ethnic particularists unworthy of self-determination rights.

These two arguments, about being a historically constituted community, and having a consciousness of nationhood and self-determination, cannot be reduced to a single logic, and national movements have appealed to one or other according to circumstance. Neither of these claims is uncontested. Some opponents regard historic rights as an irrelevance at best, a recipe for reaction at worst. Others dismiss the idea of collective self-determination as a violation of the primacy of the individual. For them self-recognition and self-determination are at best an extension of individual rights, under which any group of people can constitute themselves as a self-governing

[3] Cairns (2000: 28) is thus right to see the significance of the assumption of the term 'nation' on the part of Canada's aboriginal peoples, that 'it distinguishes them from the category of ethnic minorities, places them in terms of status on a level with the two "founding" British and French peoples...justifies...Aboriginal participation at the constitution-making table'. Later in the book, though, Cairns perhaps invests the term 'nation' with an excessively separatist meaning. Carens (2000) reads the same significance into the use of the term 'First Nations'.

[4] Kymlicka (1995) is incorrect to say that Switzerland is not a nation because of its cultural diversity. This is once again to confuse cultural identity, ethnicity, and nationality. Kymlicka does not say whether the 'nations' within Switzerland correspond to the language groups or the cantons. In fact, Switzerland has three sub-national cleavages, by language, by religion, and by canton, which do not always correspond.

community (e.g. Beran 1998). At worst they are a recipe for anarchy, inviting the proliferation of spurious nationality claims or 'balkanization'. Many critics have claimed that national self-determination is an unworkable proposition since the number of nations or potential nations in the world runs into thousands (Gellner 1983; Buchanan 1991). These objections are usually based on a fundamental category error, which identifies nations with ethnic groups,[5] an error I have discussed at length elsewhere (Keating 1996a, 2001a; see also Miller 1995 and Tamir 1991). There is a similar confusion between stateless nations and national minorities (Seymour *et al.* 1998). The latter are groups located territorially within a wider nationality but who do not identify with it, often because they identify with a group elsewhere, including one in another state. They have thus not constituted themselves as a distinct group claiming self-determination.

Nationality may overlap with these categories, but it involves much more by way of social structures and claims to self-regulation. Primordial assertions regarding the antiquity of nations are easy to debunk,[6] yet nations cannot merely be wished into existence, but are built, often painfully, over time. They require a minimum of credibility in order to mobilize support, sustain a campaign, and get attention and recognition within and beyond the state. Nor are nationality claims for the frivolous. Renan (1992), who rejected primordialist explanations of nationality, made clear that they require a constant work of creation and renewal. This is costly and diverts energy from other tasks. While claiming the right of self-determination might appear a pure benefit, it entails a psychological cost and tolerance of uncertainty and ambiguity, as we see, for example, in contemporary Quebec. Nation-building is not for the frivolous or those who prefer the quiet life. The failure of the Italian Northern League to create the nation of Padania, despite the available raw material, illustrates the problems of inventing nations (Biorcio 1997). Nations are not mere cultural communities but also socio-political entities with a wide range of social institutions and a shared political identity (Seymour 1999), though these do not need to cover the whole range of state-like activities. Fears of balkanization may also be overstated. It may be that it is precisely the international norm against disrupting states and the pressures brought by host states themselves that convinces stateless nationalists that their project is too costly—a more permissive attitude to national claims would encourage them to proliferate. Yet this would still require nationalist leaders to offer benefits to their followers in the form of material rewards or psychological satisfactions, and there is no reason to believe that this would always

[5] Even scholars who can see that nation-states are not necessarily ethnically homogeneous often insist on applying the ethnic label to stateless nations as a matter of definition rather than empirical finding, thus concluding that they could not be the basis for political order.

[6] This is not the place to enter into the old argument about primordialism versus construction in nationality.

succeed.[7] Secessions are costly matters and are more likely to stem from dire threats or crises than from mere opportunism.[8]

So nationality claims are to be taken seriously as a form of politics, but there is no universal formula for addressing them. Every nationality claim will have a different balance of elements, which may change over time and according to circumstance. Indeed, part of the nationality claim itself is usually based on the supposed uniqueness of the nation. The diversity of both cases and claims may confound universalistic or a priori reasoning; yet in a liberal and demo-cratic society we cannot simply abandon universal values. Such consider-ations indicate the need to look at claims on their own terms but also their compatibility with other claims and principles, including those of the state. This form of reasoning is similar to Tully's (1995) conception of constitution-alism which, drawing on Wittgenstein, emphasizes interpretation, conven-tion, and pluralism, while recognizing overlaps, similarities, and general types. By examining nationality claims and constitutional practice, we also avoid inventing unnecessary problems like wondering how we could cope if every 'ethnic group' in the world was allowed its own state, or how a universal principle of self-determination could produce a definitive outcome. As we shall see, in the four states discussed here there is a reasonably clear distinction in practice, if not in principle, between stateless nations and other identity groupings. Taking nationality claims seriously in their own terms also frees us from an intellectual incubus that has increasingly prevented understanding, that is the myth of the nation-state. The integrated nation-state has for some 200 years monopolized our understanding of constitutionalism and forced other claims to justify themselves in relation to it; and it has encouraged the identification of self-determination with the constitution of a separate state. Neither claim is valid in a longer historical perspective, and, as the global political order changes, the state itself is increasingly demystified and decon-structed, opening up new avenues for national accommodation.

State and Nation

In a rather loose way, the terms 'nation' and 'state' are sometimes used synonymously or combined in the compound 'nation-state', a term used in

---

[7] Beiner (1998) comes close to saying that nations will be fabricated from nothing as soon as we accept the notion of self-determination. Norman (1998) claims that at least 5,000 groups in the world could take up such a right; yet he later notes that mobilizing for self-determination is the work of generations. Claims about the existence of 5,000, or whatever number, of nations or potential nations, also made by Ernest Gellner (1983) and Walker Connor (1978), confuse ethnic groups, which may under certain circumstances constitute themselves as nations and subjects of self-determination, with nations themselves.

[8] Norman (1998), in order to make the threat of infinite proliferation credible, has to imagine an international regime such as an all-powerful United Nations which could uphold the secession and, presumably, protect it from predators, a prospect he himself admits is highly improbable.

international relations to denote a sovereign entity, often without any specific reference to nationality. In the French tradition the identity of state and nation are so confounded that the terms can sometimes be used interchangeably.[9] A more common assumption is that nationality claims entail aligning the boundaries of the state and the nation where they do not presently coincide. At one time this featured among the defining characteristics of nationalism itself (it does so in Smith 1971, but disappears from his later work). Hobsbawm (1990: 9–10) is trenchant, insisting that a nation 'is a social entity only insofar as it is related to a certain kind of modern territorial state, the "nation-state", and it is pointless to discuss nation and nationality except insofar as they relate to it'. Even now there are writers, especially in the discipline of international relations, who insist that nationality claims are claims to a state and that, where nationalist leaders disavow this, they must cunningly be disguising their long-term objectives; any goal less than statehood indicates that we are dealing with mere regionalism or ethnic assertion. This is yet another attempt to force social reality into the procrustean categories of theory. It is also a piece of teleological reasoning since the claim for statehood, the end process of nationalist mobilization, defines the process itself. It rules out by definitional fiat an investigation into the circumstances in which nationalities or national movements might decide whether to go for full statehood. Perhaps most importantly of all, it refuses to recognize social realities such as the fact that virtually the entire population of Scotland recognizes Scotland as a nation while only a minority want it to become a state, or the existence of stateless nationalisms in several modern states (Keating 1997; Guibernau 1999). Canada's aboriginal peoples have assumed the term 'nation' to indicate their possession of original rights to self-determination, but quite reasonably have no interest in statehood on Western lines. As early as 1910 the Catalan nationalist Prat de la Riba (1998) complained about the 'stone age political science' which identified the nation with the independent state; in many ways we are still in that primeval era.

Sheer self-interest may induce some nations to eschew statehood. It can be a costly business and, for small nations sandwiched between large ones, a risky one, as Czechs, Finns, and Catalans know to their cost (Puig 1998). Mobilizing populations to support separate statehood and bear the risks involved is often difficult, even if nationalist leaders do wish a state of their own (Hechter 2000). In these circumstances, insisting that, in an ideal world, nationalists would like their own state is a bit like saying that we would all like to pay no taxes but still get public services; it may be a dream, but it is

---

[9] The French (Québécois) translator of my earlier book *Nations against the State* refused to call it *Nations contre l'État*, since that would appear a contradiction in terms. He also, until corrected, used the terms 'nation' and 'État' to denote state and nation, indifferently. By 2000, however, it was possible to publish a book under the title *La Nation dans tous ses États* (Dieckhoff 2000).

neither an objective nor a policy. My argument, however, goes further than this, insisting that many nationality movements do not want a state on traditional lines at all, but seek other expressions of self-determination. The extraordinary persistence of the idea that nationality entails claims to statehood shows what a grip the idea of statehood has on the modernist imagination, a grip only gradually being prised loose with the transformation and demystification of the state in late modernity.

The obverse of the argument is an equally entrenched view that states will always become nations through the fragmentation of existing states on national lines, or by the assimilation of minorities into the 'core' nation. Empirically, this is a rather weak argument, since few actual states can be said in confidence to encompass a single nationality, however that is defined (Connor 1978; Stepan 1998). More theoretical arguments centre on modernization and the needs of liberal democracy, collective action, and social solidarity. A recurrent one is that democracy requires a *demos*, that is a defined people in which sovereignty can be invested and which can engage in democratic dialogue and exchange. This does not always have to be a homogeneous ethnic group—indeed this argument is usually couched in the language of civic republicanism—but it does need markers of identity and a commitment to belonging together. If anyone can opt out at will, then collective decision-making becomes impossible. Common symbols and values and an underlying social consensus are needed to sustain trust so that social groups can accept defeat on some issues, knowing that they may win on others in the future, while a common language may be essential for social communication and debate. It was these features that John Stuart Mill (1972: 392) presumably had in mind when he remarked that 'free institutions are next to impossible in a country made up of different nationalities'. The implication, sustained in other writers, is that empires and monarchies can be multinational but that democracies must be uninational. Hence multinational states will not survive the transition to democracy. French 'Jacobin' ideology tends in the same direction, insisting on the unity of democracy, that internal and external sovereignty must equally be vested in a unitary people, and that challenges to the unity of the state are a threat to republican virtue. There is a large literature to the effect that the nation-state was the framework for liberal democracy and that, while all nation-states have not been democracies, all democracies have been nation-states (Habermas 1998). More recently, Miller (1995) (who does not, however, insist that nations must have their own states) defends nationality as a way of securing social solidarity and collective values, with the underlying implication that these should be achieved through a state, and that the state should inculcate a single national identity.

On the other hand, it is argued that nationality is a divisive principle, an affront to universal values and solidarity. So nationalism faces, Janus-like, in two directions at once (Nairn 1997). One school of thought seeks a way out of this trap by seeking to root the state in a form of civic republicanism shorn of nationalist ideology. This allows them to portray the large, consolidated state as based not on ethnic particularism but on a 'constitutional patriotism' (Habermas 1992) or 'civic nationalism'. The corollary is that minority or stateless national movements must be based on 'ethnic' particularism against modernist universalism, backward and hostile to progress. On these grounds, Dahrendorf (1995, 2000) and Hobsbawm (1992) favour the large, consolidated state against the smaller stateless nation as the basis for democracy and solidarity. There is a serious ambivalence in most of these arguments. Habermas's constitutional patriotism is, in some versions, a culturally neutral form of order; in others it is identified with civic nationalism. The former has been criticized as too thin a basis for political order and loyalty; the latter is, for all its inclusive virtues, a form of *nationalism*.[10] The conflation of these rather different concepts allows some scholars then to bundle constitutional patriotism, civic nationalism, the creation of the nation by will, modernization, progress, and national consolidation into a single principle, not only in history but as a normative guide, which might be summed up in the principle that big nations are good and small nations are bad. This prejudicial form of reasoning has a long history, recalling Engels's strictures on stateless nations or the old distinction between a good, enlightened 'western' nationalism and a tribalistic, regressive nationalism of the east (Kohn 1944; Plamenatz 1968). Civic nationalism may be a higher ideal than ethnic particularism, but to associate it with the nationality of the large states is scarcely justified. German nationality law is, despite recent changes, ethnically discriminatory, yet Dahrendorf (1995) picks on the Catalans, who were making massive efforts to integrate incomers, as an example of narrow exclusiveness. Even in more authentic cases of civic nationalism, like France or the United States, nationality may be open and ethnically inclusive, but it is not culturally neutral (Kymlicka 1995) or a mere proxy for cosmopolitanism. So civic republicanism does not necessarily lead us out of the need for nationality, and may be a mere pretext for imposing the majority nationality upon the minorities.

Lord Acton (1972) turned the argument about nation-states, liberty, and democracy on its head, arguing that the Jacobin theory of one nation–one state was a recipe for tyranny and absolutism and the enemy of freedom. This was not, as it is often presented, an attack on the nationality principle itself, since Acton sought to separate nationality from statehood and defended the multinational state as the better guarantor of democratic liberty, as well as of dynamism and social progress. 'The denial of

[10] Two Basque critics have, moreover, criticized. Habermas's concept of constitutional patriotism is excessively based on a Germany which, while exorcizing the demons of aggressive nationalism, retained a citizenship based on ethnic homogeneity and never faced up to the question of how to integrate non-European incomers into the constitutional patriotic order (Lasagabaster and Lazcano 1999).

nationality', he wrote, 'therefore implies the denial of liberty. The greatest adversary of the rights of nationality is the modern theory of nationality' (Acton 1972: 268). The argument that the consolidated nation-state is the precondition of democracy raises a further contradiction in itself. When combined with the principle of state sovereignty, it implies that democracy within the state will coexist with a complete absence of democracy in the international order (Jáuregui 2000). Given the pressures of globalization and transnational integration and interdependence, this is increasingly anomalous. So the nineteenth-century writers who sought to delink nationality from statehood find an echo in modern efforts to find new formulas such as the plurinational state (Máiz 1999; Requejo 1999*a*) in which multiple nationality claims can be accommodated within an overarching order.

The principle of self-determination has also become confused with that of the state as discussions of self-determination rapidly turn to the rights and wrongs of secession and setting up breakaway states.[11] It then becomes a simple matter to demonstrate that the principle is not universalizable since there are more nations or potential nations than there are possible states, that conceding the right would lead to permanent instability, and that agreement on borders would be almost impossible. For this reason, international law has tended to confine the right to colonial situations. Elsewhere self-determination means only the rights of existing states to their integrity (external self-determination) and the right of people to democratic institutions (internal self-determination). This is the meaning put on it by the Supreme Court of Canada (1998) in the Quebec secession reference.[12] Only by limiting its exercise thus can the principle of self-determination be kept within bounds, however contradictory it might be to insist on the self-determination of entities like Kuwait but refuse statehood to the Palestinians or the Kurds. There is, however, no logical reason why self-determination should be linked to statehood, apart from the entrenched dogmas of sovereignty discourse (Mills 1998). Another way of looking at self-determination is to see it as the right to negotiate one's position within the state and supranational order, without necessarily setting up a separate state. Indeed, this is the basis of most self-determination claims in the modern world (van

---

[11] Freeman (1999) and Moore (1998*a*) appear to treat it thus. Buchanan (1991) recognizes that there can be other forms of accommodation for cultural and territorial minorities which may also allow for self-determination.

[12] The Supreme Court's argument was, however, ambiguous. It declared that 'A state whose government represents the whole of the people resident within its territory, on a basis of equality and without discrimination, and respects the principles of self-determination in its own internal arrangements, is entitled to the protection under international law of its territorial integrity' (Supreme Court of Canada 1998, Article 130). Here self-determination seems to mean democracy and non-discrimination, implying that there can be no democratic right to secession in a democracy. On this reading, the British government is wrong to concede the right of secession to Scotland.

der Valtt van Praage and Seroo 1998).[13] Chapter 3 discusses the variety of claims made in the stateless nations of the United Kingdom, Spain, Belgium, and Canada, and their basis in popular support.

There is still widespread resistance to the idea that self-determination claims may fall short of statehood. Halliday (2000) concedes that the Austro-Marxists in the early twentieth century questioned the equation of self-determination with statehood, but fails to recognize that many contemporary nationalists follow the same line. Yet there is nothing intellectually inconsistent in the idea that stateless nations may have rights to self-government which are limited by reciprocal obligations and the rights of other nations, and so fall short of statehood. Such rights could include the ability to renegotiate their position within the state without leaving it altogether. Some writers on secession concede that it would be wise for a state to concede devolution as a means of assuaging nationalist discontent, but rarely concede this as a *right* for a stateless nation. The distinction between granting devolution as a concession from the state, and recognizing it as a right may appear slight in practice but, as we shall see, it is a fundamental point of principle for many nationalists who otherwise are prepared to forgo statehood. This is not to invite a proliferation of incompatible claims to authority. It is not a contradiction but a logical consequence of the doctrine of self-determination that its exercise be limited by the equal rights of others (Jáuregui 1997; MacCormick 1999*b*) in the same way as rights of individuals are mutually limiting.[14]

The empirical and historical arguments about the inevitability of nation-states are similarly flawed by an inadequate understanding, or simplifying assumptions about states and statehood. Perhaps the most enduring is the Westphalian myth, the notion that the Peace of Westphalia which ended the Thirty Years' War in 1648 inaugurated a system of sovereign nation-states in Europe and subsequently the world. As a result, a nation either has a state or it does not, sweeping away the ambiguous and intermediary forms of authority that had previously existed, together with the notion of universal empire, whether under imperial or papal sway. In fact, one of the achievements of Westphalia was to prop up the Holy Roman Empire for another century and a half and to perpetuate the division of Germany into a mosaic of jurisdictions of bewildering variety (Osiander 1994). The only European state to maintain the same boundaries as it had at Westphalia is Portugal, while the practical content of statehood was established in the course of the nineteenth and early twentieth centuries, with the codification of citizenship, the introduction of passports, and the doctrine that nation and state should be

---

[13] This book records the proceedings of a conference in Barcelona, including representatives of stateless nations from all parts of the world, in which there was universal agreement that self-determination did not necessarily entail the creation of a separate state.

[14] Self-determination must therefore be seen as a political principle rather than a *right*, with its absolutist implications.

congruent. Right up until 1918 most of the European landmass was taken up by multinational states and empires and for most of central and eastern Europe independent statehood was enjoyed only briefly between the wars and again since 1989. Nor does the process of modernization and economic growth necessarily entail the creation of nation-states, as once thought. Recent works have shown the viability under various circumstances of large states, city-states, and leagues (Tilly 1975, 1990, 1994; Spruyt 1994).

More fundamentally, however, theories of secession almost never discuss the nature of statehood that follows secession, treating this as undifferentiated sovereignty. Yet secession may involve taking or not taking up any number of sovereignty features. Irish nationalists fought each other in 1922–3 over whether keeping the king as head of state was a fundamental violation of sovereignty; both sides agreed that partition was an abomination (Jackson 1999). It later became clear that the issue was of little practical significance. There is now broad agreement around the world on Palestinian statehood, but there are endless discussions on what this would entail. A few years ago politicians were discussing rather calmly the break-up of Belgium into separate units within the European Union, safe in the knowledge that neither bit would have its own defence policy or currency. Quebec nationalists have consistently favoured an attenuated form of sovereignty allowing for continued links with Canada. Chapter 5 examines the panoply of opportunities for stateless nations in the emerging transnational order of differentiated and shared sovereignty.

The Sovereignty Trap

One of the greatest obstacles to accommodating nationalities and nationality claims is the doctrine of sovereignty itself. At first glance, this is an intuitively plausible idea, that there must in any polity be an ultimate source of authority, prior to and above all others. On closer examination it is a complex and in some respects internally contradictory set of propositions, many of which turn out to be either tautological or impracticable. Further difficulties are raised by its close connections to definitions of the state and to doctrines of self-determination and nationalism. Two interrelated issues in particular bedevil analysis, the distinction between external and internal sovereignty; and the difference between formal, legal conceptions of sovereignty (*de jure*), and the substantive power to act as a sovereign (*de facto*).

The doctrine of external sovereignty, that a state has no superior in the international arena, underpins the dominant paradigm in international relations or, as they might more accurately be called, inter-state relations. It is clear that this must refer to more than *de facto* independence, otherwise we would not need a separate term, 'sovereignty', with its additional normative charge. For some analysts, external sovereignty is an intrinsic property of statehood, yet, if this were all that there is to it, the term 'sovereign state' would be a redundancy, and we would merely replace one problem, how to define sovereignty, with another, how to define a state. Others see it as a formal legal or constitutional principle pertaining to certain states and not to other aspirants, with a sharp line to be drawn between sovereign and non-sovereign entities. If this definition is accepted, then there is a huge incentive for a nation to acquire its own state and sovereign status, since anything short of this would appear to be worthless. Yet it is by no means clear how such status is gained and accepted. It is all very well to talk about a state being *de jure* independent, but if there is no global legal order to accord it this status, then it is meaningless. On the other hand, if there is a global legal order to determine claims, then it, and not the states, must be the ultimate and thus sovereign authority. Membership of the United Nations might be taken as an indication of statehood, but this is too recent an invention to stand as a general principle and is subject to essentially political conditions. If the criterion is recognition by other states, we are back to a purely practical condition, again determined by politics, and the difference between *de facto* independence and *de jure* sovereignty again disappears.

Another feature of external sovereignty is that it is usually said to be inalienable. So a state might agree to lend its sovereignty to a supranational body but will always be able to take it back. This appears to be the basis of most states' membership of the European Union, although there is no procedure for withdrawal in the treaties. Yet the experience of decolonization shows that states can surrender external sovereignty permanently. The Statute of Westminster (1931) abolished the UK Parliament's right to legislate for imperial dominions, and in 1982 Westminster surrendered its right to change the Canadian constitution. Even before abolition, it should be said, these powers had by convention effectively lapsed. There are those who argue that European Union law has its own sovereign character, or that the 1997 referendum means that the Scottish Parliament is entrenched against Westminster's sovereignty pretensions (MacCormick 1999*a*; Walker 1998*b*). So advocates of the doctrine of external sovereignty are again thrown back on arguments based on the practicalities of power and politics. This, however, is to convert the concept from an absolute to a relative one, since a state could have more or less ability effectively to exercise its autonomous authority. While there are about 200 'sovereign' states in the world, they vary greatly in their substantive independence. Indeed we can imagine cases in which an entity could have more effective control as part of a wider federation than it would if exposed to the vagaries of a hostile world and forced to become a satellite of a great power.

The doctrine of unitary internal sovereignty has been presented as a defining characteristic of the modern state, contrasted with the complex and differentiated order of the Middle Ages, in which power was divided among the estates and between church and state. It is often attributed to

Bodin, who, starting with the principle that sovereignty is indivisible, extrapolated this to a doctrine of monarchical absolutism. A tendentious reading of history and contemporary practice allowed him to assert that the parliamentary constitutions of places like Aragon or England did not modify monarchical absolutism (Bodin 1992). Bodin did, it is true, believe in moral limits to the power of the ruler, who was to be subject to natural and divine law, but this did not imply a correlative right of the subjects to defy him where he broke the moral code. A ruler could and should contract with the subjects, including estates and orders, but reserved the right to change the laws under which these were made where this was appropriate (Franklin 1992). Other interpretations see the assertion of sovereignty as something new, a feature of the modern state. Artola (1999*a*, *b*) distinguishes between monarchies, which may consist of various autonomous territories with their own systems of law, and kingdoms, with a single system of law. The latter becomes the foundation of the modern state with its unitary conception of authority. Nationalism and democracy served to reinforce it since, if sovereignty is transferred from the monarch to the people, then state absolutism acquires democratic credentials. If that people is, furthermore, construed to be a nation, then the state becomes the means of expression of a Rousseauian 'general will'. This easily leads to the conclusion that popular sovereignty requires centralization and uniformity, the Jacobin principle of unity. Others draw less drastic conclusions, arguing that the state can and should decentralize and disperse power in many ways, but that it still retains ultimate authority including the authority to change the rules. This is the 'unionist' argument, which we encounter in states like the United Kingdom or Spain.

Yet the argument for unitary authority stands in contradiction to the example of federal states in which there are coordinate systems of authority, neither fully sovereign and neither superior to the other. Defenders of the sovereignty principle, in reply, fall back on two arguments. The first is the doctrine of external sovereignty, which still applies to federations since these rarely allow their units to secede (Hoffman 1998). This, however, is really another question since secession is only one expression of self-determination and a limiting case. Anyway, to permit secession for component parts would imply that they were sovereign and would merely be another way of formulating the unitary or 'ultimate' doctrine of sovereignty. Shared sovereignty is a different matter, implying that neither level has unlimited unilateral options. The second response is to fall back on the doctrine of popular sovereignty, in which both federal and federated units are subject to a single *demos* or people. This, however, raises the question of whether the unitary *demos* exists. While this might be a plausible condition in the United States, it is much more difficult to apply it to multinational federations like Canada; indeed it is difficult to apply it to multinational states generally (Fossas 1999*b*).

The tendency to link sovereignty intrinsically to the state (Hoffman 1998) is itself problematic, since the state is a historically contingent and changeable structure of authority. If sovereignty is a matter of the state, then formal sovereignty then becomes the product of modernity, while substantive sovereignty would have to be confined to the consolidated, functionally powerful state of the last century or so. It is not indeed coincidental that 'most of the (Anglo-American) jurists who are treated as canonical belong to the period 1750 to the 1990s—i.e. the relatively short period of the rise and possible decline of the nation-state' (Twining 1999: 222). Nor is it by chance that discussions about the 'end of sovereignty' (Camilleri and Falk 1992) have abounded as the state's autonomy and functional capacity is challenged. Exponents of the more formal conceptions of sovereignty tend to dismiss these analyses impatiently, arguing that they have no bearing on the issue of sovereignty in the strict sense, but this is to save the concept by emptying it of any practical meaning.

Sovereignty therefore presents a conundrum. The notion of absolute concept is 'sociologically naïve' (Walker 1998*a*) but the concept of relative sovereignty looks like an oxymoron, while to identify sovereignty with mere *de facto* power empties it of the normative content that is its essence. Yet there are other ways of thinking, and a tradition of thought that locates sovereignty in bodies other than the state (MacCormick 1999*a*) whose rights may not have been extinguished by the assertion of unitary state sovereignty after Bodin. If the term 'sovereignty' is either too restricted to the Bodinian definition or hopelessly loose, we can talk of 'normative orders' (MacCormick 1999*a*), legal pluralism, and multiple sources of law. In this way it might be possible to delink sovereignty from the state in an altogether more radical manner, by formulating it as a right of self-determination. Here an entity, whether it be a people or a territorial unit, may be sovereign where it has the right to determine its own future. The practicalities of the world, together with their own aspirations, may mean that this does not take the form of a state, as I have already argued might be the case with nations, but this would not affect sovereignty itself. This idea underlay the musings of the late Quebec premier Robert Bourassa, responding to the demand for a referendum on sovereignty that, since Quebeckers were agreed that they had a right to decide by referendum whether to become sovereign, this meant that they were really sovereign already.[15] In Chapter 2 we will see how these alternative conceptions of authority are rooted in the constitutional and political traditions of the four states.

The Territorial Conundrum

A common feature of nationality, as opposed to other group claims, is that they have a territorial base; states too are territorially constituted entities.

---

[15] This shows at least that tautological definitions of sovereignty can play both ways.

Territory may have a symbolic importance, as the actual location of the group in question, or as *terra irredenta*, a land really or mythically lost in the past. Territory also has a functional importance since the practical exercise of self-determination depends on the control of space. We thus have two structuring features of nationality claims, that of identity and that of territory, and the territorial nation-state has often been presented as the triumph of the latter over the former. One school of thought holds that in late modernity, territory has lost both its functional importance and its power to mould identities (Badie 1995). Modern communications, migration, economic and cultural globalization, and the decline of the nation-state have created a borderless world and broken the constraints of time and space. For some, this deterritorialization of social and political life represents a reversal of state-building, unleashing uncontrollable identity claims. For others, it provides a hope that the demons of nationality may be exorcized for good, and opens up new possibilities for political order beyond the state. Universal values have spread to herald, if not the end of history, then at least the end of sharp differences in the basic principles underlying the social order.

In practice, matters are a lot more complicated than this. The connections among function, representation, and institutions have been transformed, but rather than destroying territory, this has favoured the emergence of new or rediscovered territorial spaces above, below, and beyond the state (Keating 1998a). Political institutions still rest upon a territorial basis, and political mobilization and representation are still overwhelming territorially organized, whatever the theoretical possibilities of doing otherwise. Control over territory has become more rather than less important for governing and public policy for a complex of reasons which I have discussed elsewhere (Keating 1998a, 2001a). Territory has also become more important as a basis for political legitimacy with the emergence of new political spaces beyond and below the nation-state as a result of transnational integration, especially in western Europe. What has disappeared is the monopoly of the state in defining territory and its meaning, and the new dispensation presents a more complex mosaic, in which multiple territorial identities and systems of action coexist. This has provided a new context for stateless nations and cultural communities and for the interplay between identity and territory.

Late modernity has seen a certain convergence of values, if not around the globe, at least across the advanced capitalist societies of North America and Europe. Yet in a paradoxical way this has generated new forms of territorial–national conflict and resurrected old ones. Political legitimacy increasingly requires a basis in universal liberal values, rather than claims to particularism, and in consequence stateless nationalist movements have often shifted from claims based on ethnicity and distinctness, towards a more secularized, civic, and inclusive conception of nationality based on a shared territorial society. It might be thought that this shift, corresponding to the usual sociological definitions of 'modernization', would make accommodation easier and remove absolutist claims. In fact, it sometimes makes accommodation more difficult, since stateless national movements are now making general claims to self-government and autonomous social regulation, rather than specific cultural demands which might be met by policy concessions limited to the cultural sphere; they are making rival claims to be 'global societies' (Langlois 1991*a*,*b*). They are contesting the state, therefore, in its own physical territory and normative space. A new politics of nationalism has emerged in which territorial societies are reinvented and rediscovered, below, beyond, and across the state system (Keating 2001*a*). Claims to self-determination are reformulated and placed in the context of the emerging transnational order. This is a modern example of de Tocqueville's paradox in which accommodation becomes more difficult as societies become more alike (Dion 1991).

These claims are in themselves complex, and rarely fall into simple schemas. The case of the homogeneous, territorially concentrated national minority seeking independent statehood is the limiting exception—Norway and Iceland in the early twentieth century would be examples. More common is multiple identity, in which people feel attached, with varying degrees of strength, to more than one national identity. These identities may be 'nested' (Miller 2000) so that an individual may feel Scottish and British, Catalan and Spanish, or Québécois and Canadian. A great deal of intellectual effort has been put into solving this apparent enigma. Many observers have tried to find a difference in kind between the two identities, assigning them different functions and roles. So the state identity may be seen as primarily political, while the minor national identity is a cultural one. Such a division of roles is indeed found widely and may explain, for example, the integration of the Scots and Welsh into the United Kingdom for much of the nineteenth and twentieth centuries, or the accommodation of Quebec to Canada. As long as states accommodate cultural differences through public policy or allow a degree of autonomy in matters such as education, then national identities can be contained. Yet multiculturalism of a North American type does not address the issue of *national* identity, which, as we have seen is something more, carrying normative ideas of self-determination and the scope of political authority (Doyle 1999); hence the fallacy of expecting the Québécois or either community in Northern Ireland to settle for recognition as a cultural minority.[16] Another way of reconciling them is to invest political meaning in the stateless nationality, with the state being merely a political superstructure overlying nationalities below it, sustained at best by a kind of civic patriotism. Kymlicka (1995) thus claims (wrongly in my view) that the Swiss can only feel a 'patriotism' to Switzerland. Some Quebec nationalists and aboriginal activists would convert the Canadian federation into a mere holding

---

[16] An example is Derrienec (1995), who would treat Québécois identity in the way the French Third Republic dealt with Catholicism, by effectively privatizing it and taking it out of politics.

company for certain functional competences and the management of externalities.

Neither strategy of denationalization, however, does justice to the facts, and as a political strategy they fail to take account of the way in which different spheres can become politicized and repoliticized according to prevailing circumstances. In any case, few people seem to make such fine and pedantic distinctions about the functions of their various identities. Citizens are often prepared to invest in two or more politicized national identities, to which they give equal meaning and force. Further complicating matters is that these types of multiple identity are usually found only in certain parts of the state. So a person from Madrid can be Spanish only, while a native of Barcelona may feel both Spanish and Catalan. Someone from Ontario may feel Canadian and nothing else, while her compatriot in Montreal feels primarily Québécois and is Canadian only indirectly through Quebec's membership of the wider state and nation.

Yet another complication is that some stateless nationalities are territorially integrated while in others identity and territory coincide less well. At one extreme are non-territorial ethnic minorities, like European Jews, Muslims, Gypsies, or the various ethnic groups of the United States. In practice these have tended not to make broad claims for self-determination but have looked for tolerance and cultural accommodation. At the other extreme are purely territorial movements, seeking to build territorial systems of action in the face of the global market; some of these have little cultural or historical basis, and are conventionally classified as 'regional' rather than 'national'. In between are movements which combine identity and territory in three ways. In some cases, the territorial and the cultural–identity bases coincide, as in Scotland; here we have a territorially integrated nationality.[17] In others, a single territory is contested by two groups; these are the divided societies. In a third type, a single group spills over state or administrative boundaries; these are trans-state nationalities, which may be irredentist, as in Ireland, or stateless, as in the Basque Country. The claims of the indigenous peoples of North America combine ethnic principles of recognition with

Table 1.1. Support bases of territorial or nationality movements

Non-territorial groups	Territorially integrated nations	Divided societies	Trans-state nations	Purely territorial movements
One group, no territory	One territory, one identity	Two identities, one territory	Two territories, one identity group	No group identity

[17] The facile answer that such territories are 'ethnically homogeneous' is an instance of the primordialist error and begs the question of how and why they developed a territorially integrated nationality.

territorial claims and are even more difficult to fit into conventional schemes of sovereignty.

So apart from the territorially integrated nationalities, the 'architectonic illusion' (Brubaker 1998) that one can adapt the territorial state to fit the nation is a futile exercise only guaranteed to make people more unhappy with their lot. It is a well-known argument against secession that it tends to create new minorities within the seceding states. Partition of seceding territories to create ethnically homogeneous enclaves rarely solves the problem, but merely creates new minorities while violating the territorial integrity of existing units. This is yet another reason for not identifying self-determination with secession. Yet deterritorialization, allowing forms of autonomy not based on territory, does not always help either. National identities are closely tied to territory (Nogue 1991) even where the group and the territory do not neatly coincide, as the case of Northern Ireland demonstrates so vividly. So identity and territory, while interlinked do not always coincide, so that often neither purely territorial nor purely non-territorial solutions will work.

It is often argued that if a stateless nation has a 'right' to secede from its host state, then any group within it has an equal right to secede from the new state. Secessions have indeed often provoked partition of the seceding territory. Yet these are, arguably, very different issues. Partition of a seceding territory ignores the territorial principle altogether, which is a different matter from breaking up a state along existing territorial boundaries. The argument that any group has an equivalent right to secede is, further, based on the old confusion of ethnic groups, stateless nations, and national minorities. There is a big difference between a national grouping like the people of Quebec, and minorities within it which have never asserted distinct nationality claims. The independence of Quebec or of Ireland, therefore, does not find its practical or moral equivalent in the partition of those territories on ethnic lines. On the other hand, within a seceding nation there may be people whose primary national loyalty is to the host state, and these may legitimately demand continued recognition of this tie. This is another reason for avoiding the absolutes of independent statehood with its implication that one identity group has a monopoly of the territory.

Instead, we need to unpack the concepts of nation and state, and explore forms of self-determination other than classical statehood. National identities are not always monolithic and exclusive. They become so in times of political conflict and polarization, but at other times people are able to live with several identities. It is for this reason that I use the term 'plurinationalism', which includes the idea that individuals can have several identities, rather than 'multinationalism', which implies distinct national communities living together.[18] If people do indeed have plural national identities, then we

[18] Cairns (2000) takes issue with the Canadian Royal Commission on Aboriginal Peoples on the grounds that their use of the term 'multinational federation' suggests discrete nations rather

can think of building political units underpinned by national sentiment at different levels, rather than seeking to reserve the concept of nationality for just one. Just about any jurisdiction we can imagine will have national majorities and minorities, but the minorities will at some higher or lower level be able to constitute a majority. Nairn (2000) falls back on an old argument in seeing this kind of pluralistic identity as possible only in empires and not in democracies—the argument recalls the liberal case for nationalism discussed above. At best, Nairn concedes that dual identity may work for intellectuals, but not for the masses.[19] If this were true, the outlook would be grim indeed. Fortunately, however, there are other ways of thinking about the identity and about the state itself, keeping the ideas of territory and identity as fundamental building blocks, but combining them to suit the circumstances.

Rethinking the State

One alternative tradition bears directly on the issue of stateless nations and territories within the boundaries of consolidated states, although it has until recently been subject to little systematic thought or analysis, and often considered little more than a historical curiosity. Rokkan and Urwin (1983) distinguish four types of territorial regime. Two of these are uniform in conception. The unitary state is centralized and uniform; mechanical federalism divides power between the centre and the federated units, but there is still a recognizable centre and federalism is introduced from above by constitutional means. The other two are multiform. The 'union state' is a variant on the unitary structure where the centre does not enjoy direct control everywhere. 'Incorporation of parts of its territory has been achieved through treaty and agreement; consequently territorial integration is less than perfect. While administrative standardization prevails over most of the territory, the union structure entails the survival in some areas of variations based upon pre-union rights and infrastructures' (Rokkan and Urwin 1983: 181). The fourth category, organic federalism, is really the application of the same idea in federal states. It is constructed from below, the result of voluntary association by distinctive territorial structures, which retain their separate institutional outlines with wide discretionary powers. This schema, developed as the basis for a typology of European states, raises many questions. One might ask, for example, whether it is essential that mechanical federalism be introduced from above; this was not really the case in the

---

than a shared enterprise. Whether or not his criticism of the Commission is right, I agree that the term does suggest rather sharper lines of demarcation than my concept of plurinationalism.

[19] One might turn this claim on its head and argue that it is precisely the intellectuals who torment themselves with questions about whether they can have more than one identity.

foundation of the Federal Republic of Germany in 1949. We might ask whether the union state and the organic federation are two separate categories and instead choose to see the union principle as something that can operate within either federal or non-federal states. Rokkan and Urwin's approach is behaviourist and institutional, and they do not broach normative questions or issues of sovereignty. Nonetheless, they did tap into a key difference in the constitution of states and the matter of the sources of legitimacy and normative order. The idea of the 'union' state has struck a chord in Scotland, where it is consistent with earlier formulations of the United Kingdom as a 'union' or 'incorporating union' rather than a unitary state, as the Westminster doctrine would have it (Mitchell 1996). To put matters slightly differently, the dominant interpretation of the 'unitary' UK constitution as necessarily centralist is at odds with its ability to accommodate plurality and sustain asymmetrical forms of government (Walker 2000). A similar debate is under way in Spain and Canada.

An earlier formulation of the idea comes from Georg Jellinek (1981), who in the nineteenth century coined the term 'fragments of state' (*Staatsfragmente*). He criticized the dominant doctrine of the time that the only units of jurisdiction were states and provinces submitted to states, arguing that there was a wide array of entities in between. There were states, defined as territories with their own territory, subjects, and government. Some were sovereign and independent. Others were non-sovereign but counted as states because, equipped with the necessary faculties and usually possessing the title of kingdom, republic, or whatever, they could easily continue if the parent state disappeared. One such example was Bavaria. At the other extreme were protectorates, territories with their own territory and subjects but no government, such as Bosnia-Hercegovina and Alsace-Lorraine. Fragments of state were territories which had the attributes of states but only in partial form and, lacking the complete infrastructure, could not continue without the parent state. So the Austrian *Länder* had their own laws and parliaments but not executive power; Iceland had its own constitution but was governed by a Danish minister; Croatia had much of the equipment of a state, but lacked its own citizenship and its government was nominated by Hungary. Finland was more contentious since some people considered it a non-sovereign state while Jellinek saw it as a fragment within the Russian Empire. Fragments of state in turn could be divided into stronger and weaker categories, of which Jellinek outlined four. In the weakest, the centre creates and changes the constitutions of units; in the next, the units have limited powers over their own constitutions; in a stronger form, the constitutions of the units can only be changed by their own laws; in the strongest, the units have full constituent power, able to change their internal constitution at will. Fragments of state thus have various degrees of internal sovereignty. They do not have external sovereignty, but may enjoy certain of the international privileges of states such as membership of the International Postal Union.

There is much to question in Jellinek's categories, which perhaps betray an excessive legal formality, but he too is pointing to an alternative tradition of sovereignty and authority from that of the statist school. The theme is picked up by Carens (2000: 66), who writes of the institutional incompleteness of nations within multinational states since 'no nation, not even the majority, can claim all of the economic, social and political institutions as its own'. Such thinking was and still is dismissed by those modernists who equate the unitary or uniform state with progress and see such special features as quaint relics of the past, at best colourful curiosities, at worst bastions of reaction. As nation-state has come under pressure from globalization, territorial re-structuring, and privatization, however, it has been increasingly demystified ideologically and its legal underpinnings have been questioned. Jurists have rediscovered the idea of legal pluralism (MacCormick 1999*a*), and historians have entered the fray with revisionist interpretations of the process of state formation and its normative basis.

Lessons of the Habsburg Empire

Perhaps the most complete example of a complex state is the Austro-Hungarian Empire, inspiration of much of Jellinek's work. At one time it was common to characterize the empire as a 'prison house of nationalities', each wanting to escape and set up its own state. As the system faced pressures for democratization, popular politics inevitably took an ethnic nationalist form so that there could be no legitimate basis for an overarching authority. The case thus illustrates the incompatibility of the multinational federation with democracy and modernization. There is a certain amount of hindsight in this view, since the empire did indeed collapse into national states. There is also an often unconscious extrapolation from the experience of western Europe where the triumph of the nation-state over previous forms of complex order is seen as not only contemporary with, but intrinsically linked to, modernization. Now that the failure of the nation-state model in south-eastern Europe is so apparent and the model itself is more generally in question, less deterministic accounts of the history of multinational conglom-erates, including even the Ottoman Empire (Keyder 1997), have gained currency.

The Austro-Hungarian Empire was a system of extraordinary complexity and asymmetry. As in other multinational states, there was no name for the core part, which has necessitated clumsy expressions like Cisleithenian Austria (Kann 1977). Elsewhere territories had been acquired in piecemeal fashion and often allowed to keep their old institutions and privileges. These 'historicopolitical entities' or 'crownlands' thus maintained a degree of ori-ginal sovereignty (Jellinek 1981), with their own estates or diets. The Prag-matic Sanction of 1712–23, providing for the imperial succession, recognized the separate legal existence of Croatia–Slavonia; the Holy Roman Empire; the Free City of Fiume; Transylvania; and Hungary, all under the overarching 'real' or dynastic union (Kann 1977). Estates also survived in the Czech lands of Bohemia, Moravia, and Silesia. Hungary was treated as a separate kingdom, with its own tariffs and railway system and administration in the hands of county boards. After the failed revolutions of 1848 there was a phase of centralization, but from the 1860s Vienna started to relax control. *Diets* were restored in 1861, although reduced to local government status. The *Ausgleich* of 1867 gave the kingdom of Hungary a large degree of independence, and in 1869 a measure of home rule was extended to the Polish region of Galicia (Wank 1997). A similar compromise within Hungary recognized the autonomy of Croatia, with complex provisions for affairs concerning the whole kingdom to be made by the Hungarian parliament augmented by a Croatian delegation. Proposals for a similar compromise in the Czech lands, however, failed to progress until it was too late. The Austro-Hungarian union, a form of 'sovereignty association', allowed Hungary to run its own affairs while the common affairs of the empire were managed by joint commissions. Although Hungary's treatment of its own minorities was less than generous, the settlement allowed the Hungarians more power and influence, as well as a larger territory, than they could ever enjoy as an independent state, as events after 1919 showed. The union, indeed, has often been referred to as a possible model for other binational states and was the first preference of Sinn Féin in the early twentieth century.

These self-governing estates and *diets* were based only loosely on ethnic affiliation since their origins were historical and dynastic. In any case, ethnic criteria for self-government would have been difficult to apply in a region and at a time when ethnic identities were rather fluid. The Hungarian patriot, Kossuth, was of Slovak origin, even if he did claim that he could not find Slovakia on the map. At the Social Democratic Congress held in Prague in 1913, the leader of the Czech faction was called Németh (which is Czech for 'German') while the leader of the German faction was called Czech (Macartney 1934). Ruthenians could be classified as Poles, Russians, or Ukrainians, depending on strategic considerations. Some groups, like the Slovenes, on the other hand, maintained a sense of identity without institutions of their own; lacking the status of a 'historicopolitical entity' they had no defined territory or capacity for self-government. Over large parts of the empire nationality groups were mixed, or else one might predominate in the cities and another in the countryside. Language was another matter and caused some serious conflicts in an age of increasing education and expanding literacy, but there were ways of handling this short of secession, as was shown with the establishment of separate school boards in Bohemia (1873) and Moravia (1991).

There is a widespread tendency in the literature to see these arrangements as doomed to failure because they were pre-modern, undemocratic, and an obstacle to progress. This argument, which finds a parallel in western Europe and elsewhere (see Chapter 2) takes several different forms. For some, estates systems are inherently tied to social privilege and incompatible with modern administration. A. J. P. Taylor (1948: 113) noted that the non-historic nationalities 'lacked an urban middle class and everywhere accepted the alliance of the local nobility. Even the Hungarian movement talked a historic, legal language repellent to modern liberalism.' This found an echo in the enlightened despotism of the eighteenth-century Habsburgs and their efforts to centralize the empire. Yet there was a liberal tradition of crownland self-government, which was an important element in the Revolution of 1848. Others insist that democratization could only be achieved through reforming the system of self-government on ethnic lines. Given the location of the various groups, it is not clear how this could have been done without forced transfers (or ethnic cleansing, in modern parlance), and in any case it was impossible to define the groups authoritatively. Others have argued that it would have been possible to democratize the old estates systems, while providing for language and other rights for communities within or straddling a crownland. Proposals canvassed in the late nineteenth and early twentieth century involved combinations of territorial self-government, ethnic and linguistic self-government, and the principle of personal nationality in which individuals and not groups would be the basic unit. The social democrat Karl Renner proposed a system of eight territorial *Gubernia* to replace the crownlands, with eight cultural councils based in Vienna dealing with language and cultural matters across the whole of Cisleithenia.

Reform proposals were stymied not by the inherent difficulties of plurinational government, but by political sabotage. One element was a tendency for the imperial centre to manipulate ethnic and nationalist politics the better to preserve its own power. The Habsburgs played the nationalities off against each other (Stourzh 1991), and in the early nineteenth century Metternich was given to encouraging or even inventing provincial traditions to defuse opposition from both centre and periphery (A. J. P. Taylor 1948). At the same time, some of the minorities showed themselves extremely intolerant to their own internal minorities. Hungary was committed to the unitary nation-state model, constantly sought to reduce local rights, and from 1876 intensified its programme of Magyarization. The Poles of Galicia refused to recognize the rights of the Ruthenians under the compromise of 1914 (Kann 1977). The third problem was the tendency of outside powers, notably Germany and Russia, to interfere purportedly on behalf of their co-ethnics (German speakers and Slavs).

In spite of all this, separatist tendencies were contained until the First World War. While the Poles clearly aimed at restoring a national independence and statehood they had previously enjoyed, leaders of the smaller nationalities in particular saw the empire, or some form of broader federation, as their best protection in a dangerous world. Some also saw the futility of trying to draw ethnic lines on maps. Indeed, the Austro-Hungarian model was an inspiration to other stateless nationalist movements, including the original Sinn Féin and the Catalan memorial of grievances of 1885 (Fusi 2000). The Czech leaders Masaryk and Benes remained home rulers until the First World War, supporting independence only as a final resort. Until then nationalists had preferred a large degree of home rule combined with an enhanced Czech influence within the empire (Macartney 1969; Hertz 1944; Kann 1977). Prudential arguments also played a part. As Thomas Masaryk exclaimed in 1909, 'We cannot be independent outside Austria, next to a powerful Germany, having Germans on our territory' (Sked 1989: 223–4). History was to prove him right. The Slovenes, in an equally exposed position, concentrated on their cultural revival and the establishment of their own crownland. They did not press for the break-up of the empire, certainly not for independence (Sked 1989), and only late on were they drawn into pan-Slavic ideas. The social democrats feared the power of ethnic nationalism to divide the working class, and until a very late stage they too favoured keeping an overarching framework; only in 1918 did a section of them accept Bauer's proposals for national self-determination (Macartney 1969). Some contemporary observers of the early twentieth century saw matters improving (Wickham Steed 1914), and while nationality tensions were a permanent feature of political life, there was little belief in the destruction of the empire (Sked 1989). What ultimately determined the triumph of the nation-state principle was the collapse of imperial authority in the First World War and the desperate need for national leaders to gain the security of statehood, and international recognition and guarantees. Further impetus was given by Woodrow Wilson's doctrine of national self-determination, even if the doctrine itself was a little incoherent and inconsistently applied (de Blas 1994). The outcome was a series of nation-states based on the illusion that geography, nationality, and sovereignty can coincide.

Subsequent experience has shown the futility of this proposition. Czechoslovakia fell to German irredentism and later to Soviet expansionism. Yugoslavia broke up in the 1940s and again the 1990s. Poland was divided and only reinstated after the Second World War following forcible population transfers. With the end of the cold war there is a broad agreement that the future of south-eastern Europe can only be reassured through a new transnational order. There is nothing inevitable about the evolution of the nation-state, and the collapse of the Austro-Hungarian Empire does not suggest otherwise. The nation-state, an import from western Europe selectively encouraged by the victors of 1919, was a failure. There are more promising traditions within the history of the western part of Europe as well as in the central empires themselves, and there are ways of conducting politics that make nationality issues manageable without reducing them all to the question of secession and statehood.

Nations, Nationality, and the State

What emerges from this discussion is a rather fluid set of concepts and
doctrines. 'Nationality' is used in two senses: in a narrow, restricted sense
to refer to citizenship of a state; and in a weaker sense to denote a broad
cultural affiliation. This is what allows Scots to write 'Scottish' in the line in a
hotel register asking for nationality, and 'British' in the line asking for
identity of passport (to the confusion of foreign clerks, who want to write
'English' for both). Nationality in this second sense is quite compatible with
membership of a multinational state. It does carry the normative implication
of a group right to self-determination, but the exact political implications will
depend on the aspirations of the group and the political circumstances. In the
Austro-Hungarian case, these were very diverse. The idea of nationality
might also carry the freight Miller (1995) puts on it as a principle of solidarity
and reciprocity but, again, this can take a variety of forms. 'Nation' similarly
has a range of meanings, from those that identify it with the state (as in the
United Nations) to looser cultural and social conceptions (Seymour 1999).
The Spanish constitution, by definitional fiat, reserves nation for the state but
leaves nationality for the component parts, without delimiting these at all
precisely. In the United Kingdom the term 'nation' is used indifferently for
the whole state, for Britain (England, Scotland, and Wales) and for the
component parts individually. In Canada aboriginal peoples have increasingly assumed and been accorded the title of First Nations. This semantic
confusion should at least put paid to any idea that nations and states could
ever be coterminous. It has the positive advantage of allowing for the coexistence of different degrees of national consciousness within a shared polity;
indeed this semantic dissonance is an integral part of plurinationality. When
the majority nationality constitutes itself as the 'titular nationality' of the
state, or the state nationality is interpreted as unitary, then this genius is lost.
It is equally lost where the overarching framework or regime experiences a
crisis or collapse. The implosion of the Austro-Hungarian Empire in 1918–19
left nationalities little choice but to secure themselves through statehood. The
Soviet Union collapsed, not at the periphery but at the centre, but it was the
'national' republics that filled the vacuum. The final collapse of the Spanish
Empire in 1898 triggered nationalist demands around the periphery. Yugoslavia's breakdown gave its remaining nationalities little choice but secession
and statehood. What these fragments collapsed into was a form of national
sovereignty associated with statehood but resting on fragile intellectual
foundations.

Two key concepts will guide much of the remainder of the book. The first is
plurinationalism,[20] the coexistence within a political order of more than one

---

[20] I have derived this from the adjective 'plurinacional' used in the Spanish historical nations
to refer to the complexity of nationality. This might be translated as 'multinational', but that
would lose some of the meaning and richness of the Spanish original.

national identity, with all the normative claims and implications that this entails. Plurinationalism is more than multinationalism, which could refer to the coexistence of discrete and separate national groupings within a polity. Under plurinationalism, more than one national identity can pertain to a single group or even an individual, opening up the possibility of multiple nationalities which in turn may be nested or may overlap in less tidy ways. The very meaning of nationality can vary according to the group or individual and can be more or less charged with political content. From this we can explore concepts such as the plurinational state and the possibilities of democracy in a plurinational order. It follows that we cannot make a simple one-to-one correlation of nationality with the state, nor propose secession as a solution to nationality conflicts in the illusion that this will do the trick (Bashai 1998).

The second key concept is post-sovereignty, referring to the end of state monopoly of ultimate authority. The classic doctrine of sovereignty has always been intellectually problematic and, in the modern world, is becoming increasingly untenable. One reason is the ideological demystification of the state and the decline of deference. Since sovereignty, with its extraordinary claims to authority, required both deference and a certain suspension of disbelief, it has become more difficult to sustain. It has been challenged by the emergence of new normative orders above and below the state. To name but three, these would include international human rights doctrine and practice; the rise of transnational organizations; and the advance of claims from stateless nations and minorities. State sovereignty has also been put in question by a new intellectual interest in, and respect for, cultural pluralism and multiple identity. There is an increased questioning of what the post-modernists call 'meta-narratives', which tie the whole of human experience together into a single framework, and a growing interest in diversity. Prophets of the 'end of history' apart, scholars are more likely to accept that the various social and political systems of the world are not united in single teleology and do not always fit together like parts of a single machine. Finally, the erosion of the functional autonomy of the state, even as the public domain has expanded, has put in question the reality of sovereign power (Creveld 1999).

This raises delicate questions of terminology and risks interminable semantic debate. If we follow those who insist that sovereignty is indivisible and inheres only in the state, then perhaps we are in an era where sovereignty has ceased to exist. Yet to argue thus would risk losing any basis for legitimate authority. In my usage, post-sovereignty does not mean the end of all principles of authority. Rather it means that sovereignty is dispersed and divided (Jáuregui 2000). Walker's (2001) term 'late sovereignty' captures much the same idea, referring to the existence of multiple sources of legal order, without hierarchy and not reducible to a single principle. The term 'post-sovereign' also refers to political demands and movements that embrace this idea and so want not to establish a sovereign state but to insert themselves into the new complex webs of authority.

Nationality demands and nationalism can thus be less than the demand for a separate state but more than a request for devolution within a continuing sovereign state. The new context provides multiple ways of fulfilling nationality claims, once we accept that they cannot be treated as absolutes and that they must be the subject of compromise, as are other forms of politics. Post-sovereignty is not to be confused with term 'post-nationalism', although this often seems to refer to the same thing (Kearney 1997; Shaw 2000). Post-nationalism would imply that nations have disappeared, a problematic notion in a world where nationalism seems if anything to have grown in importance. What has changed is the demand that nations should always have their own states, itself a product of the high era of the nation-state during the late nineteenth and much of the twentieth century. So my term 'post-sovereignty' seems more apt.

In the remaining chapters I seek to unpack the ideas of sovereignty, nationality, and self-determination, in search of ways in which their seemingly incompatible imperatives might be reconciled. The focus is less on abstract reasoning than on political practice. For this reason, the emphasis is on four plurinational states, the United Kingdom, Spain, Belgium, and Canada, liberal democracies which have addressed the issue in different ways, and on the emerging transnational order in Europe. The need to engage in some detailed analysis precludes the examination of a larger number of cases, but I have attempted to focus on consistent themes and draw contrasts and comparisons. The lessons drawn might be of wider application, bearing in mind differences in context. The central argument is that in a world in which state sovereignty is increasingly questioned, the nationalities issue is once again posed; but that new answers are available. Before looking forward to a world beyond sovereignty, however, we must first look back, to place arguments about statehood and sovereignty in their historical context.

2

In Search of the Ancient Constitution: Historiography of the Nation

The Present Relevance of History

The previous chapter argued that nationality claims should be seen as a form of politics, to be argued, debated, and mediated, rather than as a set of absolutes which could be settled through universal abstract reasoning. This is not to take all claims as equally valid or to abandon ethical and normative considerations. Rather it is a plea to take claims on their own terms and engage in a debate around them. It also argued that nationality claims and self-determination do not necessarily entail claiming a state, since this is a historically contingent political form, and political order may take many forms. Sovereignty is a principle of normative order, which does not necessarily inhere in the state and can be divided and shared (MacCormick 1995). There may be more than one normative order within a territory, more or less integrated with or subordinated to others. Modernity and universal values are not the monopoly of the consolidated nation-state and there may be other, equally valid, ways of accessing them. This implies a radical demystification of the nation-state and a questioning of state-focused social science. If we see the state not as an immanent principle of authority nor as the unique source of political order, but as a historically formed entity, then we can rehabilitate other, non-statist traditions of thinking about political order, lost in the excessive claims of the nation-state.

It is no coincidence that the functional problems of the state, its intellectual demystification, and the challenge to sovereignty of transnational integration have sparked off new debates on the history of states and nations and a rethinking of the origins of authority, sovereignty, and rights. Social scientists have called into question received accounts of national integration, which tended to identify state-building and national integration with modernization itself. These saw market integration, industrialization, capitalism, cultural integration, and the penetration of the modern state into all parts of its territory as linked processes, which would produce homogeneous nation-states without important cultural, ethnic, or territorial cleavages (Deutsch

1966). Some modernists portray both European integration and globalization more generally as a continuation of these diffusionist trends, leaving ever
less space for particularisms. More commonly, however, European integration and globalization have served to question further the sovereign nation-
state as the sole form of political order and have provoked scholars into
looking again at pre-modern forms of authority and their similarities to the
modern post-sovereign order. In this enterprise they have encountered historians, also breaking out of state-focused approaches, to explore the complexity of political order. The sovereign nation-state can, in this account, be
seen as an exception or interlude rather than the end point of political
development. Already in the 1970s Rokkan (1980) was presenting the construction of European nation-states as a problematic and incomplete process,
leaving behind important cleavages (Rokkan and Urwin 1983; Flora 1999).
Tilly (1990) has shown how different forms of nation-state emerged
according to circumstances, and that alternative paths, based on city regions,
were in principle possible (Tilly and Blockmans 1994). Elliot (1992) presents
the consolidated nation-state as a parenthesis between the composite state of
the early modern era and the present-day pattern of diffused authority. Even
in international relations scholars have begun to question the 'Westphalian'
paradigm as a historical account (Osiander 1994; Spruyt 1994) or as an
adequate way of understanding contemporary politics (Agnew and Corbridge 1995). Elsewhere I have also sought to present the territorial state as
historically contingent, and the process of integration as at least potentially
reversible (Keating 1988*a*, 1998*a*).

The undermining of the old teleological accounts also has normative
implications. As was noted earlier, modern nationality claims tend to be
based either on arguments about the consciousness and the will of the nation
concerned, a matter to be addressed in the next chapter, or on historic
arguments about the continuing existence and rights of a people. Historic
rights as a basis for nationality claims, as advanced for example by Miguel
Herrero de Miñon (1998*a*), have often been dismissed as irrelevant or
irrational since they cannot be argued from abstract reasoning or deduced
from universalist principles. They have also been branded as conservative or
even reactionary, being derived from monarchical, imperial, or other pre-
democratic traditions. Indeed a whole intellectual tradition sees constitutionalism as a way of transcending custom and tradition in the name of progress
(Tully 1995). Certainly doctrines of historic rights raise serious problems in
democratic theory, since they seek to derive normative principles from supposed events and suggest that mere antiquity is a basis for normative authority. This is not, however, to say that they have no authority, or that they are
necessarily more conservative than state-based doctrines of normative order.
Custom and practice underlie normative orders to a greater extent than is
often appreciated (MacCormick 1999*a*). Notably, the existing states derive
more of their legitimacy from their historic existence and practice than from

abstract principle, and it is difficult to see how most of them would survive the rigorous tests set by political theorists for non-state societies to assume statehood. Yet rejection of the state monopoly does not require us to commit the opposite error, of thinking that there is a substratum of original historic rights which could provide a basis for a peaceful and democratic normative order, if only we got rid of the claims of the states. The best we can do is to question states' claims to universal authority and counterpose them with other historically rooted traditions and ways of doing politics. Once again, the emphasis is on political practice and its foundation in normative principles.

Competing Historiographies

There is nothing new in the use of history to conduct political argument. Most European nations have origin myths, typically tracing their descent either from the tribes of Israel, or from Trojan refugees. Medieval rulers employed tame scholars to invent genealogies and discover lost laws and traditions. The opening scene of Shakespeare's *Henry V* has the English monarch consulting his sages on the meaning and application of the old Salic law to sustain his claim to the crown of France. While modern historiography was supposedly more scientific, based on evidence and research, it has been scarcely less ideological, deployed in the interests of state and nation. It has rarely been completely uncontested and at times has been vigorously disputed.

To simplify, we can identify two competing historiographies in the four multinational states under discussion here, the state historiography and the peripheral one. State history is presented teleologically as a progress to national unity, with the sovereign state representing its final expression. As historians modernized and became more scientific, origin myths could be dismissed as romantic nonsense. Indeed, historians could celebrate the diverse origins of the nation as a source of its strength and its success in moulding them into one as a sign of the national genius; but the teleology is only reinforced thereby as this unity is seen as the essence of progress. The history of the state, in this tradition, is the universal history, the only one with a real claim to encompass all human experience; other histories are necessarily particularistic. The pre-modern order of Europe, with its diffused authority, is presented as an obstacle to progress and enlightenment. The estates systems, *fueros*, special laws, historic rights, and the whole patchwork of authority that characterized the pre-state order are dismissed as bastions of reaction and privilege, obstacles to the advance of capitalism, markets, and middle-class liberalism. It is not only liberals who adhere to this view, since Marxists also see the rise of capitalism and the bourgeoisie and, in so far as it facilitated these, the nation-state as an essential phase in historical development and thus a force for progress. Engels's strictures on nations without history are well known, and a modern Marxist historian like Hobsbawm can draw a distinction between large nation-states, which have a progressive potential, and stateless nations, which tend to reaction. The same attitudes are found in analyses of the failure of the Austro-Hungarian Empire, which historians have presented as doomed to failure because it was not a nation-state and could never become one (as noted in Chapter 1). This bias to the consolidated nation-state often accompanies a cultural disdain for the minority or non-state cultures and languages, which are also presented as signs of backwardness and obstacles to progress. An extreme form of this combination of statism and nationalism is the French Jacobin tradition, itself largely an invention of the Third Republic, pitched into conflict with monarchism and the church.

Peripheral historiography presents a very different account. There is often a myth of primordial innocence and primitive democracy before the alien intrusion of the modern state. Historians may present the incorporation of their territory into the state as an act of conquest, in which case it is illegitimate and was never accepted by the people. The resulting counter-history is the mirror-image of state history, postulating a united people living in primitive independence and enjoying a precious if anachronistic sovereignty. Such analyses often underpin a radical rejection of the state and an argument for secession. Alternatively, peripheral history may present incorporation as the fruit of a pact, in which historic rights were not surrendered, with the implication that the pact can be renegotiated. This underpins arguments for pactism in a plurinational order, on the lines of the union state (Rokkan and Urwin 1983) or fragment of state (Jellinek 1981; Herrero de Miñon 1998*a*). Peripheral histories have also challenged the liberal and progressive pretensions of state history. While state historians present historic institutions of the pre-state era as necessarily reactionary because they were not democratic or liberal, peripheral historians have two responses. Some present the old institutions as forms of primitive democracy in advance of their time. Others point out more reasonably that no institutions in the Middle Ages were democratic by modern standards and that there is no reason why estates, foral bodies, or guilds could not have democratized in the same way that the British Parliament did. So there was more than one potential path to democratic modernization, and the peripheries have equal claims to form part of a (more complete and authentic) universal history. As the state loses its mystique, these histories of diffused authority are refurbished as the basis for a post-sovereign political order and new forms of democracy.

This is not to say that there is a consistent counter-history yielding historic rights which could provide a new universal solution. Historiographies are in competition, and some stateless nations have more of a 'usable past' than others. Counter-histories are equally prone to fabrication and myth. Historic rights frozen in time would be of little use, of questionable moral value, and impossible to reconcile. What is important is not the precise content of such-and-such a right, but the principles of negotiated authority and of national pluralism as a way of dealing with nationality conflicts. They point to the need for intercultural dialogue and respect for difference, without violating liberal and democratic principles. By taking counter-histories seriously we can explore new ways of thinking about power and the state and put claims to state sovereignty in perspective. In an age of national pluralism and challenges to the monopolistic claims of states, they may show us ways of thinking about national accommodation better grounded both in historic practice and in the needs of the present.

The United Kingdom

Historiographical arguments in the United Kingdom go back to the Middle Ages, when the Norman Welsh historian Geraldus Cambrensis sought to justify English suzerainty over the whole of Britain, against a vigorous defence on the part of Scottish historians like Hector Boece, first principal of the University of Aberdeen (Ferguson 1998). In the constitutional conflicts of the seventeenth century, a primitive democratic English constitution was evoked, sometimes counterposed to the 'Norman yoke' imposed after the Conquest of 1066—although at other times the Normans were seen as quintessentially English themselves (Kidd 1999). For our purposes, how-ever, the most influential school of historians in the nation-state tradition were the 'Whig historians' of the nineteenth and twentieth centuries (Butter-field 1968).

A central feature of this history was its focus on England. Almost all the works were entitled histories of England, tracing British history directly from English experience, with the peripheral nations putting in only occasional appearances and joining the central narrative only after union with England. Yet the meaning and confusion of the terms England, Britain, and United Kingdom is almost never addressed explicitly and the terms are used inter-changeably. A. J. P. Taylor, known for his scrupulous distinctions among the nationalities of the Habsburg Empire, insisted that the distinction between English and British was 'a triviality of interest only to nationalist cranks' (Taylor 1975: 622). Instead the unions of 1536, 1707, and 1801 are treated as mere incidents after which English history continues. So Erskine May (1906) could entitle his book *The Constitutional History of England*, introduce it as an effort 'to trace the progress and development of the British constitution' (p. ix), and argue that 'nothing in the history of our constitution is more remarkable than the permanence of every institution forming part of the government of the country' (p. 273). Trevelyan (1926: 481), ignoring the mutual abolition of both Scottish and English Parliaments, wrote that

'The Union involved the absorption of Scotland's Parliament and Privy Council in those of England'. A logical consequence was that constitutional historians saw the United Kingdom as the product only of English constitutional practice, arguing that parliamentary sovereignty was absolute since this had been established in sixteenth- and seventeenth-century England (Dicey and Rait 1920; Dicey 1886, 1912) (for a critique of this, see MacCormick 1999*a*). Maitland (1908) does give an account of the unions and the breaks in constitutional continuity of 1688–9, 1707, and 1801, but his account of constitutional law takes in only English history and he insists that the United Kingdom Parliament has developed continuously from the old English one. Allied with Anglocentrism is an isolationist tendency that sees the United Kingdom as something apart from Europe and in opposition to it.

Pre-Union Scotland, where it featured at all, is portrayed as a materially and intellectually impoverished country, and its eighteenth-century Enlightenment and nineteenth-century industrialization are attributed to the beneficent effects of union with England. Green's (1896) *History of England* claimed that the Union opened to Scotland 'new avenues of wealth which the energies of its people turned to wonderful account . . . Peace and culture have changed the wild clansmen of the Highlands into herdsmen and farmers' (p. 130). Trevelyan (1926: 482) asserted that 'By this great act of modern legislation, England placed upon the world's highway of commerce, colonization and culture, a small nation, hitherto poor and isolated', failing to mention that blunt threats to Scottish independent commerce had been used to get the Union. Yet while recognizing at one point that the name of the country had changed, he continues for the rest of the work to refer to it as England. A profound disdain for the Gaelic culture of Scotland pervades the work of conservative historians like Trevor Roper (1983).[1] Ireland was similarly presented as a backward periphery and the rich Gaelic culture of pre-conquest Ireland largely ignored. Well into the nineteenth century Celts were seen as alien and threatening, although potentially civilizable according to English norms. By the late nineteenth century a Germanic cult presented a racial basis for constitutionalism in England, as in Stubbs's (1897) *Constitutional History of England*, whose title is for once correct but where the absent Celts are presumably beyond this civilizing and constitutional experience. Wales hardly featured in this historiography at all, for, as Trevelyan (1926) put it, 'From the Tudor settlement until the Nineteenth

---

[1] In the celebrated Hobsbawm and Ranger (1983) book on the invention of tradition he writes that Celtic Scotland could have no independent tradition since before the 17th century its people and those of Ireland were the same. It is difficult to see what culture could survive this primordialist test—certainly not England. The book is a curious invention itself, with diehard conservatives and Marxists agreeing to denigrate so-called inventions. One can only assume that the conservatives think that the only authentic practices are those that never change, while the Marxists think that only cultures made *de novo* are valid. The idea that Scottish culture is a living one and might have adapted and modernized seems not to occur. For an effective critique of Trevor Roper, see Ferguson (1998).

Century, Wales had no history, except that of slow social and religious growth'.

English national bias was closely linked to the portrayal of constitutional development as smooth, consensual, and tending ineluctably to liberalism and democracy. England was the exception in a Europe bound up in feudalism and absolutism. The medieval English parliament is presented as unique, despite the existence of parliamentary institutions in Scotland, Ireland, Wales, and Cornwall, as well as in many parts of Europe. The conservative politician Balfour (1912) explicitly argued that the superior English polity needed to triumph over the backward 'tribal' organization of Ireland and the Scottish Highlands. The Magna Carta featured strongly as the basis of English liberties, although it was arguably no more than a feudal pact of the sort common elsewhere in Europe and it seems only to have been rediscovered and given its prominence from the mid-seventeenth century (Norman Davies 1999). The struggles of the mid-seventeenth century between King and Parliament are described as the 'English Civil War', with the Irish and Scots in walk-on parts, rather than the War of Three Kingdoms (Morrill 1995; Barber 1995; Norman Davies 1999). Its constitutional implications are thereby reduced to the development of English parliamentarism. The *coup d'état* of 1688–9 which brought William of Orange to the throne was celebrated as the 'Glorious Revolution' laying the foundations for a democratic and liberal regime. Well into the twentieth century Whig historians identified liberalism with Englishness (Stapleton 1999) against challenges from within and outwith the United Kingdom. The identification of liberty with Englishness has sometimes required a bit of category-stretching, to include the likes of William of Orange or the Hanoverian monarchs, and leads to extreme anachronism and invention when treating the Middle Ages. The liberal teleology also has to pass swiftly over awkward facts such as that the United Kingdom gained universal suffrage only in 1928 and was the last state in Europe to keep a hereditary chamber of parliament.

The dominant historiography has also been profoundly Protestant (Butterfield 1968). Historians have recognized that both Catholics and Protestants persecuted each other in their interludes of power in the sixteenth century, but tend to excuse the latter because they killed Catholics not for their religion *per se*, but because of their disloyalty to the state. Since, whatever the protestations of loyalty of Catholics themselves, Catholicism was defined as intrinsically incompatible with good citizenship, this amounts to a defence of a sectarian state. The treatment of King James II and VII is particularly illustrative. James may have had many faults, but he was deposed in 1688–9 for introducing religious toleration for all, Anglicans, Presbyterians, Catholics, and Dissenters. The revolutionary regime celebrated by the Whigs withdrew toleration for Catholics and Dissenters, imposed religious uniformity in each of the three kingdoms, and promulgated the notoriously sectarian-celebrated Bills of Rights. It is not that Whig historians approve of religious persecution, but their willingness to deplore the excesses of Anglican oppression of Catholics and Dissenters does not extend to questioning the fundamentally sectarian nature of the developing British state. Trevelyan (1926) is typical: 'The outcome [of the battle of the Boyne] subjected the native Irish to persecution and tyranny for several generations to come, but it saved Protestantism in Europe and enabled the British Empire to launch forth strongly on its career of prosperity, freedom and expansion overseas.'[2] The Stuart dynasty as a whole is presented as the incarnation of continental abolutism and its defeat in the earlier Civil War is celebrated as a triumph for freedom. Davies's (1999) view that the Stuarts may have represented a form of enlightened despotism more progressive than the parliamentary oligarchy might be contentious, but it is a provocative counter-suggestion.

It would be wrong to claim that there is a coherent counter-history from the periphery. Scotland, Ireland, and Wales have their own historiographies, which themselves are rich in controversies and revisionisms. From the nineteenth century, national history schools developed in Scotland, Ireland, and Wales, challenging Anglocentrism and focused on key elements in their own political development. This picked up on earlier, pre-Union traditions. A Scottish historiography had been deployed to counter the claims of the English Crown in the Middle Ages and Scottish historians have tended to root sovereign authority in the people. The Declaration of Arbroath (1320), while embroidered with origin myths, asserts the sovereignty of the Scottish people and their right to reject not only the English monarch but also, should he betray their trust, their own king, Robert Bruce. English historians have tended to belittle the significance of this, pointing out that it was written by the monks of Arbroath and was little more than a typical medieval statement of conditional loyalty, yet its popular credentials appear better founded than those of the Magna Carta or the Glorious Revolution, and Scottish historians have emphasized its precocious annunciation of the doctrine of limited monarchy (Cowan 1998). Hector Boece's *History of Scotland* (1526) elaborated on these earlier ideas which denied absolute sovereignty and rooted legitimacy in consent and in the people, and this was pursued by George Buchanan (1506–82) after the Reformation (Ferguson 1998). Scottish historiography has also had a European bent, reflecting the continental travels and interests of scholars and the search on the part of Scottish monarchs for support in France and elsewhere against English claims.

While for centuries Scottish historiography was deployed to support claims to national independence, from the late eighteenth-century Enlightenment there emerged a Scottish unionist historiography, critical of the 'inven-

---

[2] Trevelyan (1926: 467) also includes among the sins of James II and VII the introduction into the army of 'shiploads of Celtic-speaking peasantry' whom the English were agreed in 'regarding…as foreigners and savages, whom it was the task of the Anglo-Saxon to keep docile and unarmed even in their own island'.

tions' of the past and prepared to embrace English constitutional practice as more advanced (Kidd 1993). This was founded in a Scottish form of Whiggism, also celebrating the Revolution of 1688–9 (which was a separate event in Scotland) and stressing the backward state of such Scottish institutions as Parliament, the law, and the nobility. It is this perception that explains the willingness of Scottish intellectuals to abandon their own history in favour the English Whig gospel (Finlay 1998; Pittock 1999). With the re-emergence of nationalism in the nineteenth and twentieth centuries, however, a nationalist historiography reappeared, much of it based on the contested nature of the Union itself.[3]

Scottish nationalist histories stress the corruption involved in the negotiation of the Union of 1707 and the popular opposition it aroused at the time (Ferguson 1977), thus undermining its legitimacy. Riley (1978, p. xvi) concludes that 'The union was made by men of limited vision for very short-term and comparatively petty, if not squalid, ends', and only gained broader acceptance much later, although he recognized that the alternatives might have been worse. The intellectual arguments advanced during the union debates by Andrew Fletcher of Saltoun, and his plea for a confederal order, have continued to inform nationalist scholars (Paul H. Scott 1992), and in the 1990s they even found sustenance in Fletcher for a united Europe recognizing the rights of small nations. There have been efforts to rescue the old Scottish Parliament from the bad image given it by unionist historians (Young 1998), and to stress the plurality of authority in pre-Union Scotland, divided among the Crown, Parliament, courts, and Kirk (Kidd 1993). Scottish nationalist historians have also tended to stress the democratic traditions in Scottish society, including the organization of the Church of Scotland. Scots law has featured prominently as a form of continuing legitimacy through the Union and as more rational and European than its English counterpart. From the 1990s Scottish historians have critically examined their own historiography (Ferguson 1998; McCrone 1999) and have stressed the continuation of an autonomous Scottish civil society within the union state and the regular adjustments of the terms of union (Finlay 1997; Devine 1999; Paterson 1994). Above all, non-unionist historians have sought to present the Union as a pact between sovereign nations, which could not be changed except by mutual consent. Analysts of the union debates have argued that this sovereignty was so ill defined as to leave little in the way of legal theory (Robertson 1995), but the doctrine survived and led directly to the Claim of Right of the Scottish Constitutional Convention in the 1980s, whose very name linked to historic precedents (CSA 1988). In a famous case in 1953 (*MacCormick* v. *Lord Advocate*) it was held that the Union of 1707 was indeed superior law and not changeable by the Parliament of the United

---

[3] This periodization is itself a simplification. The intricacies of historical arguments about Scottish rights are detailed in Kidd (1993, 1999) and Ferguson (1998).

Kingdom, and that, the doctrine of parliamentary sovereignty being un-known in pre-union Scotland, the UK Parliament could not have inherited it. Nearly fifty years later MacCormick's son was pointing to the 'Scottish anomaly' of Scottish sovereign rights within an ostensibly unitary Parliament and pointing to the need to resolve this within a broader European order of divided sovereignty (MacCormick 1999*a*). Needless to say, revisionists have in turn disputed this line of reasoning, arguing that the Scottish Parliament was indeed sovereign, and warning against putting modern meaning into ancient documents (Dickinson and Lynch 2000). No doubt all sides of the debate have an element of the truth, since the Scottish state, with a powerful and covetous neighbour and a weak monarchy, was a more precarious one than was England and the doctrine of sovereignty was only just crystallizing at the time of the Union. Indeed it may be that the very vagueness of old Scottish doctrines of national sovereignty served them ill in the era of emerging nation-states, but, like its Catalan equivalent, it may be more useful in more complex modern conditions.

Scottish historians for their part have stumbled over how to treat the Highlands in their own history. On the one hand, the symbols and legitimacy of the early Scottish state were rooted partly in the Gaelic culture and tradition. On the other, Scottish monarchs from the sixteenth century strove to assimilate the Highlands to Lowland norms and extirpate the Gaelic culture. The Stuarts were forceful supporters of assimilation (Hunter 1999), yet ironically it was in the Highlands that Jacobitism (the movement to restore the Stuart dynasty) was strongest after 1688.

Jacobitism after 1745 and especially in the nineteenth century was incorp-orated into a romantic view of Scottish nationalism, forming one of its enduring myths. Yet nationalism was also associated closely with the defence of the Presbyterian Church establishment threatened by the Stuart kings and secured by the settlement of 1689. Certainly Jacobitism was not the pure reaction depicted by the Whig historians: it had a popular basis and its programme included the restoration of the Scottish Parliament, while the Stuarts did have a record of religious toleration. Yet it sits uneasily with the Presbyterian myth, with its democratic forms, including the election of ministers and an ethos of social egalitarianism. This in turn provided the basis for a view of Scotland as a meritocratic society, emphasizing education and self-improvement, where the 'lad o'pairts' from a poor background could make good. These competing myths were not reconciled until the nineteenth century, sustaining Davidson's (2000) argument that Scottish nationality was created in this period. It would be more accurate, however, to say that the *modern* Scottish nation was the result of this and other syntheses. Rather than undermining nationality claims, however, this would merely show that Scotland was a nation just like all the others.

Irish historiography was complicated by the presence on the island of three distinct groups, the Old Irish of Gaelic or Celtic extraction, the Old English descended from Norman settlers of the Middle Ages, and the New English descended from Protestant settlers in the seventeenth century, many of whom were in fact Scots. All developed a distinctly Irish account of history, borrowing freely from each other's experiences while often intermarrying (Kidd 1999). After the Reformation the Old Irish and Old English were drawn together by their common Catholicism, and the historian Geoffrey Keating (1570–1644) provided the basis for a new and inclusive Irish identity by presenting the Normans as part of a continuous pattern of assimilation of incomers into Irish society. This new Irish identity was accompanied by a doctrine that Ireland had never been incorporated into the English Crown but was merely a 'lordship' whose personal head might happen to be the king of England (Kidd 1999). Seventeenth-century Irish lawyers recalled that the Magna Carta had been sent over to Ireland in a distinct form, and called for respect for the old Irish parliamentary institutions (Morrill 1995). At times of reduced sectarian tensions even the Protestant New English could buy into this Irish identity, adopting the history of the other two groups. During the eighteenth century efforts were made to deny the backwardness of pre-conquest Ireland by playing on the alternative myth of the 'land of saints and scholars', and portraying the 'ancient constitution' of Ireland as balanced and parliamentary. Others argued that pre-conquest Ireland had an advanced system of trade and commerce under its own laws (Kidd 1999). Such historical accounts legitimized the Patriot Parliament (Grattan's Parliament) in the late eighteenth century, which repudiated Poyning's law and claimed sovereign legislative power, asserting that, like the Scots, they had never been conquered, merely brought into a monarchical union. Allied to the modernizing impulse of the French Revolution, they underpinned the United Irishmen and their democratic nationalist rising of 1798.

Yet the institutions which this historiography supported remained the property of the Anglo-Irish Protestants, and the patriots never succeeded in bringing in the Catholic majority. So from the nineteenth century mainstream Irish nationalism drew instead on accounts of conquest and oppression, turning to forms of nationalism rooted in Celtic identity and Catholic culture. A whole 'Story of Ireland' genre of historiography presented a primordial vision of national continuity and separateness (Foster 1998). The corollary of this account was not a reaccommodation of Ireland within the Union, but separatism. Meanwhile in England, Scotland, and Wales racist stereotypes depicted the Catholic Irish as ignorant savages. The Scots covenant tradition was exported to Ireland but for the Protestants of Ulster, who used it as an instrument against incorporation into a home rule state. Oddly enough, Maitland, author of the unitarist account of constitutional history, in the introduction to his translation of Gierke's work on medieval political thought, identified the British problem in Ireland as their lack of a theory of authority between absolute dependence and absolute independence, although tucking this shrewd observation away in a footnote (Maitland 1900, p. x. 1).

The implication of the dominant unionist and Anglocentric historiographies is that British constitutional development is English constitutional development, that the peripheral nations have left no contribution to it, and that the British Parliament is the heir to the unitary English state tradition. In the absence in the United Kingdom of either a successful absolutism or a Jacobin republican tradition, this provides the intellectual underpinning for an uncompromisingly unitary state. Yet in the last fifteen years or so an alternative historiography has developed, in parallel with the renewed political mobilization in the periphery, challenging both the Anglocentric 'History of England' school and the practice in the four nations of sustaining separate national histories (Ellis 1995). This new approach sees the histories of the (British) Isles as linked in complex ways with each other, and as part of a wider European history, and regards the final outcomes, with one secessionist state, one union, and a disputed territory between, as far from inevitable (Pocock 1975; Colley 1992; Brockliss and Eastwood 1997; Ellis and Barber 1995; Hugh Kearney 1995; Norman Davies 1999).

This is accompanied by a revisionism within peripheral historiographies, notably in Ireland, where it began to counter the nationalist accounts from the 1940s, and by the 1980s had produced an overtly anti-nationalist history (Foster 1989, 1998). The emergence of Irish nationalism in the eighteenth century is put in a broader European context, it is not anachronistically projected back to the Middle Ages, and its ultimate triumph is not taken for granted. Ireland is also seen as part of a wider Isles community, its elites linked into developments in the other kingdoms, and the common history of northern Ireland and western Scotland is recognized. Other scholars have traced the reforging of Welsh identity in the nineteenth century (Morgan 1980) and problematized the relationship of the Highlands and Islands not just with the British state but with the Scottish state and society (Hunter 1999). Even English historians are more ready to distinguish England from Islands history. Already in 1971 Sir George Clark prefaced his *History of England* by specifying that 'I mean England in the strict sense, not Great Britain or the British Isles' (Clark 1971, p. v). By the late 1990s it was possible to question not only the Anglocentric history of the United Kingdom but the unitarist account of *English* history, as in Tomany's (1999) work on the distinctiveness of political history and constitutional practice in the north of England. This historiography in turn makes it easier to accommodate Scottish and Welsh devolution, the Anglo-Irish Agreement and the Good Friday accords, and, in the peripheral nations if not yet in England, European integration. A post-nationalist historiography (Richard Kearney 1998) is thus a central element of a political order which, if not post-nationalist, is post-sovereigntist.

Spain

In Spain, too, history has become a potent weapon in modern political debate.[4] Like the United Kingdom, Spain is a multinational state forged over centuries but without either expanding into the whole of its potential geographical space (in its case the Iberian peninsula) or assimilating its component nationalities into a single identity. Like the United Kingdom, it has a dominant state historiography challenged by competing historiographies in the periphery, which themselves have been more vocal at times of national tension, such as the late nineteenth century or the period since the 1970s. The dominant historiography is based on the expansion of Castile, seen as the heart of Spain, and a teleological vision of the country attaining its natural destiny in union. The long struggles against the Moors are celebrated as the Reconquista, and the union of the kingdoms of Castile and Aragon and the later incorporation of Navarre are presented as national victories. Like the United Kingdom, united Spain remained for centuries a complex and pluralistic order, with no obvious division between the metropolis and the empire (Artola 1999*a*), but state historians saw this as symptomatic of incomplete national unity and evidence of a national malaise. They looked with admiration on France and, curiously, the United Kingdom, which, confusing it with England, they saw as a unitary national state. National historiography attributes absolute sovereignty at an early stage to the monarchical state, and insists that the traditional privileges and *fueros* of the provinces and towns of Castile and those of the Basque territories were merely gifts from the monarchy and not original rights. Castile is presented as the backbone of Spain and unification as a process of incorporation into an essentially Castilian state and law. As in the United Kingdom, this is accompanied by a contempt for cultural outliers, like unassimilated Basques (roughly equivalent to the Highlanders or Irish), and a grudging respect but resentment towards the Catalans (equivalent to the Scots). The unification of Spain is presented as the source of all its greatness and achievements, and particularism as the sign of failure (Ortega y Gasset 1975).

Yet while the dominant British historiography was inspired by a liberal teleology, Castilian-centred history has two distinct traditions, a conservative and a liberal one. For conservatives, Spain is essentially Catholic and traditional, committed to an imperial role in the world and pure in blood and spirit. All bad ideas, including liberalism, atheism, and (once it was discredited) the Counter-Reformation, came from outside and violated the true Castilian spirit. Developed over centuries, this historiography underlay such ideology as the Franco regime possessed.

---

[4] A proposal in 1998 to reform the teaching of humanities in schools to emphasize common Spanish experience sparked a fierce dispute, and the plan was withdrawn following objections from the Catalan nationalists, on whom the government depended for support. In 2000 the conservative government, re-elected with a majority, proposed to reintroduce it.

The liberal Castilian historiography is weaker than its English counter-part, although influenced in the nineteenth century by the British Whigs themselves. It sees absolutism as an alien importation from France which, under both Habsburg and Bourbon rulers, destroyed the municipal liberties of old Castile, but approves of Philip II's foreign policy for defending the nation against outsiders (Fox 1997). El Cid, used by the right as a monar-chical hero, is turned by the liberals into a popular folk hero and defender of the people's rights. It is not anti-Catholic since, unlike their counterparts in France and Italy, Castilian liberals (as opposed to the left) were not generally anticlerical, but it is critical of ultramontane Catholicism and of the Counter-Reformation and Inquisition as products of it. The incorporation of the peripheral territories of the Crown of Aragon (including Catalonia) and the Basque provinces into a unified state is presented as unequivocally good since it permitted the creation of a national market and stimulated capitalist development. Their traditional privileges and *fueros* are dismissed as mere props for dominant local power-brokers, notably landowners, and their abolition is seen as a step towards equal citizenship and democracy as well as freer trade and industry. This liberal version of a Castililanized history was propagated by the Institución Libre de Enseñanza founded in 1876 (Vicens Vives 1970; Fox 1997). For Antonio Cánovas, historian and politician, the old regime had given Castile too little local autonomy and Aragon and Catalonia too much, preventing the emergence of a unified liberal state (Fox 1997). The 'war of independence' against Napoleon is presented as a seminal moment in the construction of the political nation and the constitution of Cadiz as the basis for a legitimate national authority recognizing no internal divisions (Parada 1996). Linguistic unity through Castilian is equally seen as a sign of progress and another step on the way to true national citizenship. De Blas (1989, 1991) traces a liberal Spanish nationalist tradition to the nineteenth century, linked to modernization, democracy, and progress, contrasting it with peripheral nationalisms which often had their origins in conservatism and the defence of the *ancien régime*.

Spain indeed had its equivalent of the Jacobitism of the British Isles, in Carlism,[5] a movement in favour of a rival branch of the royal family.[6] With their slogan 'God and the Old Law' (or *fueros*) Carlists were religiously Catholic, conservative, and traditionalist, and gained their main support in Catalonia and the Basque Country, whose traditional privileges they claimed to uphold—indeed they were among the precursors of Basque nationalism. This helps the Spanish liberal national historiography to link reaction with

---

[5] Both Jacobites and Carlists were inclined to the somewhat contradictory positions of absolute monarchy and respect for traditional territorial rights.

[6] It originated in 1833 when Don Carlos, brother of the late king, claimed the throne against the king's daughter, claiming that a woman could not inherit. There were two Carlist wars in the 19th century. The Carlists threw their lot in with Franco in 1936 but by the 1980s were a minor element on the extreme left.

support for peripheral rights. While the conservative history underpinned the political right up to Franco, this liberal version was a guide to the *regeneracionistas*, the generation of reformers who sought to build a modern and liberal Spain after the defeat and final loss of empire in 1898. The outbreak of Basque and Calatan nationalism at the turn of the century was for some an affront to an already formed Spanish nation (Nuñez Seixas 1993). For others, like Ortega y Gasset (1975), it represented the failure of Castile's historic mission to build the Spanish nation. For De Blas (1989), the appropriation of Spanish nationalism by Franco, on the one hand, and the undermining of it by the peripheral movements, on the other, brought unmerited discredit on the liberal nationalist project and its potential.

There is again no single counter-history but competing histories among the peripheral nationalities and within them. Catalan writers have long stressed the peculiar constitution of the Crown of Aragon and of Catalonia within it, based on divided sovereignty, pactism, and constitutionalism (Moreno and Martí 1977; Giner *et al.* 1996; Lobo 1997; Albareda and Gifre 1999). Most Catalan historians have argued that medieval Catalonia, while not a complete state, did have a constitution going beyond a collection of mediaeval rights. This has been summed up as a state of incomplete sovereignty, but a state nonetheless (Sales 1989). Some have pointed to the lack of Arabization during the Moorish occupation of Spain, and to the weakness of the Counter-Reformation, Catalan Catholicism being distinct and more tolerant. Emphasis is placed on Catalonia's European vocation, as the border of the Carolingian empire (the *Marca Hispanica*) and a land of passage between the continent and Spain. The implication is that it has been more open to progressive European social, political, and economic ideas than has landlocked Castile. Unification under Ferdinand and Isabella did not, in this account, mean incorporation but voluntary union with each part of the kingdom retaining its sovereign rights. Some would even credit the Habsburg monarchs with respecting those rights and attribute Catalonia's woes to the Bourbon victory in the War of the Spanish Succession, which led directly to the suppression of Catalonia's self-governing institutions in 1714. Others see the Habsburgs in a less benevolent light and recognize their efforts to assimilate Catalonia in the seventeenth century and even before (Soldevila 1995).

At the same time, Catalonia is seen as part of the wider Spanish or Iberian community, participating fully in its development except when shut out by Castilian centralism. Vicens Vives (1970: 54), looking back to the earliest Spanish kingdoms, regrets the failure of the Catalan vision to triumph, 'The cancellation of the imperial phantasm, the birth of a viable Spain forged with a Portuguese, Castilian, and Catalan–Aragonese trident—such were the unquestionable merits of Ramón Berenguer.[7] He propounded a pluralism

---

[7] Count of Barcelona and prince of Aragon, founder of the Aragonese–Catalan confederation.

that never excluded an awareness of unity of purpose in Hispanic affairs'.[8] Prat de la Riba (1998), one of the founders of modern Catalan nationalism, similarly laid stress on the pactist tradition. This pluralistic conception of Spain and vision of divided authority has informed Catalan nationalists to this day, giving rise to a debate on the multiple meanings of, and paths to, sovereignty (Puig 1998). Catalan historiography also presents Catalans as inherently more commercial, hard-working, and entrepreneurial, portraying the typical Castilian as Don Quixote. This self-stereotype is perpetuated into the nineteenth and twentieth centuries and underpins Catalan visions of its place in Spain and Europe.

Serious Catalan historians recognize that there is a strong element of mythology in all of this, since the Catalan revivalists of the nineteenth century often resorted to an idealized and nostalgic vision of the past (Riquer 2000; Pallach 2000). Yet, while avoiding essentialist or primordialist accounts of Catalan virtue, they have sought to show that the persistence of pre-modern ideas of pactism and difference was not a sign of retarded development but the basis for an authentic political tradition. The result is a more pluralistic vision of Spanish history, a rejection of the Castilian teleology and a challenge to essentialistic views of Spanish nationhood, although often marred by an insistence that Spain was the only state in Europe to experience this trajectory.[9]

Basque history is more contentious and internally divided. One tradition sees the Basques as the original Spaniards, the most Spanish of the Spanish, drawing on their long presence in the territory and their prominent role in Spanish military, religious, political, and economic affairs (Monreal 1985). Another tradition, which overlaps with this, is provincialist, stressing the ancient rights of the 'historic territories' of Vizcaya, Guipúzcoa, and Alava, enshrined in their *fueros*, and of the kingdom of Navarre. Conservative in politics and deeply Catholic, this tradition fed into Carlism in the nineteenth century, with its slogan of God and the Old Law. This made an easy target for liberals, who could now equate defence of the old territorial pluralism with reaction and obscurantism. Basque nationalism itself was a product of the modern era, distilled by Sabino Arana from Carlism and the old folk tales, fortified by the sense of ethnic identity and continuity (Garmendia 1985). Given the lack of a literature in Basque (in contrast to Catalonia) much of the tradition was based on oral legend, and this was especially susceptible to manipulation by nineteenth-century romantics, either to support or discredit Basque claims. Anti-nationalists like Jauristi (1998) have attacked Basque historic rights discourse as little more than a farrago of folk

[8] Vives' book restores Catalonia to a prominent place in Spanish history but is silent on the Basques. He also consistently uses the term 'England' for post-Union Britain.

[9] Riqueri Permanyer (2000), for example, attack the dominance of the French model of nation-building among historians, but seem to accept it as valid for other countries, insisting that Spain was the only west European state that in the 20th century emerged as plurinational.

tales, many of them invented or borrowed from the history of other peoples. What is certain is that Sabino Arana himself took great liberties with history, to convert a tradition of foral rights into a history of sovereign independence, first for Vizcaya, then for the Basque territories as a whole. According to this account, the Basque provinces had been sovereign states whose ruler merely happened to be the king of Castile and then Spain (PNV 1995). This stands at the opposite pole from Castilian centralists, for whom the *fueros* were privileges granted by the sovereign Crown, but both doctrines share the nineteenth-century belief in a single national sovereignty. Consequently, Basque nationalism has had a much stronger separatist tendency than has its Catalan counterpart although moderate nationalists emphasize the tradition of shared sovereignty and pactism that can adapt to changing circumstances. The Basque Nationalist Party (PNV) refused to support the Spanish constitution of 1978 since the restored autonomy and fiscal privileges of the Basque provinces were presented as the product of the constitution and not the other way round. With the PNV recommending abstention, the constitution thus failed to gain the endorsement of a majority of Basques in the referendum, leaving a lasting legacy of bitterness and a problem of legitimacy.

For Arana, Basque sovereignty was equally rooted in racial differentiation and superiority and the fundamental incompatibility between the Spanish (in which he included the Catalans and the Galegos) and Basque personalities. Purity of race and cleanliness of blood (*limpieza de sangre*), ideas used widely in Castile against the Moors and Jews, were refined in Basque terms and used against all other Iberian peoples. A doctrine of universal nobility rooted in Basque custom and tradition also served as a badge of racial superiority. Modern Basque nationalism is altogether more liberal and has a strong progressive element. Doctrines of racial purity have been abandoned, and while Sabino Arana is still revered as the founder of the PNV, his racism and extremism are the source of some embarrassment.[10] There is also an effort to distance themselves from Carlism by arguing that the Carlists were really centralists who cynically used the foral argument to gain support in the Basque Country but, when the Civil War came, showed where their true loyalties lay by backing the Spanish absolutism of Franco (Sorauren 1998). Lacking the racial or ethnically exclusive arguments, modern Basque nationalists rely more heavily on institutional traditions and historic rights as embodied in territory. They discern elements of primitive democracy in the old Basque society. Universal nobility is less about Basques being superior to Spaniards and more about them being equal among themselves. The *fueros* are interpreted not as gifts of the Spanish state but as original rights, not as sources of privilege within Basque society but as a form of limited

---

[10] The fact that Arana died young after apparently recanting his more extreme anti-Spanish sentiments helps.

government and contractualism. To condemn them as not yet democratic is anachronism equivalent to attacking the English Magna Carta for not providing universal suffrage since they could have evolved into modern democracy, just as the early English Parliament did (Sorauren 1998).[11] Lorenzo (1995) argues that, while the abolition of the *fueros* allowed a capitalist take-off, the immediate beneficiaries were the bourgeoisie, and the losers were the common people. The foral regime, he admits, protected not only Basque sovereignty but the rule of the oligarchy within it, but the former could have been preserved while undermining the latter through foral modernization and democratization.

A problem facing all modern Basque nationalists is that of the unity of their country and whether to base their claims on the rights of a Basque people or of the seven historic territories (three of which are in France). Arana himself moved from provincialism to pan-Basque nationalism, and the unity of the people is a theme in all nationalist doctrine, yet the autonomous Basque government functions as a federation of three provinces (or historic territories) and it is the provincial *diputaciones* who, in view of their historic rights, have the key revenue-raising powers. Alava has been the least nationalist of the three provinces in the Basque autonomous community and tends to a provincialism hostile to pan-Basque ideology, represented in the 1980s and 1990s by the conservative Unidad Alavesa. Even more vexed is the issue of Navarre. Until 1838 Navarre had the legal status of a separate kingdom although it had been conquered by Castile and not incorporated by pact. It lost most of its rights in 1841 and 1876, but it kept its own fiscal regime and, unlike those of Vizcaya and Guipuzcoa, this even survived under Francoism, thanks to the support of Navarrese Carlists for the cause. So there is a strong argument from continuous historic rights for Navarrese autonomy. Culturally and linguistically Navarre is partly Basque, which has led Basque nationalists to call for its incorporation into the Basque autonomous community. Some Basque nationalists try to reconcile these principles by arguing that Navarre was historically a Basque kingdom extending to the other Basque provinces and beyond and its practices rooted in a form of early constitutionalism (Lasagabaster 1999; Sorauren 1998). Other scholars observe quite logically that, if the three provinces of the present autonomous community preserve historic rights, then there is nothing to stop them federating and exercising them together or to stop Navarre joining them (PNV 1995; Herrero de Miñon 1998*a*).

More recently Basque nationalists have been seeking in the doctrine of historic rights a justification for divided sovereignty and contractual order within a wider European order. New historiographical work is under way that would eventually allow the Basques to adopt a world-view based on the post-sovereigntist discourse of the Catalans. The divisions of the society and

---

[11] Sorauren, too, confuses England with the United Kingdom.

the competing visions of Basqueness, however, make this a formidable challenge.

The historians' wars in Spain have been particularly bitter, without much middle ground. Recently, however, Javier Tusell (1999) has outlined a possible Spanish history based on pluralism and the notion of the state as a 'nation of nations'. This moderate position corresponds rather closely to that of the new British Isles historians, but the venture has a long way to go.[12]

Canada

While Canada is a much younger society than the United Kingdom or Spain, it too has competing historiographies, which are at the centre of contemporary political debate, notably over the place of Quebec and the native peoples in the constitutional order. Canada does not have as clear a founding moment as the United States, nor a developed doctrine of popular national sovereignty. It does, however, have a nationalist historiography, serving the cause of nation-building since the last century. This presents Canada as a liberal nation with a British constitutional tradition, demarcated from the individualist society of the United States. French Canadians are presented as a part of this society that has been treated liberally for the most part, with the lapses from tolerance (such as the refusal to implement bilingualism in Manitoba) as deplorable exceptions. Quebec nationalism is portrayed as intolerant, ethnically exclusive, divisive, and disruptive but is generally downplayed or treated as an occasional lapse or even a recent invention. Nineteenth-century Quebec, in this view, was rather a quiescent society dominated by a reactionary Catholic Church, based on pre-revolutionary France; the main concern of the French Canadians was survival as a linguistic group, and neither then nor now have they been motivated by political nationalism (Cook 1995). This view has been challenged in recent years by a revisionist history that takes issue with the nationalist teleology of the Canadian vision and emphasizes the pluralist nature of the society, with its multiple social cleavages. Such a perspective is in tune with postmodernist deconstructionism and with the multicultural policies and demands that have emerged since the 1970s and, like them, does not recognize a special place for either Canadian or Québécois national narratives.

Countering both of these is a Québécois historiography, itself divided into distinct schools. Most share the vision of Quebec as a distinct national society and of the Conquest of 1759 as a defining moment (Bouchard

---

[12] It is also disappointing that Tusell insists that Spain is the only country in Europe with this problem and, like so many of his compatriots, does not appear to understand the difference between Britain and England. At one point he rejects the comparison because Ireland was never 'part of England'. The point, of course, is that Ireland (like Scotland) was part of the United Kingdom, and it is the *United Kingdom*, not England, that is the functional equivalent of *Spain*.

1999). One is more nationalist and separatist in inspiration, denying that Quebec ever was part of a wider Canadian political society (an example is Ferretti and Miron 1992). Sometimes this is linked to a form of victimology, in which the legitimization of Quebec's demands is provided by a list of historical grievances, summed up in the slogan 'Je me souviens' on Quebec vehicle licence plates (Létourneau 2000*b*). The tradition of *survivance* depicts the Quebec people as reduced to a struggle for survival, enclosed within their own world and social institutions (Bouchard 2000; Cantin 2000). Sometimes this is accompanied by a 'collective melancholy' in which the Quebec people are seen as traumatized by the conquest, trapped in an inferiority complex from which they can only be rescued through independence and a new founding moment (McClure 2000). Gérard Bouchard (1999) has placed Quebec's history in comparison with that of other 'new collectivities' derived from European colonization, seeking to avoid the exceptionalism of other accounts. Yet even he operates within a nationalist framework in which Quebec's failure to become a full sovereign state is an anomaly to be explained.

The other version of history is rooted in the vision of 'two founding nations' (or, as was sometimes said, 'races') both of which form essential parts of the Canadian fabric. As Laforest (1995: 7) puts it, 'Historians, politicians and intellectuals in Quebec are just about unanimous in believing that two founding peoples, two nations, two distinct societies, two majorities, gave birth to Canada in 1867. This belief is deeply anchored in the Québécois people'.[13] Létourneau (2000*a*) criticizes both the postmodernist pluralist history of Canada and the nationalist teleologies, insisting that there are structuring features of the Canadian experience, one of which is the existence of two peoples and their efforts to find an accommodation. Like Laforest (1995) he sees this tradition as indicating the need and the potential for the two societies to live together. Such accounts are the basis of the compact, or 'two nations', theory of the Canadian federation. Kenneth McNaught (1988), from a Canadian nationalist perspective, dismisses the doctrine as a modern invention, unwarranted from a study of the debates of the 1860s. Quebec intellectuals tend to insist that, whatever the details of these debates, confederation has always been treated as a pact (Erk and Gagnon 2000; Dumont 1997). There is in fact abundant evidence of the two nations theory from the days of the conquest, although it seems to have been formulated as a constitutional doctrine in the 1880s as a response to Quebec's problems within confederation (McRoberts 1997; Romney 1999*a*). Romney (1999*b*) goes further than most in arguing that not only the French Canadians but also the Anglophones of Upper Canada (Ontario) sought a decentralized confederation in which the constituent provinces would retain elements of

---

[13] Radical separatists Ferretti and Miron (1992: 17) denounce the 'pernicious sophistry of two founding peoples with equal rights in a federal state composed of two equal nations'.

their original sovereignty, in spite of the pressures from John A. Macdonald and a few others to build a centralized state. Certainly by the late nineteenth century leaders of the Anglophone provinces were also speaking of confederation as a pact, but between equal provinces of which Quebec was just one, creating a difference of opinion that has bedevilled accommodation ever since. This was not in itself incompatible with the two nations theory as long as the province of Quebec was seen as the guardian of the French tradition, but by the 1980s the equality of the provinces doctrine was being used to deny the specificity of Quebec. Romney (1999*a*) argues that the rise of Canadian nationalism and the interventionist state from the 1930s produced a historical amnesia which led English Canadians to neglect both versions of the compact theory.

There are also conservative and progressive versions of the Quebec narrative, with the latter increasingly in the ascendant. The conservative vision, associated with the abbé Groulx and Catholic particularism, sees Quebec as a bastion against the evils of modern society, including liberalism and socialism. As expressed in the Tremblay Report of the 1950s, 'the French Canadians are almost all of the Catholic faith... The French Canadians are of French origin and culture... the French Canadians are the only group whose religious and cultural particularism almost exactly coincide. Only French Canada, as a homogeneous group, presents the double differentiating factor of religion and culture' (Tremblay Commission 1973: 6). The Conservative regime of Maurice Duplessis between the 1930s and the 1950s fostered this isolationist and conservative vision, providing objective allies to those in English Canada who saw Quebec nationalism as inherently anti-modern and reactionary. The Quiet Revolution, the programme of social and political reform that succeeded Duplessisme, did not challenge this view of the past in all respects, since the new intellectuals were intent on discrediting the old Quebec institutions to legitimize their new policy prospectus. They did, however, rediscover liberal traditions in Quebec political culture and a genuinely Québécois progressivism which had been frustrated by political oppression; key historical markers are the rebellion of 1837 and Papineau's fight for responsible self-government in the name of Canadiens (Bernier and Salée 2001). The liberal tradition is also more pan-American, seeing Quebec as part of a wider continental society and free of anti-Americanism. This in turn plays into contemporary support for free trade as a way of weakening the Canadian frame and presenting an outward-looking and cosmopolitan vision of the nation. More recently the myth of the Quiet Revolution itself has been questioned as Quebec is presented as a normal political society which has evolved in its own way to modernity. Recent work has even sought to show that the Duplessis era was not the Grande Noirceur of legend but in many ways an evolving liberal society (Gagnon and Sara-Bournet 1997; Beauchemin 1997). Quebec in this account does not suffer from an ingrained ethnic virtue (for the conservatives) or pathology (for the liberals) but must be seen as a complex society in its own right, with all the internal conflicts and ambiguities in dealing with Canada that this implies. For Létourneau (2000*b*) this ambiguity is the essence of the Canada–Quebec relationship, which can never be resolved once and for all on nationalist terms, whether Canadian or Québécois, and provides the historical basis for Quebeckers' apparent ambivalence on federalism and sovereignty.

Some of the fiercest disputes, however, centre on a recent piece of history, the patriation of the Canadian constitution in 1982 by Pierre Trudeau's government, without the consent of the Quebec National Assembly or people. Canadian nationalists note that Trudeau consistently won election victories in Quebec and that opinion polls at the time showed that most Québécois supported patriation. According to Ramsay Cook (1995) this would have been the end of the matter had not Brian Mulroney foolishly reopened the constitutional dossier by negotiating the Meech Lake Accord and seeking the recognition of Quebec as a 'distinct society' within Canada. Québécois scholars see matters very differently. 1982 was not only a betrayal of Quebec but a repudiation of the very principle upon which the Canadian federation rested, that of the union of two peoples, who both needed to consent to anything as momentous as a new constitution. This interpretation was sustained by the Supreme Court, which ruled that, while legally patriation was constitutional, it did break with the historical conventions that had governed Canadian practice hitherto. McRoberts (1997) agrees, arguing that the Trudeau approach fundamentally misconceived the nature of Canada as a historical political society, while Romney (1999*b*) and LaSelva (1996) see the court decision not to enshrine Quebec consent as a *legal* principle as fundamentally wrong.

The historiography of the aboriginal peoples of Canada has been particularly contentious (Cairns 2000). Partly this arises because the oral tradition and histories in indigenous culture, which link the past with the present, can easily be dismissed by Europeans as another instance of 'invention of tradition' or fabrication, missing the point of these stories in the construction and renewal of communities.[14] Written histories, on the other hand, tended to be the property of Europeans and strongly influenced by the assimilationist strategy which was the centrepiece of policy towards native peoples for a hundred years after Confederation.[15] Assimilationism was underpinned by

[14] The Royal Commission on Aboriginal Peoples (Canada 1996) perhaps missed the point here in drawing a sharp distinction between oral aboriginal history and scientific Western history as though these were two competing paradigms. Native oral histories can have a role in community-building quite independent of the quest for scientific truth. On the other hand, there is a serious and scientific history of the native peoples which does not depend on the prejudices of European colonizers. Perhaps the parallel is between Western religion, which is generally considered now to be compatible with science, since the two are not trying to explain the same things.

[15] This is not the only difficulty. Historical controversies in North America are also bedevilled by the issue of who 'owns' whose history and the frequent assertion that the only people qualified

a teleology which saw native cultures and customs as inherently inferior or underdeveloped, so that the way to progress was their extinction and the absorption of the indigenous peoples into European society. Native political arrangements were primitive or non-existent, preventing them from assuming responsibility for their own affairs or sharing in a universal history on their own terms. Such history has been increasingly challenged by counter-histories that focus on the pre-colonial independence of the aboriginal peoples and their indigenous forms of self-government, thus raising them to the status of nationhood, with equal political standing to the Europeans.

So important is this issue of historiography that the Royal Commission on Aboriginal Peoples (Canada 1996) devoted a lengthy first volume of its report (entitled *The Ghosts of History*) to it. As usual, some of the counter-history is romanticized to portray an age of innocence destroyed by incorporation into an alien state, but there is also a serious attempt at recovery of a past which has been distorted by colonial perspectives. As in many of the European peripheral histories, the principle of pactism and negotiation is given greater weight than the concept of unitary state sovereignty and even presented as a precursor of federalism (Hawkes 1999). Indeed the intricate practices of the Iroquois confederacy has been recognized as an important source of inspiration for the constitution of the United States. There is an emphasis on the role of negotiation and treaties on a nation-to-nation basis in the early history of contact with the Europeans, and on the importance of the Royal Proclamation of 1763 in which the British Crown recognized the rights of the indigenous peoples. Only later, when the Europeans' interest shifted from fur-trading to land colonization, did they seek to dominate and subordinate the native peoples; the implication is that the tradition of mutual respect and independence can be recuperated. The respect, in an oral tradition, for verbal agreements and understandings is contrasted with Europeans' insistence on narrow literal meanings of written treaties; and of course the frequent breaking even of the letter of treaties is recorded. As in Quebec, these revisions of history produce a new conception of the issue. It is no longer just a question of devolving powers to aboriginal communities, but of recognition of original right—the terminology of nationhood is an essential part of this. Hence the native demands to be a subject of self-determination and to participate in negotiating their own future. On the other hand, since the Western concept of sovereignty has no place in aboriginal traditions, it does not underpin a demand for a nation-state on European lines (Turner 2001), although some aboriginal politicians are more separatist than others.

These problems, rather than arguments over the distribution of competences, remain at the heart of the Canadian constitutional debate. Many people in Quebec and among the native populations have invoked their own

to write a history are those sharing the ascriptive characteristics of those involved, including ethnicity and gender.

past in defence of limited sovereignty, contractualism, and divided authority. Canadian nationalists, perhaps because of the threat to Canadian sovereignty from globalization and North American integration, have responded with a very traditional discourse. This has bedevilled efforts to find an accommodation based on recognition of original rights and plural national identities (see Chapter 4).

Belgium

The case of Belgium is particularly interesting, since before the Napoleonic era this territory had not been incorporated into a nation-state and retained the diffused sovereignty and complex political order of the old imperial system. Under Burgundian, Spanish, and then Austrian suzerainty it retained traditional rights of autonomy, although the northern provinces broke away in the seventeenth century to form a nation-state. The ancient Joyous Entry ceremony confirmed both the provinces' loyalty to the sovereign and their own privileges and rights. Wils (1996a, b) notes that at the end of the nineteenth century the future Belgium was a true *ancien régime*, having largely fended off the modernizing initiatives of the enlightened Austrian despotism. Yet both progressives and traditionalists were prepared to defend these rights against the enlightened despotism of the Austrians (Deprez and Vos 1998) and during the protests of the late eighteenth century developed the idea that these were full national constitutions (Roegiers 1998) just as Basque nationalists were to do a century later.

Belgium was created by an internal event, the Revolution of 1830, and an external one, the support of the Great Powers, and both factors have featured in its historiography. While some have viewed it as little more than a buffer created by the Great Powers to keep the French and the Germans apart, Wils (1996a, b) sees a form of unity among the pre-state entities, and it does appear that the Revolution of 1830 was supported in both language groups so that Belgian identity was not the pure fabrication of official propagandists (Stengers 1995). Belgian official national identity after 1830 was rooted in myths of ethnic continuity back to Roman times, and, while historians might not have taken them seriously, they were not challenged in political debate until the rise of the Flemish movement. Henri Pirenne (1929), the most distinguished of the Belgian nationalist historians, recognized that Belgium was a compound of peoples but followed a teleological line in tracing its realization from Roman times. Other observers go to the other extreme, recognizing that Belgium is plurinational in composition but seeing it as the meeting point of the two neighbouring state cultures, rather than a historical mélange in its own right (Lynch 1996; Kymlicka 1995).[16]

[16] Lynch (1996: 107) describes Belgium as 'an amalgamation of fragments from two different countries'. Kymlicka (1995: 15) sees Belgium as 'a federation . . . of two European cultures',

The territories of Belgium do have their own complex history, but the influence of the French Revolution and Napoleonic domination, including a period of annexation by France, had served to destroy the old provincial and urban traditions so thoroughly that they did not feature in the new Belgian state, which was resolutely unitary. So while there was some occasional Flemish nostalgia for the old Burgundian regime, this past was based on provincial and municipal autonomy and so has not been available to the emerging Flemish and Walloon nationalist movements of the twentieth century. Flemish identity, as far as it existed, underpinned this Belgian nationality (Wils 1992, 1996a) which was further reinforced by memories of the Peasants' Revolt of 1798, presented first as a conservative reaction against the secularizing French Revolution, and then by liberals as a nationalist rising against France itself (Raxhon 1998). So for a long time the Flemish could see themselves as the true Belgians, much as the Québécois of the early nineteenth century could saw themselves as the real Canadiens. There were, from an early stage, complaints about Francophone dominance in the state, but only later did the concepts of Belgium and Flanders themselves come into conflict.

As the Flemish movement developed in the nineteenth and twentieth centuries, it developed its own myths, but the movement was rooted in linguistic solidarity and economic concerns and largely failed to develop a historic rights doctrine. It did, on the other hand, construct its own myths and historical revisions (Morelli 1995). The Battle of the Golden Spurs (1302) was reinterpreted as a saga of Flemish resistance to Francophone dominance, where previously it had represented the triumph of a precocious 'Belgian' resistance to the claims of the king of France. A myth of a prosperous, industrious Flanders is also counterposed to an image of Wallonia as poor, declining, and dependent, linking the medieval era to the present but passing quickly over Wallonia's era of industrial splendour during the nineteenth and early twentieth centuries. For their part, Walloon leaders, in the absence of a Walloon institutional history, have focused on the existence of the linguistic group or the links to France (Kesteloot 1993).

So despite a history of divided and diffused authority that might equip Belgium for the post-sovereign era, historic claims about legal and constitutional rights are almost entirely lacking to the Flemish and Walloon movements. Perhaps the strongest claim that can be made is that history has left to Belgium a relatively weak sense of national identity and that, unlike in France, elites failed to build a unified and culturally prestigious nation-state, so that the transition to a post-sovereign political order in Europe has been less painful as a result.

although all the survey evidence shows a considerable commonality of values across the two communities of Belgium, distinguishing them both from the Netherlands and from France (Chauvel 1995).

The Usable Past

It is a commonplace that getting history wrong is a requirement of all nationalist movements (Renan 1992). Historical inventions and accounts of continuity feature widely, even among such unlikely candidates as Padania (Oneto 1997). The aim of this chapter is not to argue for a knowable 'right' history to put against this, nor to debunk ethno-histories or draw attention to the manifold falsifications perpetrated by state historians and their adversaries. It has been to show, rather, that most claims to sovereign authority are rooted in historical accounts and that the unified nation-state is just one contender. It has also shown that the statist accounts are not the only ones with universalist, liberal, and democratic credentials. In fact the counterclaims about original sovereignty, whether rooted in medieval or nineteenth-century inventions, are less interesting than the history of divided sovereignty, plurinationality, and accommodation. It may be true that stateless nations have developed doctrines of limited sovereignty because they never had the force to assert more complete sovereignty; this does not detract from the validity of those doctrines (Battle 1988). We cannot simply read off from history a set of principles for managing multinational states since we could not simply return to the past, even if we knew for certain what it had been. Revisionists and counter-revisionists will argue for ever about whether people in the past really understood their constitutional practice in the way we understand it. Herro de Miñón (1997, 1998*a*) sums up the argument by saying that historic rights are perhaps less a matter of *having* than of *being*, that is they help define the subject of claims to self-determination. Nieto (1999) similarly argues that historic rights are less useful as literal codes to what can be permitted than as a general permission to be different. Historic rights discourse is, furthermore, only one basis for political authority, which does not have to trump elementary liberal-democratic principles or the rights of others. It does not therefore justify ethnic groups seeking to reconquer territories long lost to other peoples, as certain historic claims do (Moore 1998). Historic rights ideas can help question the idea of unified state sovereignty in the search for other principles and discourses equally rooted in custom and practice, but this does not mean that the solution will be to hand or that accommodation will become painless. Indeed, now that both sides are seeking the same moral ground in liberal-democratic norms and universal histories, the controversies might only become greater; this is another instance of de Tocqueville's paradox, referred to earlier.

Historic arguments are more easily made in some cases than in others, since some stateless nations have more of a usable past and some accounts have a firmer basis in practice. Catalan pactism, pragmatism, and divided sovereignty, while only part of the complex history of that country, fit the emerging European order quite well. A return to the pre-1714 status as a self-governing community within complex layers of overlapping authority appears more like hard-headed realism than impractical utopia. So does Scotland's tradition of popular but limited sovereignty, although Scotland was a nation-state, if a weak one, before 1707, and the official policy of the Scottish National Party favours a Europe of the states. Basque society can also invoke a practice of limited and conditional sovereignty, although the meaning and authenticity of this are more contested than in the Catalan case. The Belgian cases are more difficult given the even greater lack of correspondence between historic units and present claims, but Belgium is perhaps a trendsetter in its linking of national disintegration with European integration. There is a story to be told about Europe itself, an enterprise just begun to save it too from national historiography (Bartlett 1993; Norman Davies 1997). An old saw holds that, while Europe has too much history, Canada suffers from an excess of geography. Yet, for all its youth, Canada does sustain competing historiographies. These might form the basis for an accommodation in mutual respect of the three cultural groups, but at present the trend seems to be towards a reaffirmation of the traditional state-building strategy rather than an embrace of the old and new ideas.

3

What do the Nations Want? Nationalist Aspirations and Transnational Integration

Nationality and the Transnational Order

Nationality, then, does not necessarily entail statehood and there are alternative traditions of thinking about self-determination and autonomy. Contemporary trends to globalization and transnational integration have given new life to these traditions, neglected in the heyday of the sovereign nation-state. The connection between globalization and territorial restructuring within states is the subject of a large literature (Allen Scott 1998; Keating 1998*a*), as are the opportunities which this presents for stateless nations (Martin 1996, 1997; Lange 2000; McGarry and Keating and McGarry 2001). Transnational free trade areas or regimes such as the North American Free Trade Agreement (NAFTA), the European Union (EU), the North Atlantic Treaty Organization (NATO), or the Council of Europe are particularly rich in such opportunities, as we will see later (Chapter 5). It is not surprising, then, that stateless national movements should have rethought their aims and strategy in the light of these developments, often drawing on older traditions in the process. Nearly all stateless national movements in our four states have embraced free trade and transnational integration, but they have drawn different conclusions regarding the implications. There are, broadly, three positions. Firstly, there are those who believe that their respective transnational regimes permit sovereign independence at a lower cost than in the past. Market access is assured, there are guarantees against unilateral trade sanctions, thus protecting smaller states, and a series of costly and dangerous issues, including defence and security and even the currency, will be externalized. There is, within this group, a division of opinion on how far transnational integration can go without fatally damaging their own prime objective of self-determination and autonomy. Some insist that transnational regimes should remain strictly intergovernmental, while others are prepared to accept drastic limitations on sovereign authority. A second strand of opinion is less overtly separatist and holds that some continuing link with the original state will be necessary in order to manage interdependencies and minimize risks. This 'sovereignty-association' position is more likely where the transnational regime does not provide the full range of external solutions to the problems posed by independence, hence its greater attraction to nationalists in Quebec than in the European cases. The third position is the radical 'post-sovereigntist' one adopted by those who have embraced globalization and transnational integration to the point of believing that sovereignty in the classic sense has little meaning any more. They are more concerned with maximizing the degree of autonomy and influence open to the nation than with the trappings of sovereignty, and are usually ambivalent as to their ultimate aims, preferring to see how the world evolves before they commit themselves.

Along with the acceptance of transnational integration and the limitations to sovereignty, there has been a move among most of the movements to a more inclusive definition of the nation and a conscious adoption of a 'civic' nationalism (Keating 2001*a*). Such a de-ethnicization has enabled nationalists to extend their appeal as well as burnishing their liberal credentials. It is also connected to the move away from classical separatism and towards plurinational accommodation, since the evidence shows that the ethnic core of nationalists are most inclined to separatism, while less radical forms of national affirmation can gain the assent or active support of broader strata of society (Keating 2001*a*). These ideological transitions have not always been easy and in some cases have proved conflictual and painful. They have struck different responses among their target voters, who themselves often show preferences that cannot be contained within the conventional categories of statehood.

The United Kingdom

Stateless nationalism in the United Kingdom has taken different forms in each of the constituent parts of the state, reflecting historic traditions and modern circumstances. It has proved most conflictual in Ireland, least powerful in Wales. Separatists have vied with home rulers wishing to recast the state as a plurinational federation. By the late twentieth century European integration provided a new framework for the debates and there were signs of a new, post-sovereigntist discourse among the political parties, with some echoes in the electorate at large.

From the late nineteenth century, when the issue of Scottish home rule was placed on the agenda, it was in the context of a putative United Kingdom or imperial federation. In the early twentieth century the self-governing dominions provided the model. Only from the 1930s, with the establishment of the Scottish National Party (SNP) (1928) and the Statute of Westminster (1931) was the idea of a separate Scottish state brought into the centre of political debate, and even then there was some ambiguity about whether this would

remain part of a functioning empire (Finlay 1992). After the Second World
War the party clarified its preference for outright independence, although
there was always a moderate element willing to settle for a large degree of
home rule and to cooperate in all-party ventures to gain it (Mitchell 1996). In
the 1950s there was a generalized support for European integration as a
framework for a self-governing Scotland, but, as British membership in the
European Economic Community (EEC) became a real prospect, SNP opinion turned against it. From the 1960s the nationalists opposed European
integration on principle as an assault on sovereignty, although by the 1975
referendum the official position had softened to one of waiting until independence so that the Scottish people could take the decision on European
Community (EC) membership themselves. Scottish nationalists looked with
envy and admiration to the Scandinavian democracies, all except Denmark
outside the EC and enjoying a high standard of living and advanced welfare
state, and practising an outward-looking diplomacy. There was some talk of
an association of British states or of the islands, loosely modelled on the
Nordic Council.

During the 1980s, as European integration entered a new phase, the party
began to reconsider its stance under the influence of figures like Winnie
Ewing, who had been elected an MEP in 1979, and Jim Sillars, who had
led the short-lived Scottish Labour Party, which emerged after the 1975
referendum with a platform of independence in Europe (Keating and Waters
1985; Lynch 1996; Mitchell and Cavanagh 2001). One influence here was
certainly the Thatcher government's increasingly strident anti-Europeanism,
together with the move towards Europe by the Labour Party and the trade
unions. By the 1990s Europe occupied a prominent place in the SNP platform, including a commitment to the single currency and further measures of
political integration. Ireland, the 'emerald tiger', has replaced Scandinavia as
the model. Below the surface unity, however, lurked the old division between
radicals and gradualists. The former were suspicious of further political
integration while the latter were moving towards the post-sovereigntist position analogous to the Catalans or Welsh, and which provided possibilities
for convergence with some of the more nationalistically inclined people in the
Labour and Liberal Democrat parties.

Labour, meanwhile, had embraced both home rule and European integration. In their eagerness to discredit the Conservative government of the day,
the Labour Party, including almost all its MPs, signed the 1988 Claim of
Right, declaring that sovereignty rested with the Scottish people, although it
soon became apparent that this did not go as far as self-determination in
Europe. Labour's 1998 Scotland Act made it quite clear that devolution was
a gift of the UK Parliament, which was in turn the only subject of European
policy; but by this time public opinion was already moving ahead. The pro-
European stance of Labour and the SNP, together with the sharp decline in
Conservative fortunes, has produced a broad elite consensus on Europe in

Scotland, in contrast to the divisions in England. Labour, while cautious on independent Scottish action in Europe, has been conscious of the links between home rule and European integration, and its local government leaders have been active in the Europe of the Regions movement.

Scots have long been comfortable with the idea of dual identity, although there are some fluctuations across time. Figure 3.1 shows that Scottish identity prevails, but that most people combine this with a British identity. Scottishness does not, however, always have political implications, partly because national identity is so pervasive and well grounded (Alice Brown *et al.* 2001); only when it seems to be challenged can it be mobilized behind political objectives. There is some evidence that British identity declined in the 1980s and 1990s under the Conservative governments, whose base in Scotland gradually shrank, while the political image of Scotland was refashioned as a bastion of social democracy; and that Britishness may have recovered after 1997.

Polls in Scotland from the late 1960s to the late 1990s asked a rather consistent series of questions about autonomy, with three options: status quo; a Scottish assembly or parliament within the United Kingdom; or independence. In the early years the second question was sometimes divided into two, corresponding to weak devolution or full federalism, but no serious violence is done to the series by merging them. Since the late 1980s some surveys have distinguished between independence within the EU and independence outside it. Again these categories can easily be merged, although it is sometimes useful to distinguish them. The first point that strikes one about the data for over twenty years is the remarkable stability of opinion.

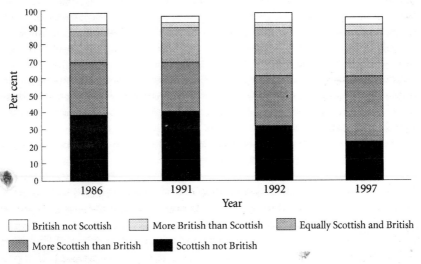

Fig. 3.1. National identity, Scotland, 1986–1997.
Source: McCrone (1998).

From the mid-1970s until the mid-1980s support for independence runs at about 20 per cent, the same level as in early polls from the 1960s and, as far as one can gather, back to the 1930s. It increases to a little over 30 per cent in the mid-1980s, probably as a result of the collapse of Conservative fortunes in Scotland and the poor prospects for a change of government at the UK level. The European factor might also be an influence, although the increase seems to pre-date the SNP's full conversion to Europe and adoption of the slogan 'independence in Europe'. These years also see an increase in support in Scotland for European integration, as Labour and SNP electors followed the lead of their parties in switching to a pro-European position.

It is often claimed that the issue of devolution is of low salience to Scottish voters, when compared with substantive issues like unemployment or health. This is perhaps an unreasonable comparison, since devolution is clearly seen as a means of delivering policies in substantive fields (Alice Brown *et al.* 1999). Yet, even compared with these pressing issues, devolution scored relatively strongly throughout the 1990s, usually as the third, fourth, or fifth most important question. According to MORI polls, it consistently scored more highly than law and order, education, privatization, and even housing. Only unemployment, health, and, for a few years, the poll tax consistently outranked it. At the time of the 1992 general election it ranked second to unemployment as the issue most cited; and in 1997, 50 per cent of voters declared that it had been an important issue in deciding their vote (Scottish Election Survey). Since 1997 the main issue has shifted from union- ism versus home rule, to devolution versus independence. When the usual question is asked, there still appears to be a great deal of stability in opinion (Figure 3.2). Yet when electors are asked how they would vote on a referen- dum on Scottish independence, without comparing this with other options, support for independence increases to about half (Figure 3.3).[1] While SNP voters are the most likely to support independence, surveys over the years have shown substantial support for independence among Labour voters. Indeed, adding these figures up shows that most prospective independence voters are supporters of the union parties. Support for independence tends to be stronger among younger voters, the working class, and, to a lesser extent, men. Surveys asking what Scots would like in the long term also show high levels of support for independence, even when this is compared with the devolution option.

These apparently contradictory findings suggest a widespread liking for independence as an idea, but a willingness to recognize realities and settle for less. In the years preceding the establishment of the Scottish Parliament

---

[1] An NOP poll of April 1999, on a fairly hard question, showed that 44% would vote for independence and 49% against. ('If there was a referendum tomorrow on Scotland becoming an independent country, separate from the United Kingdom, how would you vote?') Independence supporters included 78% of SNP supporters, 35% of Labour supporters, 26% of Liberal Demo- crats, and 8% of Conservatives.

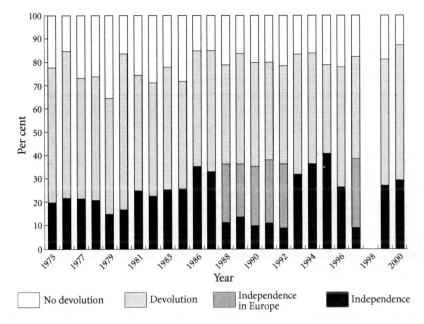

Fig. 3.2. Support for constitutional options, Scotland, 1975–2000.
Source: Various polls, 1975–2000.

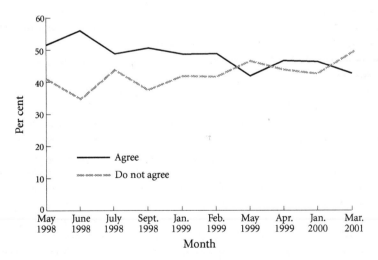

Fig. 3.3. Support for independence, Scotland, 1998–2001. Question: 'In a referendum on independence for Scotland, how would you vote? I agree that Scotland should become an independent country. I do not agree that Scotland should become an independent country.'
Source: ICM polls.

the high level of support for independence could be put down to dissatisfaction with the old regime and a feeling that independence would be better than the status quo. Since the devolution referendum of 1997, however, the default option has been a Scottish Parliament within the United Kingdom, the option which commands broad support in the other surveys. This suggests that we need to look more carefully into the meaning of these various categories. We do not have a great deal of evidence on how Scots interpret these since pollsters have assumed that they were rather clear. One revealing poll from ICM in February 1999 asked whether, if Scotland became independent, it should continue to be defended by the British armed forces: 82 per cent responded yes and just 14 per cent no. Apparently, many Scottish nationalists do not have any problems with the British army, an institution that is among the most consciously British[2] (as opposed to English) in the state. Like the monarchy, the army has long been careful to cultivate a British image in which the Scottish component is clear.[3] This poll also suggests that Scots' conception of independence falls short of classical statehood. Further evidence of a blurring of the devolution and independence categories is provided by polls on Scotland's role in Europe. A poll in June 1999, shortly after the establishment of the Scottish Parliament, showed 63 per cent, against 34 per cent, in favour of the proposition that Scotland should conduct its own negotiations direct with Europe, rather than through the United Kingdom.

The independence vote does not seem to be based on economic expectations, since only about a fifth of voters usually claim that they or Scotland would be better off independent. On the other hand, only about a third seem to believe that they would be worse off, and even some of these appear to be prepared to pay the price. So, while the economic issue is a factor, it is unlikely that the anti-independence parties would be able to scare Scots into voting no because of the economic consequences. This might suggest that the guaranteed market access provided by the EU is a factor in people's thinking, especially since the SNP has emphasized the issue.

Yet the elite consensus on Europe has only gradually penetrated Scottish society. Polls show that Scots are somewhat less hostile to Europe than voters elsewhere in the United Kingdom and considerably more open to the idea that in the years to come the UK state will be radically transformed both by Europeanization and by devolution. In the referendum of 1975 support for staying in the EC was 58 per cent, against 69 per cent in England and 67 per cent in Wales. This reflected prevailing fears of peripheralization together with the hostility of the nationalists and the bulk of the Labour Party in Scotland. By 1992, after nationalists, Labour, and the trade unions had all

---

[2] I say British in a very precise sense, since its status in Northern Ireland is quite different.

[3] Polls have shown that Scots still support the monarchy, although with somewhat less enthusiasm than the English.

Table 3.1. Long-term aspirations for Britain in the European Union, 1997 (%)

	England and Wales	Scotland
Leave the EU	17.3	12.2
Stay and reduce powers of EU	43.4	40.2
Leave things as they are	14.3	15.3
Stay and increase powers of EU	9.6	13.6
Work for single EU government	6.6	6.9
Don't know or no answer	8.4	11.6

Note: Figures are rounded.

Source: Scottish Election Study, 1997.

come round to support for Europe, the Scottish Election Study found higher, but not dramatically higher, levels of support for Europe in Scotland than in England or Wales. Only 29 per cent of Scots thought that Britain should leave the EC or reduce its powers, against 44 in the south of England; 46 per cent of Scots and 35 per cent of those in the south of England wanted the EC to increase its powers (Alice Brown *et al.* 1996). By the 1997 election Euro-scepticism had increased in all parts of Britain, and the best that can be said is that Scots were slightly less Eurosceptic than the English or Welsh (Table 3.1). Given a straight choice against the status quo, 31.4 per cent of English voters and 22.7 per cent of Scottish voters would leave the EU (Scottish Election Study 1997). On a thermometer of feeling towards the EU the most pro-European sentiment gained 13.2 per cent in Scotland and 9.2 per cent in England and Wales. The most anti-European position gained 23.9 per cent in England and Wales but 17.7 per cent in Scotland (Scottish Election Study 1997). Surveys have also showed support for Europe to be higher in the central belt of Scotland, especially the Labour heartland of west central Scotland, than around the periphery (e.g. *Eurobarometer*, 45, (Spring 1996)). In the Highlands and north-east Scotland there is a lot of opposition to European fisheries policies, which the SNP proposes to scrap, although the designation of the Highlands and Islands as an Objective One area for regional aid in the last period of the Structural Funds served to give the EU a more positive image.

British opinion from the late 1990s turned massively against the European single currency, while Scots were a little less hostile. According to the 1997 Scottish Election Study, 57 per cent of Scots and 60 per cent of English and Welsh wanted to keep the pound as the only currency. A simultaneous survey, from ICM in January 2000, showed Scots opposed to entry into the single currency by 58 to 30, while UK voters as a whole were opposed by 69 to 22. Scottish voters do, however, support eventual entry, though by fluctuating margins (between 50 and 60 per cent in 1999 polls).

Opinion in Scotland perhaps stands out most not on aspirations for the future, but on expectations. Polls from the late 1990s asked how likely people think it is that Scotland will become independent, and these show electors as having a rather open mind. About a quarter of voters expected Scotland to be independent within ten years, but a majority expected it in the longer term.[4] Of course these numbers could simply represent the sum of independence and anti-devolution supporters, both of whom think that devolution is a slippery slope to independence. Yet the fluctuating numbers suggest something more indeterminate than this, and a lack of clarity in the categories themselves suggests that independence is not always seen as a critical step but just another move along the home rule path. In an ICM poll of February 2000 only 19 per cent declared devolution to be the 'settled will of the Scottish people' against 68 per cent who thought it needed further change. In the immediate aftermath of devolution there was a high expectation that the Scottish Parliament would become the centre of political life (MORI poll, September 1999) but expectations later declined somewhat.

Similarly, Scots voters are more open to the idea that European integration will progress. A January 1999 Gallup poll showed that 80 per cent of British voters thought that the Euro would eventually be adopted. This feeling is stronger in Scotland, where two polls in 1999 showed 89 per cent and 86 per cent thinking that membership was inevitable. The Scots also see this as a more immediate possibility, with 86 per cent and 67 per cent in the two polls respectively thinking that it would occur within ten years. Two polls of UK voters in 1999 (by ICM) showed only 36 per cent and 42 per cent believing that they would have adopted the Euro within ten years. This suggests that Scottish voters follow the Labour line of adopting the Euro as soon as practicable, while in the United Kingdom as a whole the Conservative policy of putting it beyond political horizon is more popular.

Scottish opinion, then, appears to be committed to self-government as a process. There are strong aspirations to national autonomy, and Scotland is seen as more than a self-governing region within the UK state. There is an appreciation that the constitution is evolving, with both Scottish and European levels being strengthened, but an unwillingness to specify the end point of this evolution, at least just yet. Opinion has escaped the old categories of sovereignty but, like the social sciences, has not found new ones to replace them.

Plaid Cymru, the Welsh nationalist party, has traditionally been less separatist and less statist than the SNP, preferring to talk of the values of self-government and communitarianism, which it saw as part of the cultural heritage of Wales. Under the influence of Saunders Lewis in the 1930s and 1940s it believed in a united Europe, which Saunders combined with a neo-medievalism strongly informed by his own Catholicism and hostile to the concept of state sovereignty (D. Hywel Davies 1983; Lynch 1996). Like other

---

[4] A Gallup poll in May 1996 showed 38% agreeing that a Scottish Parliament would make independence more likely, against 42% disagreeing. In February 1999, 44% (against 50%) agreed with a harder question, that a Scottish Parliament was bound to lead to the break-up of the United Kingdom.

stateless nationalist parties it looked with interest on the idea of European unity in the post-war years and from 1949 was associated with the Union Fédéraliste des Communautés et Régions Européennes. By the time of its revival in the 1970s it was more committed to a form of independent state and firmly opposed to the European Community, which it portrayed as a remote, technocratic body dominated by the big states and out of sympathy with the needs of a small, peripheral cultural nation (Jones 1985). During the 1980s this attitude was gradually softened, and by 1983 Plaid was prepared to accept continued British membership of the EC as a form of protection against Thatcherism. By the 1990s the party was enthusiastically pro-Europe, linking this with a post-sovereigntist stance that drew on the party's earliest traditions. At the 1999 elections for the Welsh Assembly, Plaid astonished much of the political world by declaring that it no longer favoured a separate Welsh state, but was more interested in exploring the place of Wales within the emerging European order.

As Figure 3.4 indicates, the Welsh have a weaker sense of distinct identity than the Scots. A larger number declare themselves to be British not Welsh, no doubt as a result of the large number of English-born people living in Wales who have not adopted a Welsh identity. Given that these amount to about 20 per cent of the Welsh population, though, there does appear to be some assimilation. At the other extreme, rather few people describe them- selves as only Welsh, with the great bulk of the population opting for the intermediate categories. Polls on independence and devolution in Wales are not as regular as in Scotland, and, with the massive rejection of a Welsh Assembly in the referendum of 1979, there was less interest in conducting them. Support for devolution did increase during the 1990s, and, while the 1998 referendum passed by less than 1 per cent on a low turnout, this represented a considerable change since 1979. Polls have shown no more than about 10 per cent support for independence in Europe, but after

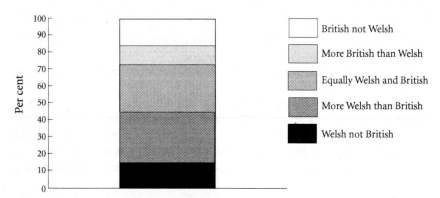

Fig. 3.4. National identity, Wales, 1997.
Source: British Election Study, 1997.

devolution the support for centralization with no Welsh Assembly fell considerably to about 20 or 25 per cent.

Northern Ireland is, in contrast to Scotland and Wales, a profoundly divided society, created by the partition of 1921. Politics has revolved around the national question, which has smothered social and economic cleavages. Within the nationalist and unionist blocs, however, matters are more complex. Irish nationalists base their case on the right to self-determination of a territorially defined Irish people whose will was maliciously frustrated by partition. Yet nationalism has long been divided into an intransigent, 'physical force' sector and a moderate and constitutionalist one. The former have been represented by Sinn Féin, political wing of the Irish Republican Army, and the latter, since the 1970s, by the Social Democratic and Labour Party (SDLP). Sinn Féin was, until the peace process of the 1990s, committed to the overthrow of the political regimes both in Northern Ireland and in the Irish Republic, and the creation of a united Irish state, without regard to the wishes of the unionists in the north. The SDLP has always been committed to Irish unity but has argued the need for consent from the people of both parts of the island, a prospect which it accepts is likely only in the long term. In practice, this means a recognition that the unionists have a veto over the process. In the meantime, it has supported power-sharing arrangements to give the nationalist community a share of influence within Northern Ireland, and the promotion of as many links as possible with the south. These divisions were paralleled in the south, where Fianna Fáil, while opposing political violence, refused to accept the legitimacy of a unionist veto over unity, while Fine Gael, descended from the pro-treaty party of 1921, accepted that unity could come only by consent. Like the SDLP, they have recognized the unionists of the north as a national minority possessing some collective rights to recognition if not self-determination. These positions began to shift in the course of the 1980s and 1990s, with a gradual recognition of the distinct national identity of the northern unionists, first by the SDLP and Fine Gael and later by Fianna Fáil. Finally, in the Good Friday Agreement of 1998, Sinn Féin accepted that Irish unity could come about only by consent and that in the meantime there must be provision for the recognition both of the Irish identity of nationalists in the north and of the British identity of the unionists (Ivory 1999).

Europe has in the past been a divisive force in Irish politics. The Irish Republic tied its European strategy to that of the United Kingdom, being rebuffed in 1961 and 1967 and going in along with the British in 1973. In the longer run, however, European membership has allowed the Republic to diversify its trade, reducing its dependence on the UK market, and to adopt a more independent diplomacy as a small member state of a larger union. While there was much misgiving to begin with regarding the threat of Europe to Irish sovereignty, and there are persistent fears about the contagious effect of European secularism, the Republic has over time become a stronger supporter of integration. Europe has also come to be seen as a new framework for addressing the national question. From an early stage, the SDLP supported European integration as an instrument for internationalizing the Northern Ireland question and for transcending the border, and by the late 1990s was promoting a Europe of the Regions as a new opportunity for Northern Ireland. It presented Europe as a model for reconciliation among former enemies and as a framework for new forms of sovereignty (Mitchell and Cavanagh 2001). Sinn Féin has traditionally opposed European integration, arguing for economic protectionism and self-sufficiency (Aughey *et al.* 1989), and by the late 1990s had modified this stance only to the point of accepting a strictly intergovernmental Europe, in which a thirty-two county Ireland would be a sovereign player. It has continued to condemn the existing EU as a creature of the large states and multinational corporations, and Sinn Féin totally opposed European defence cooperation and NATO, insisting on strict Irish neutrality.

Like nationalism, unionism comes in various forms, with different historical traditions overlaid with religious, nationalist, and class concerns (Cochrane 1997). Unionists long regarded two priorities as intimately linked: maintaining Northern Ireland within the United Kingdom; and sustaining the integrity of the Protestant–unionist community within Northern Ireland, usually in the form of Protestant supremacy. Intellectually there was always a tension between these two. Support for the Union was predicated on the idea that Northern Ireland is part of a single British nation, with the Republic of Ireland as a foreign country and nationalists as disloyal citizens. Self-maintenance of the Protestant community, however, required that the Northern Ireland Protestants be a distinct people with the right of self-determination within their own territory. This would permit them to resist both incorporation into the Republic, and the abolition of their own institutions in favour of British norms of universal democracy. From the 1970s, as the old Unionist Party crumbled under British pressure for reforms, these logics came increasingly into conflict, although majority unionism was slow to accept the idea and continued to insist on a return to something like the old Stormont system of devolution, with majority rule within the province. Sections of unionism, emphasizing the need to sustain the community, dreamed from time to time of an independent Northern Ireland state. Others began to demand integration into the United Kingdom, on the grounds that Northern Ireland should be treated no differently from other parts of what they saw as a unitary British nation. This has developed into an argument on the part of liberal unionists that the problem in the past was the denial of citizenship rights to Catholics and that the solution is the forging of a new non-sectarian British 'civic' identity in which both communities can share (Aughey 1991). Yet one of the bases of the whole problem is that British identity is not acceptable to one part of the community, any more than Irish identity is to the other; civic identity is not the simple answer when there are two civic communities competing for loyalty (Doyle 1999). In any case, British identity is itself not simply available on demand. Outside England, British identity is filtered by local national identities and there is no standard model for the various parts of Britain, which have always had their own specific relationship with the state as a whole. Integrationists seem to have been arguing that Northern Ireland should be treated as though it were part of England, which it clearly is not. A section of unionism was prepared to accept devolution accompanied by power-sharing with nationalists, but was leery of the all-Ireland institutions which tended to be part of the various power-sharing proposals. Finally, there have been unionists prepared to go further, sharing power with nationalists within Northern Ireland and accepting links with the Republic, as the price for keeping British support for the Union. This was the basis for the Sunningdale Agreement, disowned by most unionists and brought down by the loyalist workers' strike in 1974, and for the Good Friday Agreement of 1998.

Unionists have tended to be anti-European, seeing the European project as a threat to their precarious British identity and, in many cases, expressing suspicions about the weight of Catholic countries within the European Union. There were some pro-European elements within the Ulster Unionist Party, but, as the party broke with the British Conservatives, these were weakened (Aughey, *et al.* 1989). By the late 1990s, however, the Ulster Unionist Party had accepted Europe and was keen to see a Northern Irish presence in the British delegation to the Council of Ministers. Extreme unionists, such as the Democratic Unionist Party of Ian Paisley, which regards Europe as a Catholic plot and a surreptitious way of uniting Ireland, and the UK Unionist Party, remained stridently anti-European.[5] As a member of the European Parliament, Paisley objected strongly to efforts to bring the Northern Ireland question into the European sphere.

Surveys of opinion in Northern Ireland have generally confirmed the party alignment, polarized around the absolutes of Irish nationalism and British unionism. So Catholics see themselves as Irish while Protestants see themselves as British or from Ulster. In Rose's 1968 survey only 15 per cent of Catholics labelled themselves as British, and further questions revealed that most of these used the term purely descriptively, to recognize a juridical fact, rather than as a badge of pride (Rose 1971). Only 4 per cent of people were the product of mixed marriages, although the proportion may have risen since then as a result of secularization. Yet there are considerable differences within Northern Ireland, depending on class and locational factors, from the working-class communities of Belfast, where identities are highly polarized, to the middle-class and coastal areas, where there is an easier coexistence. Political conflict has served to increase social polarization, which has fallen in

---

[5] The UK Unionists' web site has the slogan 'United Europe', with the 'Europe' crossed out and replaced by 'Kingdom'.

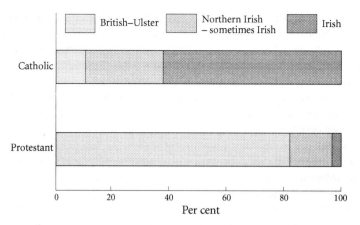

Fig. 3.5. National identity, Northern Ireland, 1994.
Source: Breen (1996).

times of peace. So the Troubles since 1969 have served further to polarize the two communities, whose members are less likely to live in the same neighbourhoods or to form friendships. British identification among Northern Ireland Catholics and Irish identity among Protestants have fallen (Moxon-Browne 1991). Figure 3.5 shows a divided community, with relatively few people choosing the middle-ground option of 'Northern Irish/sometimes Irish'.

The political implications of identity, however, are less stark and becoming ever less clear as new political opportunities open up with the Good Friday Agreement and the advance of European integration. There has always been a sizeable section of the Catholic community which does not consider itself nationalist, although almost the whole of the Protestant community considers itself unionist (Evans and Duffy 1997). In the early 1990s, about half of Catholics identified themselves as nationalists (Breen 1996).[6] In the aftermath of the agreement, however, the proportion of Catholics prepared to label themselves as nationalists increased to 70 per cent, exactly the same as unionist identification within the Protestant community (NILT 1999). If taken with evidence about constitutional options (see below), this suggests not an increase in polarization as might appear, but rather that in the wake of the peace process and its new possibilities nationalism has begun to lose both its association with political violence and its absolutist implications. Only 1 per cent in the Catholic and Protestant communities considered themselves unionists and nationalists respectively. Over a quarter of the whole population, and more than half of those without a religious affiliation, considered themselves neither.

[6] The figures varied between 40% and 54% in the years 1991–4 (Breen 1996).

Surveys on separation or irredentism are notoriously susceptible to the wording and context of the question. There is a tendency for Catholics to favour Irish unity, while Protestants overwhelmingly and vehemently oppose it. Yet surveys since the 1960s have shown northern Catholics as more concerned with non-discrimination, power-sharing, and material issues than with reunification (Rose 1971; Moxon-Browne 1983). On a very soft question in 1995 just 53 per cent of Catholics preferred Irish unity, although only 13 per cent were opposed (Breen 1996). A 1996 survey showed 15 per cent of Catholics in favour of remaining within the United Kingdom, while 34 per cent wanted to join the Republic (Evans and O'Leary 1997). Protestants, on the other hand, consistently come out as massively opposed to Irish unity. This may reflect a sense of realism in the Catholic community, since Irish unity is a remote prospect, but it may also show that the British state, with its more extensive welfare provisions and public services, is not automatically rejected, and that Catholics will respond to initiatives to improve their immediate position. This has made Catholics much more amenable to solutions such as power-sharing or shared sovereignty which have been tried over the last twenty-five years. Yet support for Irish unity as an alternative also increased over that time, because of the intractability of the conflict and community polarization. The Good Friday Agreement, by raising a real prospect of unification, may have raised support further. A 1999 poll showed 48 per cent of Catholics in favour of a united Ireland, against 16 per cent wanting to remain in the United Kingdom, and 18 per cent favouring an independent Northern Ireland (an option not available in most surveys) (NILT 1999). By contrast, 87 per cent of Protestants preferred to remain within the United Kingdom.

All this would suggest a considerable support base within the Catholic community for solutions falling short of unity and national independence for Ireland. This is not to suggest that Catholics are only concerned with material issues and that they could easily be assimilated into a non-discriminatory unionist order, since all the evidence shows that they do not subscribe to a British identity or unionist ideology. Rather it suggests that they may be open to new ways of expressing identity, short of a unified Irish state.

As in Scotland, however, constitutional change has opened minds to alternative futures. By 1999, 40 per cent of electors in Northern Ireland thought that a united Ireland was likely within twenty years, with Catholics only slightly more likely than Protestants to hold this view (NILT 1999). Moreover, electors showed a surprising degree of willingness to live with this. Of those against Irish unity, only 19 per cent felt that a united Ireland would be impossible to live with. This included 29 per cent of the Protestant unionists but only 1 per cent of Catholic anti-unity electors. Conversely, 68 per cent of those wanting either to unify with the Republic or to declare an independent state could happily accept a majority decision never to unify with the Republic, and only 2 per cent would find this impossible to live with.

These results may be difficult to interpret, but they do suggest that belief in the absolutes of British and Irish sovereignty is rather weak, especially on the Catholic side.

Northern Irish public opinion was long lukewarm about European integration. In the 1975 referendum on British membership of the European Community, Northern Ireland mustered a bare majority in favour on a low turnout, while the yes side won comfortably elsewhere.[7] By 1999 opinion was much more favourable to Europe, with opinion on the single currency almost evenly divided, in contrast to the massive opposition elsewhere in the United Kingdom. The denominational division was marked and symmetrical, with 60 per cent of Catholics in favour and 60 per cent of Protestants opposed.

Northern Ireland has often been presented as a most intractable case, pitching the absolutes of identity against each other, with rival conceptions of the locus of sovereign authority and legitimacy. Yet a careful analysis shows that the absolutes are not as solid as appears, that nationalism and unionism, far from being monoliths, come in a variety of forms, and that there is some political space for new and post-sovereign solutions like the Good Friday Agreement (discussed further in Chapter 4). There seems to be more room on the Catholic–nationalist side than on the Protestant–unionist one, as shown by the results of the 1998 referendum, in which the former overwhelmingly endorsed the Agreement, while the latter was evenly split. Over time, however, it is likely that more of the unionist community will see that preserving their culture and tradition requires more than loyalty to a UK state which shows ever fewer signs of accepting them as full co-nationals. For their part, nationalists in both north and south have accepted that unity will come about only by consent and that, just as nationalists in the north can now express an Irish identity, so unionists in a future arrangement will be able to maintain their own distinct identity, whether this be British or Ulster.

A notable feature of the UK studies is the weakness of a countervailing British nationalism in the dominant nation. Polls of English opinion on Scottish devolution are not frequent, but all have shown a similar breakdown of support for the main options as in Scotland itself. We even find the same paradoxical support for Scottish independence when presented as a single option.[8] Polls over the years have also shown a majority within Great Britain in favour of Irish reunification. There have been some signs of an emerging English nationalism. The British Social Attitudes Survey of 1999 showed an increase in the number describing themselves as English and not British, and that these were more likely to support the independence of Scotland and Wales (Curtice and Heath 2000). These unambiguously English voters

---

[7] In Northern Ireland 24% of the entire electorate endorsed EC membership, compared with 44% in England and Wales, and 36% in Scotland.

[8] An ICM poll of February 2000 showed English voters in favour of Scottish independence by 46% to 36%. In response to another question in the same poll, they broke out 14% for independence, 54% for devolution, and 24% for centralization.

were also more likely to be anti-European and anti-immigrant. There have been sporadic efforts by sections of the Conservative Party to capitalize on this English nationalism, but this is at odds with its historic support for the Union, so that no clear message has come across. In any case, the evidence shows that most English voters are content with the post-1999 constitutional settlement, although there is support for regional government in some areas, notably the north-east of England.

Spain

The context for nationalist claims in Spain differs from that of the United Kingdom, since central governments have not conceded the plurinational status of the state itself and have certainly not agreed on the right of self-determination of its constituent parts. It has therefore been important for the stateless nationalists not merely to put forward constitutional claims, but to defend the existence of the nations themselves.

Catalan nationalism has, from its inception in the nineteenth century, tended towards moderation and to disclaim separatism. The early nationalist ideologue Prat de la Riba (1998) disowned separatism in favour of a plurinational state and empire. Francesc Cambó was so committed to playing the Spanish political game that he threw his lot in with the dictator Primo de Rivera, wrongly imagining that he would give recognition to Catalonia. The Catalan left has always had a more independentist element, but only under extreme conditions of civil war did it seek to realize its goal. On the fall of the monarchy in 1931, Francesc Macià proclaimed an independent Catalan state but declared it to be a member of a non-existent Iberian confederation. Since the restoration of democracy in the late 1970s the dominant formation has been Convergència i Unió (CiU), both of whose components are committed to a staunch but moderate and non-separatist nationalism. Party leaders and policy statements have repeatedly and consistently declared that Catalonia's vocation lies within Spain, but a Spain converted into a plurinational confederation, with symbolic and substantive recognition for the stateless nations. The historical reference point is the pre-1714 constitution with its concentric circles of power and opportunities for Catalonia to act within and beyond the Spanish state. Europe has become a key element of the strategy, and CiU is firmly in favour of European integration, while seeking a special place within Europe for regions and stateless nations. When pressed to define their ultimate goal, spokespersons refuse to place a limit on Catalonia's aspirations, insisting that, as Europe evolves, so can its constituent nations, so that a future of independence in Europe on SNP lines is not completely ruled out.

The key to CiU ideology is the idea of the plurinational state, a confederation of self-governing nations voluntarily united on the basis of self-determination (CDC 1997; UDC 1997; McRoberts 2001). Spain or the Castilian-speaking territories would, in this schema, be a constituent nation, although it would not necessarily organize itself separately.[9] Sovereignty would be shared and divided, with Europe occupying a large role. There would be a high degree of symbolic recognition of plurinationality, in the name of the state, identity documents, sporting team, flags, and anthems. The constitution would be interpreted in light of the distinct status (*hecho diferencial*) of the nationalities and would be asymmetrical in principle and practice. Catalonia would have exclusive powers on matters of culture and language, and would have its own fiscal regime in imitation of the Basque *concierto económico*, allowing it to raise most taxes and pass on an agreed share to Madrid. It would have its own system of courts, and with the other nations would have the right to nominate members of the Constitutional Court. The Senate would be reformed as a chamber of territorial representation, and the nations would have a right of veto on matters affecting culture and language. The nations would have an external presence by right, especially in cultural matters, where they would be sovereign; so they would have their own delegations in Unesco. For other purposes, they would have a guaranteed place in Spanish delegations abroad and especially in the representation in the European Union. The programme reflects three preoccupations: symbolic recognition of nationality; preservation of the language and culture; and the feeling that Catalonia is contributing too much to the Spanish treasury. It is a list of radical demands, but far from a recipe for national independence.

Catalonia's second nationalist party, the Esquerra Republicana de Catalunya (ERC), did come out for independence in the early 1990s but has since then subordinated this to the arrival of a Europe of the Peoples, in which the states have disappeared. This is a post-sovereigntist position akin to that of Plaid Cymru and quite different from independence in the classic sense. The Catalan socialists, for their part, have a strong 'Catalanist' streak, which leads them, while deploring nationalism, to support the national affirmation of Catalonia and advocate a federal Spain with more power for its component parts. Catalonia's post-Communist alliance, Iniciativa per Catalunya, has also incorporated nationalist elements into its programme, producing a divorce with the Spanish-level Izquierda Unida. Outside the main parties elements supporting 'sovereignty' or independence for Catalonia have persisted, but this has invariably been placed in the European context and normally accompanied by an insistence that this would not represent statehood in the classical sense (Congrés de Cultura Catalana 2000; Serra and Ventura 1999; Seroo *et al.* 2001).

---

[9] Some Catalan nationalists still seek to dilute the presence of Spain further by advocating an Iberian confederation, with Portugal as a fifth element. There is no support whatever for this in Portugal.

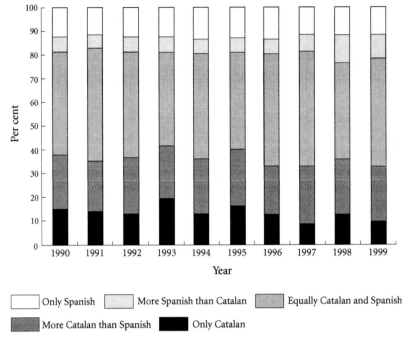

Fig. 3.6. National identity, Catalonia, 1990–1999.
Source: ICPS polls, 1991–2000.

Surveys show that Catalans largely adopt dual Spanish and Catalan identities (Figure 3.6). Native-born Catalans and Catalan speakers are more likely to identify as Catalans, yet there is a tendency for assimilation in the second generation, so that Catalonia is not a sharply divided society. Yet while Catalan consciousness seems high and growing, only a third of the respondents in 1996 considered Catalonia to be a nation, a proportion that seems to have declined over ten years.[10] Support for constitutional options is clustered around the moderate positions of autonomy and federalism within Spain (Figure 3.7). Support for independence does tend to be related to Catalan identification and to the belief that Catalonia is a nation (Moral 1998; Table 3.2). It is also unsurprisingly related to partisanship. In 1998, 60 per cent of ERC supporters favoured independence, while CiU provided a home for much softer nationalists, with only 27 per cent of its voters in favour (ICPS 1998*a*). There are, as in the other nations, ambivalences about all of this. Less than 20 per cent support independence against the other options, but when asked a softer question as to whether they are favourable to the concept of Catalan independence, about a third

---

[10] We need to be cautious here, as surveys are not always perfectly comparable and responses can be influenced by immediate events.

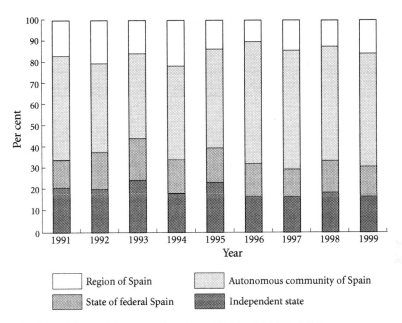

Fig. 3.7. Support for constitutional options, Catalonia, 1991–1999.
Source: ICPS polls, 1991–2000.

consistently respond positively (ICPS polls, 1992–8). Similarly, a 1996 survey found 34 per cent of Catalans answering yes to a question about whether they were in favour of Catalonia being independent, and a third said that they would like a Catalan rather than a Spanish passport (Moral 1998). An earlier survey with a very soft question showed 44 per cent, including 60 per cent of native Catalans, in favour of independence (Estadé and Treserra, 1990).[11] Support for the idea of self-determination is markedly higher than in other parts of Spain apart from the Basque

Table 3.2. Level of support for independence option and national identity in Catalonia, 1998 (%)

Identity	Level of support
Only Spanish	3
More Spanish than Catalan	6
Equally Spanish and Catalan	9
More Catalan than Spanish	25
Only Catalan	52
Don't know or no answer	9

Source: ICPS (1998a).

[11] The question asked 'If there were a referendum to initiate a gradual process towards the independence of Catalonia, how would you vote?'

Country and Navarre, but less than half of Catalans identify this with independence.

Moral (1998) explores the ambivalence of Catalan and Basque attitudes to independence by dividing them into six categories, from coherent *independentistas* to coherent *españolistas*, using the criteria of support for independence, regarding their community as a region, and wishing to have a Catalan or Basque passport. Intermediate categories are ambiguous *independentistas*, who want independence but only qualify on one of the other criteria, and Spanish *independentistas*, who want independence but qualify on neither of the other criteria. Correspondingly, there are ambiguous *españolistas*, who reject independence but meet one of the other criteria; and integrationist nationalists, who reject independence but want Catalan or Basque passports and consider themselves to belong to a distinct nation. As Table 3.3 shows, the proportion of coherent separatists in Catalonia is about a fifth, while the total *independentista* pole amounts to about a third. Some 60 per cent of the electorate are pro-Spanish in their orientation, but some 30 per cent have ambivalent views.

As in Scotland, it has taken the elites some time to persuade the electorate of the link between nationalism and Europeanism. According to the European Values Study of 1990, Catalans, while broadly in favour of Europe, were somewhat less enthusiastic than people in other parts of Spain, apparently viewing Europe more as a neutral political space less hostile to their aspirations than positively as a new form of identity (Andrés and Sánchez 1991). On the other hand, evidence from the mid-1990s shows Catalans becoming more European. On a decimal scale, Catalans' identification with Europe, at 7.48, was higher than the Spanish average, and well above that of the Basques (Sangrador García 1996). Similarly, Catalan favourable attitudes to Europeans were higher than the Spanish average and again much higher than the Basque figure. Catalans in the majority continue to feel both

Table 3.3. Typology of independence supporters in Catalonia and the Basque Country, 1996 (%)

Attitudes to independence	Catalonia	Basque Country
Coherent *independentistas*	20.6	29.5
Ambiguous *independentistas*	6.6	10.9
Spanish *independentistas*	7.6	4.7
Total *independentistas*	34.8	45.1
Coherent *españolistas*	42.6	22.8
Ambiguous *españolistas*	9.7	17.2
Integratist nationalists	7.4	5.6
Total *españolistas*	59.7	45.6
No opinion	5.5	9.3
TOTAL	100.0	100.0

Source: Moral (1998).

Spanish and Catalan, but the European identity is ever more salient and, among native Catalans, is now equal to Spanish identity (Sangrador García 1996). Catalans are also more likely to feel European the more Catalan they are, although these attitudes might to some degree represent two sides of the same attitude, a rejection of Spain. The percentage feeling close to Europe increases steadily from 30 per cent of those feeling only Spanish, to 66 per cent of those feeling only Catalan (ICPS 1998*b*). ERC voters stand out for their pro-European attitudes.

Elite and public opinion in the Basque Country are much more polarized between integration and separation and among competing parties (Gillespie 2000), but there is an emerging post-sovereigntist option. It is a founding belief of Basque nationalism that original sovereignty lies with the Basque people and that any link with Spain can come only from mutual agreement. There is also a strong separatist streak, although within the Basque Nationalist Party (PNV) are many moderates who would settle for less. All are agreed that the Basque *fueros* constitute fundamental law prior and superior to the Spanish constitution. For this reason, the PNV refused to accept the 1978 constitution and recommended abstention in the referendum. They did, however, participate in the negotiation of the Basque Statute of Autonomy and campaign for its acceptance in the referendum. This history gives a very different starting point for discussions on autonomy from that in Catalonia. In recent years, while not abandoning the historic rights doctrine, they have placed more emphasis on the sociological basis of the nation, the fact that the Basques consider themselves a people, and the existence of the nationalist parties themselves. Basque nationalism has an international and European dimension going back to the Second Republic, and after the Second World War the PNV was drawn into the European orbit by its membership of the Christian Democratic International, and has long stressed the idea of a Europe made up of 'natural' peoples rather than artificial states. After a highly conflictual period during the negotiation of the autonomy statute and the establishment of the Basque government, there was a period of consolidation in which the PNV, governing for much of the time in coalition with the Socialists, sought to build its fortunes. While the PNV maintained an ambivalence about its ultimate aspirations, the implication of statehood was there, notably in the logo it adopted after Spain's entry into the European Community, a flag with thirteen stars, implying that Euskadi would be the next member state.[12]

In contrast to CiU, the moderate Basque nationalists must compete with a radical alternative, Herri Batasuna (HB), committed to the complete independence and unity of the seven Basque provinces, including Navarre and the three provinces in France. As the political arm of the terrorist group ETA,

---

[12] It is perhaps a comment on the particularism of the PNV at this time that the thirteen stars implied that they would be the only stateless nation to enter.

they can make no compromise and, indeed, must constantly radicalize their demands in order to maintain the tension on which ETA feeds. After the transition the PNV distanced itself from ETA and for some years participated in an anti-terrorist 'democratic front' with the other parties, under the pact of Ajurea Enea. From the mid-1990s there was something of a radicalization as the PNV launched a campaign for the full application and extension of the statute, and for recognition of the right to self-determination. This corresponded to changes within the party itself but also to the decision to seek a way out of the prevailing terrorist violence by incorporating the radical nationalists of HB into the political process. This was to produce a change of alliances in the late 1990s and, following the ETA truce of 1998–9, a united nationalist front, based on a shared demand for self-determination. Inspired by the peace process in Northern Ireland, moderate nationalists argued that only by conceding the right of self-determination including secession could the democratic parties bring HB back into the fold, since it would show that their objectives were, at least in theory, attainable by democratic means.[13] From this point the PNV demanded a radical break with the old statute of autonomy rather than its evolution, and a round table of all Basque political representatives to produce a home-made solution based on the principle of self-determination, without the participation of Madrid. This could then be negotiated bilaterally with the Spanish state. The alliance with HB was brutally shattered by the ending of the ETA truce in 2000, leaving the strategy of a nationalist front and rupture with the statute in ruins.

Over time the PNV has laid ever greater stress on Europe as a framework for self-government. This stemmed from its own traditions and evolution and had nothing to do with the rapprochement with HB, which maintained the traditional left-nationalist critique of Europe as a conspiracy of big capital and the large states. HB has made little of the European issue, and this did not feature in the pact negotiated between the PNV and HB in 1999.[14] The PNV for its part has developed an active European strategy, pursued in parallel with the more radical initiatives for self-determination. As early as 1917 it participated in the Congress of European Nationalities in Lausanne, which called for a federal union of European peoples. From the 1930s Basque nationalists like José Antonio Aguirre were committed to European federalism, an idea that stemmed both from their nationalism and from Christian Democratic ideas of subsidiarity. In exile from the 1950s, this line was developed as the Basques became involved in the European movement. While

---

[13] The possibility is purely theoretical since opinion polls do not show anything like a majority for independence. The radical nationalists want the widest definition of the Basque Country, including Navarre and the French Basque provinces, but the more widely the boundary is drawn, the smaller the support for independence.

[14] Even the highly propagandistic pro-ETA book published in English by the Welsh Academic Press (Núñez 1997) and presumably intended for an international readership contains no discussion of Europe.

their general framework is the Europe of the Peoples invoked as early as the 1950s, there are three distinct strands in this, pursued at different times and by different sections of the nationalist movement. One strand parallels that of the SNP, demanding an independent state within Europe. This was the 'thirteen stars' line, pressed by the more traditional nationalists and in the early years of EC membership. A second strand, which has become more prominent with the advance of European integration to include the single market, the single currency, and common defence and security, can be characterized as post-sovereigntist. This emphasizes shared sovereignty in Europe and the inadequacy of the nation-state model, and sees the Basque Country as part of a European vanguard of small nations exploring a new political model; there are obvious parallels here with the Catalan strategy. The third strand is to exploit the opportunities provided by the Europe of the Regions movement to join with other stateless nations and regions to enhance the role of sub-state entities in the EU. With the Catalans, the PNV has demanded participation in the Spanish delegation to the Council of Ministers, and opportunities for Basque interests to be pursued separately when they conflict with those of the state. There have been suggestions that the Spanish votes might at some time be divided to allow the stateless nations to cast their own, although this is presently not allowed under the treaties. Cross-border cooperation, bringing the Spanish and French sides of the nation together, has also been an important theme. In the wake of the Maastricht Treaty subsidiarity was invoked in favour of the smaller nations in a decentralized Europe.

Polarization in the Basque Country is also increased by the presence of stronger Spanish centralist forces than are found in Catalonia. The Partido Popular (PP) gained in strength in the 1990s as the PNV, which hitherto had attracted the votes of the conservative middle classes, radicalized. Both in Madrid and in the Basque Country itself, the PP has refused to contemplate reopening the statute of autonomy or conceding any element of self-determination to the Basque Country. The Basque socialists must straddle the nationalist–centralist cleavage, since they draw much of their support from immigrant workers from other parts of Spain. They do have a more nationalist wing concentrated in Guipúzcoa, but, like their Catalan and Scottish counterparts, must also follow the line of the central party in the state. This creates a picture of immense complexity in Basque politics, compared with the other stateless nations, with much greater distance between the nationalist and non-nationalist parties than in Catalonia. There have been attempts to find a way out of the situation, often inspired by the Northern Ireland peace process, notably by the pro-peace social movement Elkarri. These have involved putting aside preconceptions about sovereignty and pursuing the post-sovereigntist options, but they have had a limited impact while terrorist violence continues.

Public opinion in the Basque Country is similarly fragmented, with less consensus than in Catalonia. Like the other nationalities, Basques are

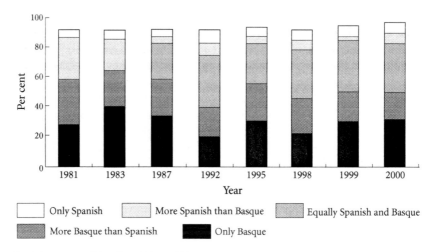

Fig. 3.8. Basque identity, 1981–2000.
Source: Euskobarómeter.

generally at ease with dual identities. Surveys back to 1981 show very few—
an average of 7 per cent—consider themselves solely Spanish, a proportion
well below the percentage of the population born outwith the Basque Country. At the other extreme, about 30 per cent of the population consider
themselves only Basque, a group dominated by the native-born and Basque
speakers. While there are fluctuations from year to year, there are no long-
term trends (Figure 3.8). This is not to say that Basque nationality is entirely
closed. Forty per cent of immigrants consider themselves only Spanish, but
the rest have some degree of Basque identity. Most of the electorate define
being Basque by voluntaristic criteria rather than ascriptive ones like being
born in the Basque Country or having Basque parents, although nationalists
do tend to be less inclusive here (Llera 1994). Opinion is divided on whether
the Basque Country is a nation, with the native-born and Basque speakers
believing that it is (Moral 1998). Similarly, Basques are evenly divided
between those who call themselves nationalists and those who do not.

Opinion on constitutional options also shows great stability (Figure 3.9),
with about 60 per cent favouring some form of autonomy within Spain and
about 30 per cent preferring independence. Support for a centralized Spanish
state has almost disappeared. As in the other nations, however, differences in
the wording and the context of the question can produce a plurality of
support for independence. A 1996 survey showed 44 per cent support for
independence, against 32 per cent opposed (Moral 1998). Asked which
nationality they would like in their passport, Basques divide almost equally
between Spanish and Basque (Moral 1998) or, on a slightly softer question,
prefer the Basque one (CIRES 1991–6). Basque electors, like those in Catalonia and Navarre, but not elsewhere in Spain, are overwhelmingly

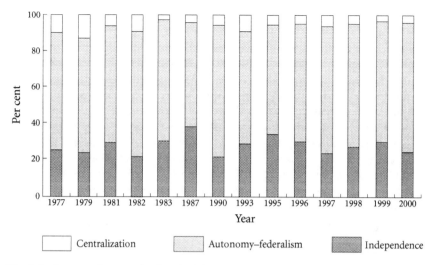

Fig. 3.9. Support for constitutional options, Basque Country, 1977–2000.
Source: Euskobarómeter.

familiar with the idea of self-determination and most of them support it, but only a third consider it the same as independence (García Ferrando *et al.* 1994; Moral 1998). Support for the Spanish constitution has increased since 1978 but is still under 50 per cent, suggesting that there is a continuing problem about the legitimacy of the state (Euskobarómeter, November 2000).

There is some evidence, then, that the Basque Country is a divided society, with nationalists and non-nationalists occupying different political worlds, but there is not a clear ethnic division based on ascriptive criteria. Not all native-born Basques are nationalists, while a substantial proportion of immigrants are, over a generation or two, drawn into the nationalist community. Nationalism has a harder edge than in Catalonia, with more support for independence. Identification with Spain among Basques in 1994 was just 5.7 on a decimal scale, against 8.26 in Catalonia and 8.8 in Spain as a whole (Sangrador García 1996). Attitudes to independence follow identification. While it is true that identification as purely Spanish or purely local is actually higher in Catalonia (Mota 1998), if we add the various measures of localism cumulatively, they tend to coincide in the Basque Country to produce a core of 'coherent *independentistas*' higher than in Catalonia, where the various measures tend to cross-cut more (Table 3.3). This means, as many of the PNV leaders are aware, that to press for independence would risk opening up the social divide between the nationalist and non-nationalist communities. The strategy of ETA, on the other hand, appears predicated on precisely forcing this social division, to increase the solidity and reinforce the boundary of the nationalist community.

Basque particularism also emerges in attitudes to Europe where the elite link between nationalism and Europeanism has not penetrated society as it has in Catalonia. The 1994 survey showed the Basque Country to be the Spanish region with least identification with Europe, while Catalonia was among the highest (Sangrador García 1996). Among native-born Basques as among native-born Catalans identification with Europe was as strong as with Spain, but in the Basque case both were at a low level. Other surveys have shown Basques less Europhile than Catalans (CIRES 1991–6). Yet opinions may have evolved during the 1990s, as the Basques seem to accept the Euro as much as do other Spaniards, which is above the European average. Like the Scots, Basques show a strong preference to conduct their own negotiations in the European Union, with about 40 per cent of them going for this.

Nationalists in Spain's third historic nationality, Galicia, can draw on a tradition of plurinational federalism going back to Castelao (1992) but, since the transition to democracy the movement has been fragmented and heterogeneous. During the 1990s the Bloque Nacionalista Galego (BNG) brought together the various elements into an electoral coalition which displaced the socialists as Galicia's second party after the dominant PP. The BNG remained a heterogeneous coalition of the far left, social democrats, and centrists, and of separatists, federalists, and post-sovereigntists, but success forced it to define its programme more clearly. The BNG's line on nationalism has also softened somewhat. They were never quite clear about the nature of the national self-government they sought, but the early rhetoric was quite radical, couched in anti-colonial terms and embracing the language of the Basque radicals, with whom they had close links. By the time of the autonomous elections of 1997 the BNG's programme referred to the model of the confederal or plurinational state and called for the transfer of more competences, especially in economic matters. It demanded the application in the long run of the Basque formula, in which the autonomous government would raise most taxes and pass on a proportion to Madrid. In the short term it called for a transfer of income and value added taxes. Yet, conscious of the weak economic position of Galicia, they continued to press for interterritorial solidarity in Spain and Europe, even while demanding, as a medium-term objective, the full fiscal sovereignty of Galicia.[15] Their 1999 programme laid a heavy stress on economic development, followed by education, language, and culture. There was nothing on independence and very little on constitutional issues generally.

Attitudes towards Europe have also modified over time. In the early years the EC was condemned as a capitalist and imperialist operation against the interests of the Galician people. This allowed the BNG to capitalize on the serious problems of adaptation of the Galician economy and on the crisis in the fishing industry, which could be blamed on the Common Fisheries Policy. In 1988–9 there was a debate over whether the BNG should present

---

[15] In fact these two demands are in the same paragraph (BNG 1997: 22).

candidates for the European Parliament, given its fundamental opposition to the institution. Eventually the BNG decided that absenting themselves would be irresponsible and called for unity around a single candidate to represent Galicia. Their programme called for a minimal reform, which would give each nation (including Galicia) direct representation with a right to veto any Community action that was against its interests. By 1998 it had accepted that the EU was an inescapable reality and that Galicia needed to be present wherever possible in its institutions. There was support for a more social Europe and concern about the democratic deficit, but the focus was on improving the EU and not destroying it. In the long term the BNG dreams of replacing the state-based EU with a Europe of the Peoples but recognizes that this will require a lengthy evolution and that in the meantime there are interests within Europe that the BNG must defend, including securing a good share of Structural Funds and agricultural spending. This more positive attitude paid handsome dividends, with a 77 per cent increase in its vote for the European elections from 1994 to 1999.

Galicia comes out in polls as having a strong sense of local and regional identity, although its people are more reluctant than Catalans or Basques to call their region a nation and more likely to see Spain as one (Moral 1998). Public opinion favours regional autonomy rather than the more radical federal or confederal alternatives, and independence has hardly featured as a salient issue. As the BNG have risen in the polls and have been drawn into cooperation with the other nationalist parties of the state, the issue of self-government is beginning to reach the agenda. In this context, the claim to be a nation rather than a mere region has given a particular significance to the debate.

The three minority nations in Spain thus present rather different sets of demands, but with some emerging consensus around the concept of the plurinational state embedded in a post-sovereigntist European order. In 1998 the principal nationalist parties issued the Declaration of Barcelona, followed by meetings and declarations in Bilbao and Santiago de Compostela, in which they set out their agreed demands. These included a recognition of the plurinational state and most of the items developed by CiU, with a strong emphasis on the evolution of Europe and the new opportunities that this provided. The declaration marked an important evolution for the PNV away from its particularist and separatist tendencies, and an embrace on the part of the BNG of the reality of the European Union. Further development, however, was stunted by the political crisis in the Basque Country following the failed ETA truce.

Belgium

The Belgian party system is fragmented on linguistic as well as ideological lines, so that all parties represent the component elements of the state and no one speaks for Belgium as a whole. There are, however, explicitly nationalist or regionalist parties, and others which believe in keeping Belgium together as a matter of principle. There is a broad consensus on European integration and an appreciation both of the limits which this places on the sovereignty of small states and nations and of the opportunities which it offers (Beyers and Kerremans 2000). To this extent, everyone has adopted a form of post-sovereign politics, but to varying degrees.

At the extreme end of the stateless nationalist spectrum is the Vlaams Blok (VB) a Flemish separatist party appealing to a narrow ethnic nationalism and hostile both to Belgian Francophones and to non-European immigrants. VB accepts European integration only in the form of an intergovernmental confederation of nation-states. There would be no supranational foreign and defence policy or European social programmes. Such a confederation would include the other presently stateless nations of Europe, but the VB's extreme rightist and racist attitudes have prevented them from making alliances with other European stateless nationalists. The Volksunie (VU) is a moderate nationalist and social-democratic party whose programme envisages a confederal Belgium with sovereignty vested in the constituent nations of Flanders and Wallonia; Brussels would be a full part of Flanders and not, as at present, a distinct unit. With exceptions for the native French-speakers of Brussels, Flanders would be unilingual, and immigrants would be encouraged to integrate into the Flemish pole. Both in its proposals for confederation and in its support for integration of immigrants through language, the VU shares much in common with moderate Quebec nationalists, and, indeed, there has been a lot of mutual learning and cooperation between the two movements. VU supports a federal Europe and is a member of the European Free Alliance of nationalist and Green parties, but it is not always clear just how a Belgian confederation would fit into a European federation. In the short-term VU wants more Flemish influence in determining the Belgian position in the Council of Ministers, and envisages dividing the Belgian votes between Flanders and Wallonia (although this is not permitted under the European treaties). In the longer term the aim seems to be Flemish independence in a united Europe and, like the Catalan nationalists, it is prepared to adjust its position to the evolution of the European Union. It believes that Europe should be more than a common market on neo-liberal principles, and favours a strengthened European Parliament and greater democratization generally. With more power for Flanders and more for Europe, the Belgian state, it predicts, will gradually disappear, but in the meantime it has been prepared to participate in the government of Belgium. The Flemish Green party, Agaleev, also pursues a post-sovereigntist strategy but without the cultural or nationalist content of the VB or VU. It believes in a Europe of the Regions transcending the old nation-states but does not want these to take the form of nation-states themselves, hence its opposition to nationalism and 'separatism'. Like the VU, Agaleev opposed the Maastricht and Amsterdam treaties because they did not go far enough towards a united Europe and were excessively based on neo-liberal principles. With important pacifist traditions, both are suspicious of military integration and of NATO.

The Flemish Christian Democrats are an officially pro-Belgian party with a strong Flemish nationalist wing. They are united in support of European integration and for a Europe of the Regions, with a particular role for strong regions with legislative powers and a cultural identity (like Flanders), and speak of Flanders as a federated state (*deelstaat*) rather than a mere region. While they are against separatism, some of their leaders are given to rather nationalistic rhetoric, and in government in the 1990s they pursued the Flanders 2002 strategy predicated on a high degree of independence. These various strands are reconciled in a Europe of the Regions discourse and a strong emphasis on the principle of subsidiarity both within Europe and within Belgium. Flemish Socialists and Liberals tend to be more pro-Belgium and not given to nationalistic rhetoric. The Liberals favour a Europe of the Regions, although more on functional and efficiency grounds than for reasons of Flemish cultural identity, and have not made a clear link between European integration and the reform of the Belgian state. The Socialists reject both Flemish nationalism and regionalism as too narrow and, un-usually among the Flemish parties, favour keeping the Belgian system of social security, which in recent years has favoured Wallonia.

Minority nationalism is distinctly weaker on the Francophone side of Belgian politics. The Francophone Christian Democrats are more Belgian-minded than their Flemish counterparts, reflecting their minority position within Wallonia and their dependence on the Belgian level. Conversely, Francophone Socialists, from their power base in Wallonia, are more region-alist than those of Flanders, arguing for a Europe of the Regions and the transformation of the Committee of the Regions into a European Senate. While this reflects some of the positions of the VU, it comes without the culturalist or nationalist rhetoric found among the Flemish nationalists.

Despite the fragmentation of the party system and the existence of nation-alist and non-nationalist parties, there do remain important shared elements in the Belgian attitudes both to devolution and to Europe. There is a broad acceptance of the limitations of independence in the modern world and a consensus on the need for European integration. Similarly, there is a shared belief in the need for decentralization and for the federalization which the country undertook in the 1990s. A minority see these two trends as leading inexorably to the dissolution of Belgium into two separate states which would be full members of the EU and other transnational bodies. Most of the political elites, on the contrary, see Europe as an important factor in keeping Belgium together in some form, by externalizing matters which could otherwise be impossible to handle together, by providing a common project for both main communities, and by sustaining a common political space in which both are equally at home. At worst, Belgian elites see Europe as providing a form of insurance policy so that, should Belgium disintegrate, it will fall into a ready-made European framework.[16]

There are survey data on identity in Belgium, but the questions asked vary and responses are particularly sensitive to the order in which the various identities are presented, producing some inconsistency in the findings (Billiet 1999). Some surveys also include the option of local identity, either framed generally or specified as the town or province, a variation not present in most of the surveys in the United Kingdom, Spain, or Quebec. Matters are further complicated by the fact that Belgians, irrespective of competing sub-state identities, are among the least nationalistic peoples of Europe (de Winter *et al*. 1998). A consistent finding is that the Flemish identify more with Flanders than the Walloons do with Wallonia, reflecting the essentially asymmetrical nature of national identities in Belgium. The Flemish movement has a strong territorial base, to the point that the institutions of the Flemish region and Flemish-speaking community have merged, while there is a big difference between the territorial movement of Wallonia and the broader Francophone movement, which includes residents in Brussels and at one time included those within Flemish territory itself (Kesteloot 1993). So Flemish electors feel a tie to the cultural–political–territorial entity of Flanders, while those in Wallonia tend to identify with the French linguistic community (Doutrelpont *et al*. 2000). It is also important to bear in mind that the origins of the Flemish and Walloon movements rested in a struggle over the nature of the Belgian state, in which the Francophones were initially the dominant force, rather than a struggle against the state itself, although there have been occasional demands for the unification of Wallonia with France; it is perhaps not surprising that, following the federal reforms, a number of scholars have, furthermore, identified a return to a more Belgian identity in the course of the 1990s (de Winter *et al*. 1998). Surveys have shown a strong local identification, which has usually surpassed identification with the other levels, perhaps reflecting the historic importance of the cities and provinces of the old Low Countries. Since the 1970s, however, this has been in decline, mainly to the benefit of the regions and language communities (de Winter and Frognier 1997). Figure 3.10 shows the contrast in national identities between Flemings and Walloons. When local and European identities are added in, the picture is more complicated. Local identity features strongly, while European identity is weaker in Flanders than in Wallonia or Brussels (Table 3.4). There is in general no correlation between European identity and the various sub-national identities (Doutrelpont *et al*. 2000). At first this might suggest once again that the Flemish elites have failed to make the connection between national affirmation and European integration, but further evidence shows

---

[16] Belief in the future of Belgium seems to fluctuate. In the mid-1990s Belgian politicians and academics interviewed nearly all believed that the function of Europe was to ensure that the break-up of Belgium would be peaceful and achieved at least cost. By 2000 belief in the future of the Belgian state had revived.

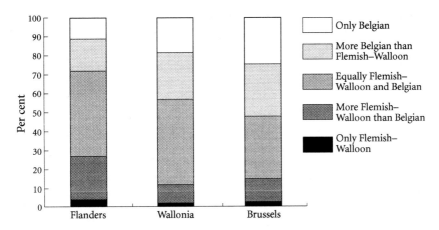

Fig. 3.10. Belgian identities, 1995.
Source: 1995 General Election Study, Belgium.

Table 3.4. Identities in Belgium, 1999 (%)

	Locality	Region	Belgium	Europe	World
Flanders	39.0	23.7	22.3	5.1	7.0
Wallonia	29.7	14.9	34.4	10.2	10.0
Brussels	20.5	19.2	27.2	14.7	16.0

Note: Totals are rounded.
Source: Billiet *et al.* (2000).

that within Flanders the VU voters have a much stronger European identification than do those of the VB or the Christian Democrats, and a weaker local identity (ICPS 1998*b*; Billiet *et al.* 2000). Residents of Brussels, perhaps not surprisingly, come out as the most pro-European and cosmopolitan. It seems that, for most Belgians, their various identities are compatible and can be mobilized in different ways for different purposes, resisting efforts to place them in opposition or even in a hierarchy (de Winter and Frognier 1997). In particular, Belgian and community identities are not in opposition at all in Wallonia and only rarely in Flanders (Doutrelpont *et al.* 2000).

Attitudes to the future of the Belgian state and its component parts are similarly fluid. There is more support for decentralization in Flanders but little support for separation. Indeed there is a strong segment of public opinion that wishes to return to the old centralized state, and there are suggestions that this element may have increased in the 1990s, in contrast to the attitudes of the elites, especially those of Flanders. The 1995 election survey asked a rather general question as to whether Flanders or Wallonia should decide everything itself or whether Belgium, Flemish, and Walloons together should decide about everything, with responses measured on a scale.

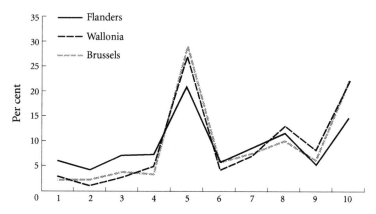

Fig. 3.11. Attitudes to autonomy, Belgium, 1995. 1 = Flanders–Wallonia should decide everything; 10 = Belgium should decide everything.
Source: 1995 General Election Study, Belgium.

Table 3.5. Typology of attitudes in Belgium, 1991 (%)

Attitudes to autonomy	Flanders	Wallonia
Unitarists	31.0	28.5
Hesitating unitarists	13.0	17.0
Neutrals	0.0	20.0
Hesitating regionalists	12.0	15.5
Regionalists	33.0	19.0
Autonomists	11.0	0.0

Source: Maddens *et al.* (1994).

As Figure 3.11 shows, there was a strong clustering around the middle range, but Flemish voters were more inclined to independence than those in Wallonia or Brussels. Even among those registering scores between 1 and 4 on support for the regions deciding everything, however, only 16.8 per cent of Flemish and 10 per cent of Walloons wanted complete independence. Maddens *et al.* (1994) capture the spectrum of attitudes in Belgium, from the uncompromising unitarists who want to strengthen the Belgian state to the autonomists who want to break away altogether. As Table 3.5 shows, there is no consensus in either Flanders or Wallonia and, while there is a greater regionalism in the former, there is also slightly greater support for a centralized Belgium. Yet while there is an underlying wish on the part of both Flemings and Walloons to retain a Belgian frame of reference, the political dynamics have served to create two quite distinct political communities. De Wachter (1996) demonstrates this dramatically by showing how Flemings and Walloons–Francophones are able easily to identify their own politicians but find great difficulty in recognizing those from the other community.

Canada

While Quebec has seen sporadic independence movements throughout its history, the issue has occupied centre stage only since the 1970s with the foundation of the Parti Québécois (PQ), which has twice staged referendums on sovereignty. During that time the issue has been surrounded by an enormous semantic confusion, as parties and political movements tried to find a formula for national autonomy. The first movement was René Lévesque's Mouvement Souveraineté-Association which soon gave way to the PQ, dedicated to negotiating a new partnership with Canada. After the failure of the 1980s referendum, which merely asked for a mandate to negotiate sovereignty-association, Lévesque changed tack, taking what was described as the *beau risque* of negotiating a renewed federalism with the federal Conservative government of Brian Mulroney, who had brought many prominent erstwhile sovereigntists (including Lucien Bouchard) into his government. These negotiations were to culminate, after the defeat of the PQ government, in the Meech Lake Accord, agreed by the Liberal provincial government of Robert Bourassa. Meanwhile, the hardliners of the PQ under Jacques Parizeau, who had resigned from Lévesque's government in protest, overthrew his successor as leader to install Parizeau in his place. The party's line was changed to one of outright independence following a future PQ election victory. After the PQ were defeated again in 1989, the line was softened once more, but by this time the US–Canada Free Trade Agreement, followed by the North American Free Trade Agreement (NAFTA), was beginning to transform the issue. Both main parties in Quebec became enthusiastic supporters of free trade as a means of loosening the Canadian federation. More generally, they adopted an active internationalism, building on the work of Quebec governments in the 1970s and 1980s in establishing a large international presence (Balthazar 1992).

Within the nationalist movement, however, there remained a division between those, like Parizeau, who believed that NAFTA and the global free-trading regime of the World Trade Organization would provide all the external support needed for an independent Quebec and those, like Lucien Bouchard, back in the nationalist fold after the failure of Meech Lake, who believed that Quebec would also need a special bilateral treaty with Canada. The result was a compromise, put to the electorate by the new PQ government of Parizeau in 1995. This asked for permission for the government to declare sovereignty, after having made an offer of association to the rest of Canada on the basis of an agreement concluded among Parizeau, Bouchard, and Mario Dumont, leader of the moderately nationalist Parti Action Démocratique du Québec. In the agreement there was provision for a Canadian common market, the continued use of the Canadian currency in Quebec, and joint executive and parliamentary institutions between Canada and Quebec to decide on matters of common interest. There would also be free movement of labour between Canada and Quebec and dual citizenship would be freely available. Following the narrow referendum defeat and his own resignation as party leader, Parizeau retreated to his hard line, insisting that a partnership with Canada was unnecessary. By 2001 the new PQ leader and premier of Quebec, Bernard Landry, was proposing a confederal arrangement on European lines between Canada and Quebec, an arrangement he dreamed of extending to the Americas as a whole. Veteran sovereigntist Claude Morin (2001) was advocating a post-sovereignty partnership to include a single market and single currency; common fundamental human rights; dual citizenship for those who wanted it; a defence accord and perhaps a common army; common norms on the environment, product standards, workplace standards, and transport, with common if not identical penal and commercial laws; and common positions in international organizations.

Meanwhile, the Quebec Liberal Party has played an equally inconsistent game. After the failure of Meech Lake, Bourassa set up two commissions to consider the possibilities of sovereignty, and unleashed the nationalist wing of his own Liberal Party to produce the Allaire Report recommending such drastic transfers of power as to amount virtually to sovereignty-association. All this manoeuvring has caused a great deal of criticism in the rest of Canada, and it must be said that the referendum questions of 1980 and 1995 were not models of clarity. On the other hand, politicians like Bouchard and Bourassa rarely strayed beyond a middle ground, vacillating between a more decentralized and asymmetrical federalism and sovereignty combined with some confederal link to Canada. Indeed federalists believing in a plur-inational state and sovereigntists favouring partnership may have more in common than the purists on either side (Seymour 2000). The difference lies perhaps more in the method, since the former involves negotiating within Canada and the latter leaving it and then trying to negotiate some way back in. Neither has proved a practical proposition given the attitudes elsewhere in Canada. They do, however, seem to correspond to the movement of Quebec public opinion, towards some form of asymmetrical arrangement within a new confederation.

The constitutional debate in Quebec has been marked by substantial semantic confusion, much of it sown by the various sides in the debate. In contrast to Scotland,[17] many of the polls are conducted on behalf of the protagonists to the debate or by polling firms close to the parties, so that findings, and in particular the wording of questions, have to be scrutinized closely. The question has changed according to the developing strategy of the

[17] Parties in the United Kingdom do conduct polls, but as far as we know they have not yet adopted the Canadian practice of placing fat contracts with selected firms when they are in government in return for free polling at election time, so party polls are much less frequent. Nationalist parties have never controlled government resources and there are no equivalents to the Council for Canadian Unity.

PQ and the international opportunity structure, notably NAFTA. We also suffer from a large gap in polling in the 1980s, when the issue was less salient.

For all these problems we can group the responses under three or four headings: federalism (with or without reform); sovereignty-association; and independence. Even these categories are very loose, as the independence question can be posed in a soft way or in a hard way, emphasizing the breaking of links with Canada. What emerges (Figure 3.12) is a fluctuating pattern of support, with the various sovereignty options moving in harmony (Cloutier *et al.* 1992; Pinard *et al.* 1997). Support for sovereignty-association or partnership is in the mid-40 per cent range for the late 1970s and 1980s, the period of the first PQ government. In the referendum of 1980 it scored only 40 per cent, rather lower than most of the polls around that time. After the failure of the referendum it falls away to the point that pollsters stop asking

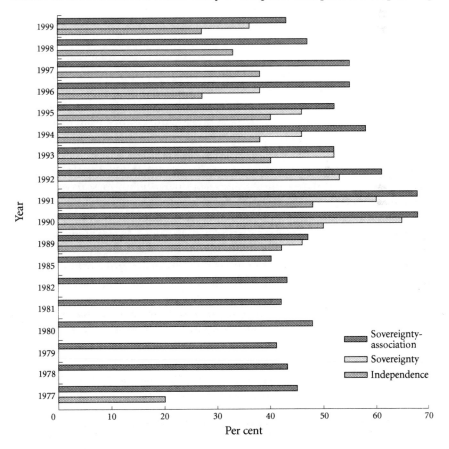

Fig. 3.12. Support for constitutional options, Quebec, 1977–1999.

Sources: Maurice Pinard; Léger and Léger; Angus Reid.

about it in 1983 and 1984. It was widely believed at this time that the issue had gone away and could be left alone, but the failure to incorporate Quebec in the constitutional settlement of 1982 rankled, and the Mulroney government, coming to power with the support of a group of erstwhile sovereigntists, sought to redress the situation with the Meech Lake Accord. The failure of Meech Lake in 1990 gave a massive boost to sovereignty, support for which was sustained for two years at 68 per cent. It then tailed away, but the election of the second PQ government in 1994 gave it a further boost. The referendum of 1995 posed a question hovering between the sovereignty and sovereignty-association options and resulted in almost exactly 50 per cent support.[18] Since then, support for sovereignty has fallen away, again feeding the belief among federalists that the battle has been won. Harder questions elicit lower levels of support. When the question of sovereignty is posed without the reassurance of association or partnership, support falls. The hard question on independence gained majority support in the polls only in the traumatic period after the failure of Meech Lake, when even the Quebec Liberal Party was threatening secession.

There is some very sophisticated analysis of the polls in Quebec, allowing us to probe the meanings of the various categories and the relationship of support for sovereignty both to socio-economic factors and to attitudes on other matters. It emerges that, while Quebeckers are able to position themselves along an axis of more federalist or separatist sentiments, they do not draw the sharp lines between independence and non-independence that observers would like. This is a source of endless frustration to federalists, who have designed a series of questions to accentuate the qualitative difference of the independence option. One finding, which they continually emphasize, is that a substantial proportion of sovereigntists think that a sovereign Quebec would remain somehow part of Canada and send MPs to the federal parliament in Ottawa. Table 3.6 is from a poll commissioned by the federal government in 1999 and shows that while 38 per cent wanted Quebec to be sovereign, only 28 per cent wanted it not to remain part of Canada. An Angus Reid poll of November 1998 showed that 47 per cent would vote yes in a referendum on the 1995 question (sovereignty with an offer of partnership); 33 would vote for Quebec independence; and just 27 did not want Quebec to remain part of Canada. A poll for the Council for Canadian Unity in 1998 showed that substantial numbers believing that a

---

[18] It read: 'Do you agree that Quebec should become sovereign, after having made a formal offer to Canada for a new economic and political partnership, within the scope of the Bill Respecting the Future of Quebec, and of the agreement signed on June 12, 1995?' The agreement in question provided for sovereignty combined with a new Canada–Quebec partnership encompassing a common market and the use of the Canadian currency, together with a joint executive for Quebec and Canada to decide on common issues, with representation according to population, and an advisory parliamentary assembly, with parity of representation. This was modelled on the EU and represented an effective return to the old sovereignty-association formula.

Table 3.6. Support for sovereignty options in Quebec, 1999 (%)

Sovereignty-partnership	Independence	Independence, separate from Canada	Don't want Quebec to remain a province of Canada
38	35	31	28

Source: CROP poll, Aug. 1999.

Table 3.7. Implications of sovereignty in Quebec

	Yes	No	Don't know, no answer
Under sovereignty-partnership, do you think			
Quebec would leave Canada and become an independent country?	50	37	13
Quebec would still elect MPs in Ottawa?	29	55	16
Quebeckers would still be citizens of Canada?	39	48	13
Quebec would still be a province of Canada?	36	52	12

Source: Council for Canadian Unity (1998).

sovereign Quebec would participate fully in Canadian affairs (Table 3.7). One could cite many more polls to the same effect, but more light is shed on the issue in a July 1997 poll for the Council for Canadian Unity. This showed that both no voters (on sovereignty) and Bloc Québécois voters (the Quebec nationalist party in the Canadian federal parliament, presumably more convinced nationalists) were less likely than the average to think that Quebec could be sovereign and remain in Canada. In between were the soft or conditional nationalists, looking for a middle ground.

The evidence suggests, then, that there is a core of separatist voters and a core of anti-nationalists (found almost entirely outside the Francophone community), but a large number of Quebeckers who are looking for a third way between separatism and federalism. It is also clear that most Quebeckers resent being forced to choose between the polar options, as they have to in a referendum. Polls before the 1995 referendum and again before and after the re-election of the PQ government in 1998 showed strong majorities against staging a referendum at all. A poll immediately after the 1998 election showed that only 24 per cent of electors thought that Bouchard should pursue his strategy of establishing the winning conditions for another refer- endum. Even PQ voters were opposed by 60 to 37 per cent (Angus Reid survey, November 1998). Yet 47 per cent declared that, if there were a referendum, they would vote yes, and 64 per cent thought that Bouchard would indeed work to create the winning conditions. Although by 2001 the federalist camp had more or less declared victory as sovereigntist support was down to about 40 per cent, this represented a rather stable core and,

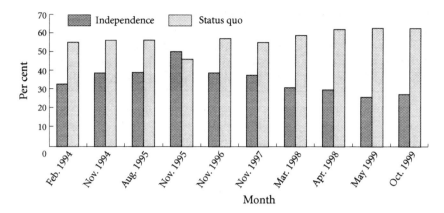

Fig. 3.13. Support for independence versus status quo, Quebec, 1994–1999.
Source: Ekos polls between 1994 and 1999.

indeed, support since 1997 had settled at about the level it had been immediately before the near-victory in the referendum of 1995 (Durand 2001). A force-distribution asking people to choose between independence and the status quo shows lower levels of support for independence (Figure 3.13).[19]

The federalist Plan B, launched in the aftermath of the 1995 referendum, builds on this sort of finding and is intended to consolidate the various sovereignty options under the independence heading. It is sustained by consistent evidence that people in Quebec want a 'clear' question and do not think that the 1995 question was clear. While the 1995 question was certainly ambivalent, however, we still lack evidence on just what a clear question would look like. The federal government's 'Clarity Bill' suggests that it would involve a hard choice on independence and could not include any reference to partnership even on EU lines. By 2000 the federalists had managed, by equating sovereignty with separatism, to push support below 40 per cent. Yet the strategy comes with risks. At the time of the 1995 referendum independence outranked the status quo in public opinion and there is a real chance that at some stage Quebeckers, if not allowed a post-sovereigntist option, would vote for complete separation.

Another way of probing the meaning of sovereignty is to ask what matters should be the responsibility of the Quebec government. Blais and Nadeau (1992) conclude that sovereigntists are primarily concerned domestic policy, notably with control of culture, education, and social policy, but are prepared to leave foreign policy to Canada. This is confirmed in more recent polls. An Environics/CROP poll of 1997 showed majority support, at similar levels, in Quebec and Ontario for more provincial control over social

---

[19] This is consistent with CROP polls showing similar options.

housing, employment training, and social services. Quebeckers, on the other hand, were much more likely to want control over health, education, language policy, and environmental protection. 31 per cent of Quebeckers wanted provincial control over immigration, a matter linked to culture and language, against just 12 per cent in Ontario. Support for other state powers is much lower.

The ambivalence about sovereignty reflects Quebeckers' sense of dual identity. After the 1960s there was a rise in a distinct Québécois identity, replacing the old French Canadian ethnolinguistic identity. This gradually became the primary identity of most Quebeckers, but did not entirely displace Canadian identity. Quebeckers divide into three groups: those who have a strong emotional attachment to Canada; those whose attachment is merely instrumental, dependent on economic advantage; and those who have no attachment at all. There has been an increase in the second and third groups. Between 1980 and 1991 the percentage feeling profoundly attached to Canada fell from 56 to 30, and this correlates with support for sovereignty (Angus Reid 6.10, 1991; 5.10, 1992; Cloutier *et al.* 1992). Pinard (1992) cites data showing that the percentage of Francophones identifying themselves as Québécois increased from 21 per cent in 1970 to 59 per cent in 1990, while those identifying as Canadians fell from 34 per cent to 9 per cent. In less fraught times there is a return to dual identity but still with a bias to the Quebec one. Another 1999 poll showed that, while people in Quebec and in the Rest of Canada (RoC) were equally attached to their provinces, 88 per cent in RoC against 58 per cent in Quebec felt strongly attached to Canada (Ekos 1999).

An approach developed by Jean-Herman Guay and applied by the CROP team identifies four indicators of support for sovereignty:[20]

1. It is not possible to reform the federation.
2. Quebec has the right to separate.
3. Quebec has the material and human resources to be sovereign.
4. Sovereignty is realizable in the short term.

The federalist Plan B has played, with considerable success, on item 2, support for which fell sharply in the late 1990s, taking with it item 4. On the other hand, item 3 fell less sharply and may be a better predictor of support for various degrees of sovereignty, if not separation, in the long run. This would be particularly so if globalization and North American Free Trade convinced Quebeckers that small nations could go it alone. One might speculate that if Quebec, like Scotland, were part of a member state of the EU, this argument would be difficult to gainsay.

As in Scotland, the argument about free trade has been linked to the constitutional issues in two ways: by the PQ, which sees free trade as permitting

---

[20] See *La Météo politique* (1998).

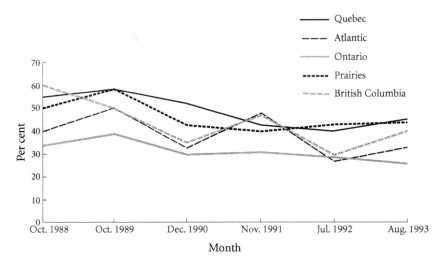

Fig. 3.14. Support for free trade, Quebec, 1988–1993.

independence; and by the Quebec Liberals, who see it as permitting a loosening of the Canadian federation and limiting the power of Ottawa. Support levels for free trade in Quebec have consistently been higher than in neighbouring Ontario, although not always as high as in the western provinces (Figure 3.14). Yet while western support for free trade can be explained on economic grounds, this is less plausible in Quebec, where it stems rather from an elite consensus in both main parties, which in turn is based on strategic–political rather than economic considerations (Martin 1995). For the Liberals this is less of a problem, linked, as they are, to the Quebec business elite. The PQ, however, has a larger working-class base and a social-democratic wing, which have tended to share the opposition to free trade of their counterparts in the rest of Canada. PQ voters are thus likely to be cross-pressured. It is perhaps this that explains why we have not been able to find a correlation at individual level between support for the independence of Quebec and support for free trade.[21] The problem is perhaps most acute for the Quebec dairy farmers, who are strongly sovereigntist, but who would lose their protected Canadian markets to US competition if Quebec were to become independent within NAFTA.[22] This cross-pressuring, similar to the fishermen and small farmers of Scotland, may again explain some of the reticence about independence, as opposed to more complex arrangements allowing for more autonomy without surrendering the Canadian framework

[21] I have correlated support for free trade with support for independence in Quebec and found a consistently positive but not statistically significant relationship.

[22] An Angus Reid poll of September 1995 showed 62% of Quebeckers in favour of Quebec dairy farmers keeping their production quotas for the Canadian market after independence, while 77% of Canadians outside Quebec were opposed.

altogether. Support for the idea of a common currency for the United States and Canada, an idea floated in the late 1990s, also splits along national lines. A 1999 poll showed that while English Canadians massively reject the idea (58 per cent), a small majority of Quebeckers are favourable (51 per cent) with supporters of the Bloc Québécois being most favourable of all (65 per cent) (Ipsos Reid poll, 3 August 1999).

Controversies about aboriginal self-government rights go back to the earliest days of European settlement but the issue has entered into serious discussion only in recent decades. The British North America Act, founding the Canadian federation in 1867, mentioned only status Indians, who were placed under the trusteeship of the federal government, with no reference to the Métis (people of mixed aboriginal and European ancestry) or Inuit. From the 1940s there was some mobilization among native peoples, but the modern history of the issue dates from the 1960s and particularly the reaction to the federal government's 1969 White Paper proposing a comprehensive assimilation policy. Early demands for self-government were focused on respect for existing treaties, the need for new treaties where they did not exist, and on land claims. The lengthy debates on repatriating the Canadian constitution and the rise of Quebec nationalism stimulated further mobilization and pointed to the need for a place for aboriginal peoples within the redesigned confederation. Canada's new constitution in 1982 did recognize, for the first time, the existence of the three aboriginal groups, but they were not part of the constitutional revision process. Nor were they involved in the negotiations on the Meech Lake Accord designed to bring Quebec into the constitution. In 1982 the Assembly of First Nations was formed from earlier bodies, as a united body for status Indians. Other bodies speaking for indigenous peoples are the Congress of Aboriginal Peoples, the Métis National Council, the Inuit Tapirisat of Canada, and the Native Women's Association of Canada. Following the defeat of the Meech Lake Accord, which was strongly opposed by aboriginal groups for not giving them equal treatment with Quebec, they were brought into the consultation process for the Charlottetown Accord, although without the status as full parties enjoyed by the provincial and territorial leaders. It was Charlottetown that first recognized the inherent right of aboriginal self-government, although the Accord was defeated in the referendum in English Canada, in Quebec, and among the native peoples.

Over the years aboriginal demands have developed from status claims to a more developed nationalism using the language of self-determination and original rights. There has been a strong identification with the colonized nations elsewhere and appeals to international bodies and the United Nations. The case is summed up in six points in the Universal Declaration of the Indigenous Aboriginal Nations of Canada (Center for World Indigenous Studies 1999):

1. We are nations. We have always been nations.
2. As nations we have inherent and fundamental rights which have never been given up and which we continue to exercise.
3. We have always had and exercised the right to govern ourselves and will continue to do so.
4. The right to govern is an expression of our right to be a self-determining nation of people within a revised Canadian Federation.
5. Our right to govern ourselves includes our right to determine our own citizens.
6. Our right to govern includes the right to determine the kind of education we want for our children, the kind of economy we need to foster self-reliance, sufficient control of our land and resources to be self-sufficient, and the right to control our land—including water, air, minerals, timber and wildlife.

This is a plea for sovereignty but of a radically different kind from classic statehood. Self-determination and nationhood are strongly asserted, and other documents show that this is placed in an international context, yet there is no demand to leave Canada. Rather, the emphasis is on reshaping Canada as a nation of nations. Aboriginal peoples are thus a founding partner in the Canadian state and entitled to a full say in how it evolved. Within this broad understanding there is a variety of views, with some emphasizing separation or parallel development, under the symbol of the two row wampum, an image of two boats going down the same river together. Others place more stress on the integration of native peoples into Canadian life, on their own terms. Further questions arise regarding the position of aboriginal peoples living in cities (up to 40 per cent of the population, depending on how they are counted). Generally speaking, in constitutional negotiations priority has been given to territorially based claims. There are also differences on the concept of citizenship of aboriginal self-governing territories. The Royal Commission on Aboriginal Peoples (Canada 1996), which had a majority of aboriginal members, recommended against ethnic criteria for membership in native self-government bodies, insisting that they should be 'political communities... Their bonds are those of culture, not blood.' Instead, it proposed three models. Nation government could be applied where a group has an exclusive territorial base, and here elements of traditional government could be incorporated. Public government would be appropriate where, as in Nunavut, an aboriginal group is in the majority but where others are present. Community interest government would be applied where an aboriginal group was not in the majority, and could not therefore dominate territorial institutions; this is of particular relevance to native peoples living in urban areas. In practice, these distinctions have not avoided the need to determine membership and status in aboriginal self-government institutions, and this has been one of the most controversial issues at stake.

Paths to Self-Determination

The stateless nations under consideration here have consolidated their national identities in recent years, strengthened their institutions and become a primary point of political reference for their citizens (Pinard *et al.* 1997; Keating 2000*b*). Their political parties have been moving towards a post-sovereignty stance, but to varying degrees and in various ways. The most advanced are in Catalonia, where this ties into a historic discourse of shared sovereignty and multiple spheres of action. Basque nationalism, having gone through a phase of classic nineteenth-century nationalism, has generally been slower to recuperate its pre-sovereignty traditions, but is moving that way under the influence of Europeanization and a new generation of thinkers (Gurrutxaga 1999). There is a strong movement within Scottish nationalism towards the post-sovereign position, but support for classical statehood remains widespread. Indeed in some ways Europe may have strengthened the latter in the short run, since it has permitted the SNP to maintain its sovereignty–independence language largely intact, merely placing it in the context of the EU. Scotland, on this view, could become as much of an independent state as the Netherlands simply by acceding to the *acquis communautaire*. Welsh nationalism, in which separatism has traditionally been weaker, has found the transition easier. Northern Irish politics is polarized around the issue of belonging to one or other sovereign state, but the sheer impossibility of reconciling the two has forced the parties into new solutions, which detach nationality, to some degree, from statehood. In Belgium, nationalist–regionalist affirmation is strongest in Flanders, but is divided among the hard-line nationalists of the VB, the moderate nationalists of the VU, and the regionalists of the other parties. All except the VB are strongly committed to European unity and accept that this entails a drastic transformation of old ideas about state and national sovereignty.

The parties in Quebec are separated on the issue of sovereignty, but if we remove this invisible but politically crucial line, then they look less far apart. Both are committed to the national affirmation of Quebec in a post-sovereign political order, with only the hard-line sovereigntists and federalists outside this broad consensus. In one sense, however, all the sovereigntists have to devise their own form of limited independence, whether by negotiating a new bilateral pact with the rest of Canada (Bouchard) or free-riding on Canadian institutions, notably the currency (Parizeau). Sovereignty remains critical in Quebec because of the absence of an overarching structure like the EU, after which the softer nationalists hanker. In Europe, as we shall see, the emerging transnational order helps to defuse the issue, hence the strong support from the stateless nationalist parties for the new European order (Chapter 5). In all the cases, there has been an increasing emphasis on the need of small nations to maintain social and cultural coherence while improving their competitive position within the global trading order (Keating 2001*a*; Latouche 1991;

Santacoloma *et al.* 1995; Parellada and Garcia 1997; Gómez *et al.* 1999). This provides a common political economy perspective on the issue. Constitutionally, matters are less clear, since there is as yet no constitutional provision for stateless nations within the EU. Consequently, nationalist parties have to play both statist and regionalist games, arguing for formal or effective independence in Europe at one time, and joining the Europe of the Regions movement at others.

Public opinion has in some respects been ahead of the political elites. National identities are increasingly pluralist, with citizens often able to identify with the local nation, the state, and the broader transnational order. Of course, measures of identity such as those cited earlier are static and give little insight into the meaning of identity and the ways it is used in different circumstances. Yet the very possession of multiple identities provides the possibility of operating in different national settings without undue stress, and it does appear that these identities are increasingly treated as politically relevant rather than simply as a form of cultural marker. It is clear, from analysis of the survey data, that the peoples of the stateless nations stand out in their dual identities and attribution of nationality to both.[23] Loyalty to the state is perhaps increasingly conditional rather than absolute, but in no case has a sense of belonging to the wider state disappeared. Again, of course, there are differences from one case to another, with the Catalans again emerging as among the most plurinational. Public opinion is also less dogmatic on issues of sovereignty and more open to new solutions. There is strong support for nationalism, much less for radical separatism. So far this has tended to remain unfocused, as the nationalist elites have taken longer to persuade their publics of the connection between national affirmation and transnational integration, partly because electors are cross-pressured by class and other questions. They have been more successful among Catalans and Irish Catholics than in the other cases, but everywhere we have seen some movement towards linking the two. In North America this overarching political framework is not available, and post-sovereigntist politics has been discouraged by the federalist counter-attack which insists that in North America there is no third way between being independent and not being independent, and refuses to allow the possibility of a sovereign Quebec nation within a Canadian confederation.

Acceptance of plurinationality by state majorities is more varied. In the United Kingdom, as already noted, there is a general acceptance of the idea of national diversity and a rather relaxed attitude, indeed indifference, on the part of the English majority towards the constitutional aspirations of the other parts of the state. This has not, however, crystallized into a coherent view of England's place in the Union and there is even some evidence that

---

[23] It should be added that the Canary Islands also stands out within Spain for its strong sense of distinct identity.

Englishness may be being appropriated by the xenophobic right. State-wide political parties have at one level accepted the right of the stateless nations to secede, but have been ambivalent on the issue of self-determination within the state. Labour, notably, accepted Scottish sovereignty in the 1988 Declaration of Right, but denied this in government. The majority populations of Spain and Canada are much less amenable to the idea of plurinationality or constitutional diversity and tend to insist on the constitutional equality of the provinces and regions. To a large degree this reflects the fact that they do not have a national identity distinct from that of the state, but it is also a result of political practice and leadership. Opinion polls in Canada have consistently shown opposition to any suggestion of special status or recognition for Quebec, of about 70 per cent in the rest of Canada. A 1997 CBC poll, typical of the series, showed that 64 per cent of voters in the rest of Canada thought that Quebec should be a province with its existing powers, while 6 per cent wanted Quebec to be totally independent. Within Quebec support for the proposition that they should be a province with the same powers was just 21 per cent.

The Meech Lake Accord never gained public support in Canada and the Charlottetown Accord was soundly defeated in the referendum. Spanish electors outside the historic nationalities similarly have little interest in constituting a plurinational state. They do not recognize the right of self-determination of the historic nationalities, although one factor here may be that they identify this with separatism. In the 1996 CIS poll support for a confederal state reached significant levels only in Catalonia, the Basque Country, and Navarre (Moral 1998). Political parties have tended to insist on the unity and sovereignty of the Spanish nation, and although at the time of the transition the Socialists did accept the principle of self-determination (de Blas 1984), they later on insisted that autonomy was the gift of the Spanish state (González, 1982). In Belgium there is no such central majority and indeed it is the Francophones, numerically the minority, who are more strongly attached to a single Belgian identity. The next chapter examines the implications of these complex identities and demands for constitutional accommodation within the state, while the following one looks at the possibilities within the emerging transnational order.

4

Asymmetrical Government and the Plurinational State

The Problem of Deep Diversity

The concept of the plurinational state, sketched out in Chapter 1, might be criticized as abstract and in violation of the secular trend to state sovereignty and unity. Yet as we have seen, there are other ways of thinking about state and nation as historically developing normative orders. The last chapter has shown that there are movements committed to new forms of national affirmation beyond statehood, rooted both in historic practice and in an appreciation of the possibilities offered by the new state and international order. This chapter considers how such demands might be satisfied within a reconfigured state, based on the principles of plurinationality and asymmetry; the following one considers solutions beyond the state.

One classic response to the existence of diversity within states is decentralization, devolution, or federalism, dividing power so as to allow territorial communities to manage their own affairs, control their own resources, and make their own policy choices. Yet, as writers from de Tocqueville (1986) have stressed, federalism seems to require a degree of national homogeneity, or at least a strong commitment to shared values, to balance the centrifugal forces of decentralization. Many have concluded that ethnic or nationally based federations will not work (Tarleton 1965; Frank 1968; Trager 1968). Elazar (1993, 1996) identifies the crucial dilemma that federal arrangements are needed for complex multinational societies but that the very nature of these societies makes it difficult to achieve. In these countries we find what Charles Taylor (1993b) calls deep diversity, the demand not merely for devolution of this or that competence, but for recognition as a distinct people, or a distinct national community (Fossas 1999a; Requejo 1999a; Rubert de Ventós 1999; Máiz 1999). To the outsider, the issues in contention here can often look merely trivial or 'symbolic' yet the symbolism takes us to the heart of political legitimacy and self-determination. While the question at any one time might be whether the term 'nation' can be used, or whether a place constitutes a 'distinct society', the larger implication is that the state contains more than one *demos*, and more than one fount of sovereignty. The issue is also one of democracy. Defenders of the uniform nation-state will insist that, as long as members of national minorities have full voting rights, then democratic norms are being respected. Yet democratic politics depends on the existence of deliberative communities (Miller 2000) or political spaces (Keating 2001*b*) in which citizen choices are debated and formed and stateless nations constitute one such community. If such communities are denied, or assimilated into larger ones, or the choices emerging from them are consistently overruled by state-wide majorities, then democracy is curtailed (Gagnon and Gibbs 1999).

Recognition of plurinationality, of the existence of nations within nations, has proved difficult, precisely because of the strong normative implications of the terms. General acceptance of popular sovereignty has accentuated the insistence that the sovereign people must correspond to the nation. So for some people and states there can only be one people and nationality is singular. In the 1980s the French constitutional court struck down an apparently innocuous reference to the 'Corsican people' on the grounds that there can only be one *demos* within the republic. Many people in Canada find it difficult to conceive of the possibility of a Quebec nation within the Canadian nation; or think that the recognition of a Québécois nation entails the denial of the Canadian one. There is a long-standing view that to accord aboriginal people the status of nations with their own citizenship implies depriving them of Canadian nationality, rather than giving them the status of 'citizens plus' (Cairns 2000). Even people who recognize the reality of diversity are tempted to find another word for the minority entity. In Spain the terms 'Spanish people' and 'Spanish nation' were often used interchangeably in the nineteenth and early twentieth century as weapons against monarchist claims but were never accepted in the peripheral nations. After fierce arguments between the Catalan representatives and the rest, the 1931 republican Spanish constitution in its general declaration avoided the term 'nation' both for the state and for the minorities, although the expression did creep into various articles (Hernández 1980). The 1978 constitution skirts the issue by insisting on the indissoluble unity of the Spanish nation and then talking about the 'nationalities' within it. The Canadian constitution of 1982 marks a step forward in the recognition of aboriginal claims, raising them to the status of 'peoples', which is getting towards nationhood but not quite reaching it. Miller (1995) wonders whether Scotland and Wales can really be 'nations' since they are also part of the British nation, but generally people in the United Kingdom can live with multiple conceptions of nationality.[1] Yet even in the United Kingdom the implication is that the term 'nation' carries connotations of the right of self-determination, and it is for this very reason that unionists have

---

[1] Failure to understand that nations can exist within nations is no doubt one factor in the infuriating tendency for many people outside the United Kingdom to refer to the whole state as England.

been unwilling to concede elected parliaments to the peripheral nations (discussed below).

The Politics of Symbols

The debate about the language of nationality or peoples might appear merely symbolic but for the normative charge of the terms. As noted earlier, the term 'nationality' is in part defined by a claim to self-determination. This does not, despite the fears of many, amount to separatism, but it does at least involve the acceptance of the political order as a pact among entities with their own original rights, hence the fierce arguments over historiography. Such a view is incompatible with the doctrine of unitary state sovereignty. Hence the traditional British unionist refusal to concede decentralization along national lines, while allowing all manner of municipal government. Hence too the position of Spanish Jacobins or Canadian federalists like Trudeau, who was unwilling to make precisely these symbolic gestures. Debates on symbolism reach deep into discussions of accommodating nationalities. Against those who have defended the consolidated state as a neutral forum shorn of ethnic or national connotations, Kymlicka (1995) and Tully (1995) have insisted that even the most 'civic' or national identities have a symbolic code, focused on the dominant group. This may be true of states in general, but within this code some states give more recognition to pluralism than do others. The symbolism involved ranges from highly political issues like the name of the state or the flag, to the 'banal nationalism' (Billig 1995) of everyday life. The United Kingdom has gone furthest here, its very name reflecting its plurinational composition, while the union flag is no more than the superimposition of the flags of the component nations. The monarchy takes care to cultivate its Scottish credentials, while the army consciously uses national and regional patriotisms in the names and recruitment patterns of its regiments. In Spain and Canada leaders have preferred to construct an overarching nationality purportedly separate from and above the components, but which has tended to incorporate the majority symbolism. The minorities are celebrated as components of the cultural diversity and richness of the country, not as individual entities in a plurinational reality.[2] Belgium is a different case again. Flemish activists complained consistently during the nineteenth century that the image of the state was a Francophone one; but the twentieth century has seen an assertion of ever greater Flemish particularism rather than the reconstruction of the state symbolism on plurinational lines. Nationalist symbolism is deployed much more in Flanders than in Wallonia, perhaps because of the Walloons' greater identification of their culture with the Belgian one (de Witte and Verbeek 2000).

[2] I myself have two passports, one of which carries the legend 'European Community. United Kingdom of Great Britain and Northern Ireland', while the other one simply has 'Canada'.

Public holidays may also be treated with respect for plurinationalism. In the United Kingdom, Canada, and Belgium there are some holidays for the whole state and others for the component parts.[3] A symbolic issue of some importance is the ability to field national sports teams. Here again, the United Kingdom has the most pluralist provision, although this owes more to historical accident and the assignment of responsibility to civil society than a conscious policy on the part of the state. Olympic teams and track and field events are organized on a UK basis (although there are separate national track and field teams in the Commonwealth games). Separate soccer teams exist for England, Scotland, Wales, and Northern Ireland, with no British or UK team. For rugby, there are teams from England, Scotland, Wales, and Ireland (north and south together), with an occasional 'British' selection (now renamed 'British and Irish'). None of this has caused any great problem or been subject to much controversy, although sporting teams are an important symbol of the individual national identities. Spain recognizes for international purposes only teams representing the whole state, although in recent years the Basque and Catalan nationalist governments have been pressing for their own selections and passed their own laws to provide for this. Generally, these have been presented as a supplement to all-Spain teams rather than a substitute, but the analogy with the United Kingdom is used to bolster the case.[4] A survey in Belgium showed only 5 per cent of Flemings in favour of splitting the Belgian national team (de Winter and Frognier 1997). Canada too has only a single selection in each sport, though the Quebec media do tend to focus on Quebec athletes in international competitions. Nationalists would of course like to field their own selections, but this has not been pressed the way it has in Catalonia and the Basque Country.

In matters of religion the United Kingdom was unusual in pre-nineteenth-century European states in maintaining two official religions. This was not a matter of tolerance or pluralism, but a settlement which allowed the Scots to have their own church, presbyterian in organization and Calvinist in doctrine, while the Church of England was imposed elsewhere.[5] In 1869 Gladstone disestablished the church in Ireland, a concession extended to Wales after the First World War, so that all parts of the kingdom had a different relationship between church and state. Secularization has greatly diminished the salience of this issue, but different forms of established religion still mark

---

[3] Kymlicka's (1995) objection that every state has a national culture because there are statewide holidays thus seems misplaced. It is possible even to go below the component nations. Municipal councils in Scotland set most of the public holidays. In England and Wales, when Sunday trading was illegal, there were special provisions for Jewish merchants, provided that they closed on Saturdays.

[4] Basques and Catalans will confess in private that they fear their own teams would not progress far in world and European competitions, and take pride in the numbers of Basque and Catalan players in the Spanish teams.

[5] This marks the United Kingdom as a clearly 'non-Westphalian' state, violating from the outset the principle of *cuius regio, eius religio*.

the United Kingdom from other plurinational states and have helped shape its distinct national identities.[6]

A question that goes beyond the symbolic concerns the educational curriculum and its role in inculcating national identities. Here too the United Kingdom has operated in a remarkably decentralized manner for a unitary state. There has never been a state-wide Ministry of Education and the 'national curriculum' developed in the 1980s and 1990s applies only in England. Wales has its own variant, which now includes the Welsh language as a compulsory element. Educational provision in Scotland has always been made separately; there is no national curriculum, but central guidance (from Edinburgh) was stronger than in England before the latter adopted the national curriculum. The Scottish educational policy community has always jealously guarded its autonomy, although there have been complaints that the syllabus has not been sufficiently Scottish. Education is an area in which the Canadian provinces have resisted federal intrusion, and this has allowed Quebec to shape its own system and curriculum to reflect its distinct society. Aboriginal peoples, on the other hand, were forced until the 1960s into the European educational system under the aegis of the federal government, with a view to eliminating their culture and assimilating them. Belgian education has always been organized in a complex manner, to accommodate both linguistic differences and the lay-secular cleavage. It is now entirely devolved to the linguistic communities, so that pupils no longer follow the same curriculum (Martiniello 1997), leading to some efforts in Flanders to use it as an instrument of nation-building. Matters are different in Spain, where a formerly centralized system has been devolved to the autonomous communities. Although the system is almost entirely devolved to the autonomous communities on the fast track, including the three historic nationalities, a national Ministry of Education still exists and the state has retained the monopoly of validating academic qualifications. This gives it an influence over the content of education and has been a source of frequent conflicts. In the late 1990s the conservative government of the Partido Popular proposed a reform of the teaching of humanities to emphasize Spanish national themes, especially in history. They had to abandon the plan as a condition of support from the Catalan and Basque nationalists, but, returning to office with an absolute majority in 2000, they declared their intention to return to the issue.

Instances of banal nationalism within the stateless nations are legion. Institutions, especially in the field of culture, are given the title 'national', a designation that does not require the endorsement of the state but which would be unthinkable in a Jacobin state like France. Outsiders need a careful

---

[6] Curiously, another example of religious asymmetry is in Alsace, where state establishment of the Catholic Church, abolished elsewhere in France in 1905, was retained when Alsace returned to French control after the First World War.

education to learn that 'national security' or the National Health Service refer to the United Kingdom, but 'national curriculum' in education refers to the component parts separately; or that the National Trust covers England, Wales, and Northern Ireland but the National Trust for Scotland refers to the Scottish nation. Scottish and Northern Irish banknotes do not denote a separate currency, but reflect the fact that the state bank (still called the Bank of England) does not have the monopoly of note issue in two parts of the United Kingdom. Catalan institutions are routinely given the designation 'national', although this does not carry great resonance elsewhere in Spain. In the Basque Country, by contrast, use of the term 'national' carries nationalist overtones and is largely confined to supporters of the nationalist parties. Quebec entitles many of its institutions, including its legislature, as 'national', but, again, this is not broadly recognized outside its boundaries since other Canadians tend to see only one nation which includes Quebec. In Flanders the term 'national' carries strong nationalist overtones and is deployed accordingly by the nationalist parties, but the Flemish government prefers the term 'region', a term which would be unacceptable in Scotland.

Constitutionalizing Difference

Recognizing the existence of multiple nationalities within the state may be the first step to addressing the problem, but resolving it requires that this be given practical and institutional expression. Paradoxically, most states have found it easier to countenance secession than to recognize internal pluralism. This became clear in Canada in the late 1990s. Following the 1995 referendum, the federal government made a reference to the Supreme Court of the right of secession under Canadian and international law, and the conditions under which this would be possible. The court found that there was no right of secession but that, if Quebec were to vote yes by a clear majority on a clear question, then Canada would have to negotiate (Supreme Court of Canada 1998). This was a clear breach in the doctrine of the integrity of the state and was initially welcomed both by federalists and by many Quebec nationalists, as well as drawing international attention for its weaving of legal and political, as well as domestic and international, considerations (Oliver 1999). The apparent clarity of this judgement, however, soon dissolved into wrangling over what constituted a clear question and a clear majority. Arguments about the majority pitched the Parti Québécois, which favoured a rule of 50 per cent plus one, against the federal government, which insisted that some sort of qualified majority would be necessary. There was also a wrangle about the rights of minorities within Quebec to remain within Canada. The issue of a clear question is even more intractable since, as has been argued at length here, sovereignty itself is a difficult and changing concept in the modern world. The federal government's line was reflected in a bill of December 1999 (the Clarity Bill) laying down procedures for secession but extending these to provinces in general. This would allow negotiations on secession only if there were an undefined super-majority, and if it were clear that the seceding province would cease to be part of Canada and not linked by any form of economic or political association with it. This had the merit of providing some basis for federal responses to future referendums, but arguably posed a serious danger to the unity of the country. We have seen that most Quebec elite and public opinion does not seek a complete break but recognition within a plurinational state. With this inter-mediate solution ruled out, except in the form of mild concessions from the federal level, Quebeckers were effectively being invited to secede altogether, or have their bluff called. What the Supreme Court was not asked to address is the question that really appears to concern Quebeckers, whether they, as the subject of self-determination, have the right to renegotiate their position within the Canadian federation without having to secede. Yet by conceding the right to secession, they were admitting the limitations to national sover-eignty, if not accepting the full implications of the plurinational state.

Similarly, in the United Kingdom, unionists, who have never denied the multinational character of the United Kingdom, have claimed to have fewer problems with secession than with asymmetrical devolution (Townsend 2000; Dicey 1886; Dalyell 1977). There is no constitutional provision for the secession of Scotland, but political leaders of all parties have made it clear that there would be no obstacles placed in Scotland's way if that were its clear will.[7] In the case of Northern Ireland there was a clause in the Ireland Act of 1949 providing that Northern Ireland would remain within the United Kingdom as long as its people and Parliament wished it, indicating the provisional nature of the union. In 1998 this was changed to a more positive right to join the Republic of Ireland should a majority of the voters in a referendum so wish. Belgium's constitution does not provide for the seces-sion of its component parts, but there is an understanding among the political elites that there could be a time when the union might be dissolved; given the bilateral nature of the union, the separation of one part could not leave the rest of the state intact. There is, however, no agreement on how Brussels could be dealt with in such an event. The response has been less generous in Spain, where historical experiences have made separatism a taboo for the central elites. The constitution of 1978 affirms the indissoluble unity of the Spanish people and successive central governments have refused to concede even a theoretical right of secession to the Basque Country.

Short of secession, most answers to the question of diversity have focused on federalism. If it were simply a matter of recognizing the difference between

---

[7] In 1993 Conservative and staunchly unionist prime minister John Major (1993) declared in relation to Scotland that 'each of the constituent parts of the United Kingdom has entered into Union with the others by a different route' and that 'no nation could be held irrevocably in a Union against its will'.

the nation and the state and the existence of several nations within the state framework, then a multinational federation might address matters well, with a division of authority between the constituent nations and the overall federal level. Plurinationalism, however, is more complex, encompassing the very asymmetries of national identities themselves so that, where there is a minority nation, there is not always a majority. Canadians have to resort to expressions like 'the Rest of Canada' (RoC) or 'Canada hors Québec' to capture the collectivity that does not recognize itself. Spain has no expression for the country outside the periphery. Stateless nationalists themselves often try to imagine their adversary as a unitary actor, using names like 'English Canada', which might be a linguistic, an ethnic, or a historic category, or reserving the word 'Spain' for the central parts of the Iberian peninsula. This, however, involves stretching reality to try and forge a symmetry that does not exist. The United Kingdom might seem easier, since England is clearly a historic nation, and a stateless one at that, but most of the inhabitants of England do not see matters this way, easily confounding England, Britain, and the United Kingdom. The Flemish, too, lack a corresponding nation on the other side since, while all Walloons might be Francophones, not all Francophones are Walloons. The French population of Brussels have their own complex identity, which does not fit into any easy scheme. So it is not possible to solve the problem by devolution all round, converting the state into a federation of nations, since the majority often do not want this, and may see their own future in a unitary state, combined with local or regional devolution.

Yet partial devolution, only to the conscious and vocal nationalities, raises its own problems, since it involves recognizing two orders of authority which do not match each other clearly. Indeed, there is a persistent argument to the effect that it is precisely in states with such component nationalities that it is dangerous to devolve power, since this would mean putting control of the governmental machinery in the hands of a body claiming a direct element of sovereignty or with national or 'ethnic' underpinnings (Duchacek 1970). This is a strong version of the argument that multinational federations will not work since devolution, unbalanced by any overall plan of federation, would so destabilize the state that secession would be preferable, leaving the rest of the state as a unitary entity. Opponents often argue, indeed, that the inevitable effect of asymmetrical devolution will be separatism, since two orders of authority cannot coexist unless they are balanced in a federal arrangement. It is also argued that conceding special status for particular groups will lead to a competition for status and an unmanageable explosion of claims for special status (Breton 1993; Diekhoff 2000). There is some evidence for this, for example in the politics surrounding the Charlottetown Accord in Canada and the spread of autonomy movements in Spain, but the argument as a whole seems to confuse two issues: the recognition of plurinationality, which I have argued is limited to a particular type of case, and the more general recognition of cultural pluralism or functional decentralization, which does not involve claims to original sovereignty or plurinationality. Recognizing the plurinationalism of the state does not imply raising all other claims to recognition to the same level. On the contrary, this would defeat the very purpose of the exercise.

More problematic, perhaps, is dealing with nationality claims in the right order. One issue is usually more pressing than the others—Ireland in nineteenth-century Britain, Catalonia under the Spanish Second Republic, Quebec in Canada in the 1980s—and other minorities may resent their first claim to attention. Aboriginal peoples have resented being placed behind Quebec in the queue and were prepared to hold up progress on Quebec in order to force their own needs onto the agenda. On the other hand, stateless nations may see any move towards plurinational recognition as positive, opening up opportunities for themselves, as Scottish and Welsh nationalists did towards Ireland in the nineteenth century. Since the 1980s constitutional reformers in England have looked favourably on Scottish and Welsh devolution, not because they want to advance national claims of their own, but because devolution opens up the constitutional issue more generally.

None of the states considered has been as intransigently opposed to the recognition of internal nationalities as has France. Yet none has fully embraced the plurinational principle. Instead they have followed one track and then the other, without much consistency. Forced to concede the distinct political personalities of the stateless nations, they have then tended to cover up the concession with unitary formulations of various sorts. Rejecting the idea of negotiating with the constituent nations as holders of original rights, they have usually tried to present concessions as a matter of general principle and so been forced to extend them to the whole state or accord recognition to claims of another order altogether. So doing, they have tended to encourage precisely that explosion of claims against which critics of asymmetry have warned.

Recognizing Diversity

For over a hundred years these principled objections to asymmetry provided the intellectual basis of British unionist opposition to home rule, firstly for Ireland and then for Scotland (Dicey 1886, 1912; Wilson 1970). Unionists have rarely denied the right of secession to the stateless nations but insisted that, short of taking up this option, they must respect the untrammelled sovereignty and unity of Parliament. Governments of the centre left have sometimes been more accommodating, conceding asymmetrical home rule under the Liberals in the late nineteenth and early twentieth centuries and under Labour in the 1970s and 1990s. Had William Ewart Gladstone's programme been carried through, or the First World War not intervened to stall the programme of the Asquith Liberals, the United Kingdom might have been transformed into a rather asymmetrical federation of nations. Yet, even as they conceded the substance, centre-left governments have been as diligent as their Conservative opponents in not conceding the principle, insisting that home rule is no more than devolution of powers, which Parliament could in future take back. Gladstone (1886) went out of his way to distinguish his home rule scheme from Daniel O'Connell's earlier repeal campaign, which would have restored the old Irish Parliament. Labour governments in the 1970s and again in the 1990s inserted clauses into their Scottish devolution legislation to the effect that none of this would affect the sovereignty of Parliament, although the very fact that such clauses were seen as necessary suggests that parliamentary sovereignty was indeed at risk.[8] The Scottish Labour Party managed to face both ways on this, signing the declaration of the Scottish Constitutional Convention that sovereignty was vested in the Scottish people, and then insisting during the 1997 election and subsequently that devolution in no way affected the sovereignty of Parliament. Labour's decision to hold devolution referendums in Scotland and Wales, whatever the political motives at the time, also carries a recognition that the people of those nations have some charge of their own destiny (Walker 1998*b*). Winifred Ewing, a nationalist politician, may have been stretching constitutional interpretation when she declared in 1999 that the Scottish Parliament was now reconvened (after being prorogued in 1707), but Westminster is surely equally deluded in believing that its sovereignty is no more abridged than when it sets up a municipal government. Nairn (2000) is in no doubt that the Scottish Parliament has inherited the unbroken sovereignty of the Scottish people. British governments have also shown inconsistency in dealing with Northern Ireland, as opposed to other parts of the United Kingdom. Throughout the 1980s and most of the 1990s Conservative administrations sought to restore self-government to Northern Ireland on the basis of power-sharing arrangements negotiated with local politicians, while setting their faces against any negotiation with the dominant political forces in Scotland, which were united in their demand for home rule.

The same problem has arisen in Canada with efforts to accommodate Quebec and, later, the native peoples into the constitution. The rise of Quebec nationalism from the 1970s might have provided an opportunity to refurbish and update the 'two nations' doctrine, expanded to include the native peoples, but this proved difficult because of three obstacles. The first was the decision to base a new Canadian nationalism on individual citizenship, enshrined in a Charter of Rights and Freedoms at the federal level. This was seen in Quebec as a challenge to its collective identity, not because

---

[8] The relevant clause was struck out of the 1978 Scotland Bill by an unholy alliance of nationalists who wanted to limit parliamentary sovereignty and unionists who did not. The government finally decided that, since Parliament could not abridge its own sovereignty, it did not really matter (Keating and Lindley 1981).

Quebeckers are necessarily more collectivist than other Canadians, but because they have tended to base their citizenship claims in the Quebec as much as the Canadian collectivity (Coulombe 1992). It also undermined the old intergovernmental mechanisms for managing relationships between Quebec and the rest of Canada. Trudeau's uniform view of Canadian national citizenship is captured in his remarks on aboriginal self-government in 1969 that is was 'inconceivable . . . that in a given society one section of the society [could] have a treaty with the other section of the society. We must all be equal under the laws and we must not sign treaties amongst ourselves' (Cairns 2000: 52). The second obstacle was the doctrine of the equality of the provinces, pushed hardest by the provinces of the west, who have traditionally resented domination by Ontario. As we saw in Chapter 2, there is indeed a historic doctrine about Canada as a pact among provinces, but this is separate from the doctrine of the pact between two nations, now extended to three. Alberta might have strident demands to make on the federation, but these do not amount to a doctrine of national self-determination. The third obstacle is the doctrine and practice of multiculturalism in Canada as a way of integrating its diverse peoples, including immigrants, while recognizing the value of their traditions. Again, this is a separate issue from the rights of founding nations but has become confounded with it, so that demands for recognition of Quebec or the native peoples give rise to demands for recognition of a plethora of other status groups who have made no claim to national self-determination. This is resented in Quebec as a ploy to dilute their own nationality rights.

These debates came to a head with the failed ratification of the 1987 Meech Lake Accord between the federal government and the provinces. Meech Lake conceded the minimal demands of Quebec, including a limitation on the federal spending power in areas of provincial jurisdiction and the right to nominate members of the Supreme Court, but its most controversial clause was one that recognized Quebec as a 'distinct society'. These two words, defended in Quebec as a substantive concession and in the rest of Canada as harmless symbolism or a mere sociological fact, were subject to endless exegesis. Many critics in English Canada believed that Quebec's substantive grievances about social discrimination and powers had been resolved, and that such a clause would merely fuel further nationalist agitation. For the west and the smaller provinces it was a blow to the doctrine of equality of the provinces, and conferred special 'privileges' on Quebec. 'Charter nationalists' complained that it would undermine equal citizenship rights by allowing the courts to interpret them differently in Quebec. Women's groups in English Canada complained that it would undermine gender equality in Quebec, a charge denied by feminists in Quebec itself. Multicultural groups opposed it as giving special status to Quebec's culture, which they saw as being on a par with their own. Finally, aboriginal groups opposed it, not so much on principle but because Meech Lake had focused on Quebec and not addressed the issue of native self-government. Meech Lake collapsed technically because a single native member of the Manitoba legislature filibustered the ratification hearings,[9] but it is clear that it did not command general assent outside Quebec and that the stumbling block was the 'distinct society' clause. Similar objections have been raised to aboriginal self-government, which is criticized for giving 'special status' to one section of society, notably by the Reform Party (now the Canadian Alliance), who cling to the old assimilationist belief.

A second agreement, the Charlottetown Accord, included the 'distinct society' phrase but accompanied it with stronger language on Canadian unity, and a series of concessions to other groups, including aboriginal peoples, women, and the disabled. Since, apart from the aboriginal peoples, these were not national communities but status groups, this effectively destroyed the implicit recognition given in the 'distinct society' clause.[10] The clause itself was subordinated to a 'Canada clause' to keep proponents of national unity happy. Charlottetown was put to a national referendum, conducted separately in Quebec and the rest of Canada, but soundly defeated in both, showing the gulf in public opinion. Following the near victory of the 1995 referendum on sovereignty, the federal government and the provinces returned to the issue, passing non-constitutional resolutions recognizing Quebec as a distinct society with the support of erstwhile opponents of Meech and Charlottetown. The circumstances of this manoeuvre deprived it of conviction and, being too little and too late, it made little impact on the debate. The same was true of the 1997 Calgary Declaration agreed by all the provincial and territorial leaders except for Quebec, and which attempted to please all sides at once. It recognized the aboriginal peoples, but alienated them by putting them in the same sentence as the multicultural immigrant community. It sought to accommodate Quebec by recognizing 'the unique character of Quebec society', but in the next clause insisted that powers given to one province must be available to all. It was not, in other words, an endorsement of the plurinational state.

Matters are no clearer in Spain. Governments have not been as ready as those of the United Kingdom or Canada to contemplate secession or admit that they could not stop it if it occurred in a democratic way. They have been at pains to insist that sovereignty lies with the unitary people and that devolution is a gift of the unitary state (González 1982). Even the effort to find a specific language for the minorities by calling them nationalities within the Spanish nation came unstuck when the Spanish government banalized the term by allowing Aragon and the Canaries to incorporate it in their amended statutes of autonomy. Yet to call Catalonia, the Basque Country,

---

[9] Newfoundland, under its new premier Clyde Wells, had rescinded its previous ratification, but it is not clear that Newfoundland would have held out alone if all others had ratified.

[10] To dilute the clause even further, there was even at one point a proposal to recognize all the provinces as distinct societies.

and Galicia nations would be to concede the emotive and normative charge of the term, and their right to a measure of self-determination. The same urge to uniformity affected the process of devolution during the transition to democracy. Political circumstances forced the governments of the transition to allow self-government to Catalonia and the Basque Country, with Galicia making up the third historic nationality, but, in an effort to make this look like a general policy, they laid down routes to autonomy for all of Spain's regions (discussed below). In the face of pressures to uniformity, the stateless nations have been insisting on their distinctiveness, or *hecho diferencial*. Like the United Kingdom, Spain has also effectively entrenched autonomy rights by requiring them to be endorsed by local referendums. The result of this series of political compromises is a constitution which can be read as permitting a high degree of asymmetry and recognition, as the Catalans would argue, or as requiring uniformity, as others would insist (Blanco 1997).

In Spain much controversy has centred on the historic rights of territories as incorporated in their *fueros*. The issue is particularly acute in the Basque Country (Chapters 2 and 3), and it was failure to recognize the *fueros* as original rights that prevented the Basque Nationalist Party from endorsing the constitution of 1978. Instead, they were incorporated into an annexe of the constitution, thus suggesting that they were subordinate to it, a position sustained by most Spanish jurists (Solozábal 2000). The annexe operates like the proposed Canadian 'distinct society' provision, as an interpretative clause whose precise status is not clear. Catalan nationalists have put less stress on historic rights and more on the need for recognition of the *hecho diferencial*, based on the historical and sociological personality of the people and implying the right to difference without spelling it out in detail. Outside the historic nationalities, Miguel Herrero de Miñón (1996, 1998a, b) has presented the most elaborate defence of the principle of historic rights, starting with the theories of Jellinek on fragments of state (Chapter 1). Herrero argues that only with a recognition of the principles of plurinationality and difference can the constitution be stabilized and the constant counter-bidding for status and recognition be arrested. The argument is not a reductionist one, but builds on a number of legal and political principles which together constitute an argument for recognizing the special status of Catalonia, the Basque Country, Galicia, and Navarre. These territories have foral law, and, while other territories do as well, it is only in these ones that the Council of State has recognized the autonomous communities as titular holders of these rights. Voting for statutes of autonomy in the 1930s also constitutes a historic right in the present since it established a principle which cannot unilaterally be overturned.

Rubio Lloriente (1993) and Blanco (1997), on the contrary, dismiss the idea of historic rights as a self-serving invention, arguing that they cannot be defined and it is not clear to which territories they apply. Herrero's argument is that the principle is a living one, not just a reference to some outdated principles of the past. The principle constitutes the historic territories as the subject of self-determination in negotiation with the state, and updating the old laws does not invalidate their source. Similarly if three Basque provinces, the depositories of the *fueros*, choose to confederate into a new autonomous community, as they have done, this does not prevent the new body from inheriting the historic rights of the old; although Herrero does think that abolition of the historic territories in favour of a unitary Basque Country (as favoured by some nationalists) might invalidate them. Rubio Lloriente (1993) shares the general opinion of jurists outside the historic nationalities that the distinction between nationalities and regions, even supposing that we know which is which, refers to a sociological fact and not a principle of rights. Any differences in status or powers would, according to this view, be a breach of the principle of equality of all Spaniards. Parada (1996), arguing directly against Herrero, insists that Spain is a single nation, with one source of popular authority. Herrero is dismissed as a 'Carlist straggler' dedicated to a pre-modern, pre-liberal view of the polity. In 1998 the Socialist presidents of Andalucia, Castile–La Mancha, and Extremadura published their Declaration of Mérida, rejecting the existence of any 'natural right, either previous or posterior to the Constitution, that could be invoked to justify privileges among territories or inequalities among Spaniards' (Fossas 1999*a*: 293).

Asymmetrical Government

In practice, constitutional asymmetries have been considerably larger than one might think, given the reluctance of states to admit the principle. There are two dimensions to this: the existence and powers of sub-state governments, and the representation of the stateless nations, as opposed simply to undifferentiated citizens, in central institutions. Figure 4.1 (p. 122) shows that in practice there are some notable asymmetries in the constitution and competences of sub-state governments in the four cases. Asymmetries of functional decentralization in turn need to be divided into those that are entrenched constitutionally or legally, and those that arise because not all units choose to exercise all the powers open to them (Fossas 1999*b*). The most asymmetrical is, since 1999, the United Kingdom, where there is a Scottish Parliament and a Northern Ireland Assembly with extensive legislative competences, and a National Assembly for Wales with administrative powers only. Officially the justification for giving the Scottish and Northern Ireland bodies legislative competence is that there are already systems of law in place there, while Wales is governed almost entirely by English law, but it is widely accepted that an important reason was the lesser demand for devolution in Wales. The allocation of competences also differs between the Northern Ireland Assembly, where the centre was careful to reserve powers to do with security matters, and the Scottish Parliament, where the centre was more concerned with maintaining the British social and economic union (Keating 2000c). English domestic affairs are subject to legislation by Westminster (which is also the legislature for UK matters) and are administered by UK departments, many of which are largely English by default, though none has responsibilities exclusively limited to England. Even the internal operation of the three devolved systems differs radically. Scotland has a system of responsible Cabinet government on the Westminster model, while in Wales the executive function is officially lodged in the Assembly committees. In practice a Welsh cabinet of secretaries has been formed as an executive, but they still have to work closely with the Assembly. Northern Ireland's executive is formed on a power-sharing basis to include all the parties.

Belgium exhibits asymmetries of a different sort because of the need to accommodate both linguistic and territorial cleavages and the situation of Brussels, a French-majority city surrounded by Flemish territory. Powers are devolved to regional councils for Flanders, Wallonia, and Brussels on 'territorial' matters, while 'personalizable' functions like health, education, and social services are devolved to three linguistically based communities, the Flemish, the French, and the small German community. The regions of Flanders and Wallonia are unilingual, while Brussels is bilingual. The language communities also have territorial boundaries, corresponding to the regions except in the German area and in Brussels, citizens getting their personal services from the appropriate linguistic community. In practice, the Flemish regional and community institutions have merged, with special provision for Brussels participation in community issues. The French community has not merged with the Walloon region, because the people of Brussels do not consider themselves Walloon. Instead, the French community council is made up of the elected members of the Walloon and Brussels regional councils. There have, however, been some moves to bring the two institutions together, with many of the French community services contracted to the regions, and from the late 1990s there was an effort to promote 'Brussels–Wallonia' as a unit to international investors and visitors.

Spain's system of autonomous governments is the result of contradictory pressures for differentiation, coming from the historic nationalities, and for uniformity, coming from the central state. At the transition in the late 1970s, as under the Second Republic in the 1930s (Hernández 1980), the state parties saw the political necessity to concede autonomy to the nationalities, but wished to contain the process and avoid the dissolution of central authority in a federal arrangement. The idea was to have a symmetrical framework, which would permit asymmetries *de facto*. The first ploy was to establish two tracks to full autonomy, a fast and a slow one. The fast track would be available to regions that had voted for autonomy under the Second Republic, meaning the three historic nationalities. Other regions would have to make do with a slower process with, at least initially, fewer powers, unless they could manage an extremely complex and difficult procedure involving an initiative of three-quarters of the municipal councils and a referendum with a qualified majority of 50 per cent of the entire electorate in each province of the region. The statute then had to be approved by the senators and deputies for the region, an absolute majority of the central parliament, and a second referendum in which only a simple majority was required. In the event only Andalucia managed the feat.[11] The central parties then adopted a twin-track strategy of limiting the powers of the fast-track regions through the Ley de Armonización del Proceso Autonómico (Law to Harmonize the Autonomy Process, LOAPA) while encouraging the spread of autonomy to the other regions. Although many of the key provisions of LOAPA were struck down by the constitutional court, the process of harmonization has continued to produce what critics call *cafe para todos* ('coffee for all'). The most striking element of asymmetry remaining is the *concierto económico*, the special fiscal regime applying in the Basque provinces and Navarre, which allows them to raise almost all their own taxes and pass on a negotiated share to Madrid. This is part of the historic privileges, modified but retained in the nineteenth century and which Franco had abolished in Bizkaya and Guipúzcoa because of their support for the Republic. There are some differences in systems of traditional civil or foral law, notably in Catalonia. Other asymmetries are, at least in principle, transitional since all autonomous communities can aspire to the same powers in time.

Canada similarly has a formal equality of constitutional status among the provinces, with various *de facto* asymmetries, depending on how powers are exercised. Provinces generally enjoy the same powers, although, as each was incorporated separately, there are numerous small special provisions. Quebec's civil law is guaranteed under a clause allowing it to opt out of the consolidation of civil law in Canada, as are the religious schools in Quebec and Ontario.[12] What is striking in the Canadian case, however, is the different use which the provinces have made of their powers. Quebec has chosen to legislate a complex system of language normalization, and to establish its own income tax and pensions regimes (Watts 1999). It has negotiated an arrangement with the federal government allowing it to select its own immigrants. It is this type of flexibility on which federalist spokespeople like Stéphane Dion[13] insist when arguing for federalism as a means of accommodating Quebec's distinct needs.

---

[11] Technically, it missed out since, while there was a large yes vote everywhere, in one of the provinces it failed to reach the required threshold of 50% of the entire electorate. The central parties eventually allowed the proposals to go ahead, while pressing on with the LOAPA proposals.

[12] Newfoundland required an amendment to the Canadian constitution to merge its six systems of denominational schooling. Other oddities are also entrenched, like the railway service on Vancouver Island.

[13] Political scientist and Minister for Intergovernmental Affairs in the federal government of Jean Chrétien.

Implementation of aboriginal self-government has also had to go forward outside the framework of constitutional change, although not without a constitutional basis. As long ago as the Royal Proclamation of 1763, the rights of aboriginal peoples were recognized, although this meant little during the decades of suppression and forcible assimilation. In 1982 the Constitution Act again recognized the status of the three groups of aboriginal peoples and, although it did not provide for self-government, some legal scholars have taken it as a basis for proceeding with treaty negotiations. Conferences in the following years attempted to clarify the idea and come to a consensus. The failed Charlottetown Accord had stronger wording, proclaiming an 'inherent right of self-government', but, with the failure of the accord in a national referendum, the process had to proceed piecemeal, given some impetus by the report of the Royal Commission on Aboriginal Peoples (Canada 1996) which strongly backed the idea. A major breakthrough was the Nisga'a treaty in British Columbia, ratified in 2000 and providing for self-government on a territorial basis, with fairly wide jurisdiction. There is Nisga'a citizenship, although Nisga'a continue as full Canadian citizens, subject to the federal criminal code and other federal and provincial laws in matters not devolved. Extensive provision is made for the application of Nisga'a civil law. The treaty provoked massive controversy on the grounds that it created a special class of citizens, based on racial criteria.[14] It is true that the grounds for Nisga'a citizenship are based on descent, but there is also provision for non-citizens to participate in elected bodies that affect them; but for the most part Nisga'a laws will apply only to Nisga'a citizens— it is reasonably assumed that non-citizens will not wish to place themselves under Nisga'a civil law, for example. There is also provision for individuals who might face imprisonment under Nisga'a law to opt for trial in the Provincial Court of British Columbia. Moreover, agreement provides for the eventual elimination of the tax exemption which Nisga'a enjoyed as Status Indians under the Indian Act.

While the process has been extremely complicated and conflictual, this is an example of asymmetry in practice, which seeks to provide for self-determination without destroying Canadian citizenship or leading to separation. By 1997 the federal government had come a long way, stating its principles as follows (Canada 1997):

- The inherent right (of self-government) is an existing aboriginal right recognized and confirmed under the Canadian Constitution.

---

[14] This provoked a fierce outburst from Reform Party leader Preston Manning, who objected to the ethnic criterion for Nisga'a citizenship on the self-governing lands but, inconsistently, complained that off-reserve Nisga'a were not included (Speech in House of Commons, 26 Oct. 1999). Manning was on stronger ground in criticizing the Liberals for conceding to the aboriginal peoples a form of special status they had refused to Quebec, but I would draw the opposite of Manning's conclusions from this.

- Self-government will be exercised within the existing Canadian Constitution. Canada's recognition of self-government does not mean sovereignty in the international sense.
- Aboriginal people will continue to be citizens of Canada and the province or territory where they live. However they may exercise varying degrees of jurisdiction and/or authority.
- The Canadian Charter of Rights and Freedoms will apply fully to aboriginal governments as it does to all other governments in Canada. The current provisions of the Charter that respect the unique aboriginal and treaty rights of aboriginal peoples will continue to apply.
- All federal funding for self-government will come from the reallocation of existing resources.
- Where all parties agree, rights in self-government may be protected in new treaties under Section 35 of the Constitution Act, 1982. They may also be protected through additions to existing treaties, or as part of comprehensive land claims agreements.
- Federal, provincial, territorial and aboriginal laws must work in harmony. Certain laws of overriding federal and provincial importance, such as the Criminal Code, will prevail.
- The interests of all Canadians will be taken into account as agreements are negotiated.

Representation at the Centre

The other dimension of substantive recognition concerns the representation of the constituent nations in the central institutions of the state. It has often been argued that the most appropriate mechanism for representing territorial interests or national minorities formally in federal or federal-type systems is through a second chamber of the state parliament. Yet, in spite of all the proposals, three of the four states have not yet done this. Canadian senators notionally represent provinces but are nominated by the federal prime minister. An elected senate with equal representation of all ten provinces was the principal demand of the western provinces in the constitutional negotiations of the 1990s and formed part of the failed Charlottetown Accord, but this reflected the doctrine of Canada as a compact of provinces not nations, and was not regarded with favour in Quebec. Proposals for reforming the British House of Lords have been circulating for over a hundred years with no great result, apart from the elimination of most of the hereditary peers. The Spanish Senate is supposedly the chamber of territorial representation, but there has been no agreement on giving effect to this. Most senators are elected from the provinces (the same electoral constituencies as for the lower house) with only a minority nominated by the parliaments of the autonomous communities. Belgium has reformed its Senate to represent the regions and communities. Forty senators are elected directly from the three regional constituencies used for European elections, with provision for linguistic balance between Flemish and French speakers. Twenty-one are nominated by the three linguistic community councils, and ten are co-opted by the other senators. The Senate has powers over constitutional matters, international relations, the organization of the courts, and relations among the federal government and the regions and communities. While Belgium has thus incorporated into its constitution a mechanism to represent the federated units, critics have noted that it does not provide equal representation but recognizes the overall Flemish majority, although providing for concurrent majorities on a variety of culture-related issues (Brassinne 1994).

The lack of interest in reforming second chambers on a territorial basis certainly owes much to the reluctance of central governments to see their power curtailed, but there is also a lack of urgency on the part of minorities, given that second chambers are often seen as a second-best form of representation. So, curiously, there is often more provision for differentiated representation in the popularly elected chambers and the executive. On the representation of nations in the central Parliament, the United Kingdom is again the most explicitly plurinational. There are separate parliamentary boundary commissions for England, Scotland, Wales, and Northern Ireland, none of which traditionally has had a fixed number of seats to allocate. Scotland, Wales, and Northern Ireland were, however, guaranteed a minimum, which meant that, in practice they have been over-represented. Scotland, which has lost population relatively, had a marked advantage (McLean 1995; Rossiter *et al*. 1997). Although this was arguably little more than a historic accident, it was subsequently defended as a concession to the stateless nations in compensation for lacking self-government (Keating 1975). The Scotland Act of 1998, establishing a devolved Scottish Parliament, contained provision to reduce the proportion of Scottish MPs down to the English level. The Canadian constitution stipulates that no province shall have fewer MPs than senators, or fewer MPs than it had in 1976, with the result that an Alberta MP represents three times as many people as one from Prince Edward Island. A provision of the Charlottetown Accord sought to compensate Quebec for the equal Senate by guaranteeing it at least a quarter of the seats in the House of Commons in perpetuity, and another one talked vaguely about guaranteed aboriginal representation. In Spain the nationalities are not taken into account in drawing parliamentary constituencies, but there are nevertheless asymmetries in representation. MPs are elected by province but with a minimum of two per province, ensuring that the smaller ones are over-represented and that the electoral system is far from proportional. In the Basque parliament all three historic territories are equally represented, despite massive disparities in population. Surprisingly, these disparities in representation have rarely been a matter of political contention in any of the countries concerned. There seems to be a general consensus that representation is a function of both population and territory, allowing more for small territories or historic entities. The outcome, however, seems to owe more to chance than to planning or reason.

Provisions for representation in the central executive have similarly developed over time in response to circumstances. The most elaborate are in Belgium, where consociational traditions have been incorporated into successive constitutional revisions, providing that there should be equal numbers of Flemish and Francophone ministers in the Cabinet (the prime minister excepted). In the United Kingdom there has long been a system of territorial ministers for Ireland (1800–1922), Northern Ireland (since 1973), Scotland (since 1885), and Wales (since 1965), whose task is both to translate central policy to the peripheral nations and to represent them in the central government. The strongest has been the Secretary of State for Scotland, who by firm convention has always been a Scottish MP and who, until 1999, headed a substantial administration dealing with a range of matters which in England would be the responsibility of functional departments (Midwinter *et al.* 1991). Irish secretaries, by contrast, have always been sent over from mainland Britain and do not have any political base locally. Canada has a system of regional ministers who, while being in charge of functional departments, also manage the government's political affairs, including the distribution of patronage, in the various parts of the country. It is always important to maintain some degree of regional balance in the Cabinet and to have a credible team of ministers from Quebec. It has been suggested that there is a form of consociationalism between English Canadian and Quebec elites but, if so, it is of a very weak form and does not provide the veto power one would expect under consociationalism. These considerations are less important in Spain, although there are usually prominent Catalans and Basques in the central Cabinet, and between 1993 and 2000 successive socialist and conservative governments in Madrid had to bargain for support with the Basque and Catalan nationalist parties.

A recurrent issue in constitutional arguments has been the demand for representation of constituent nations in supreme and constitutional courts. The Meech Lake and Charlottetown Accords met a persistent demand for a guaranteed Quebec representation on Canada's Supreme Court, which has responsibility for constitutional adjudication; at present there must be three Quebec judges, but these are nominated by the Canadian government. Charlottetown also provided for a consultative role for aboriginal peoples in the nomination of judges. In Belgium the Arbitration Court, which has responsibility for ruling on the competences of the various governments, has equal numbers of French- and Flemish-speaking judges, nominated in turn by the Belgian federal Assembly and Senate. Catalan and Basque leaders have consistently asked for a role in the appointment of judges to Spain's constitutional and supreme courts, but without success. Nor in the United Kingdom is there provision for Scottish, Welsh, or Northern Ireland representation on the Judicial Committee of the Privy Council, the final authority on devolution matters.

These different conceptions of state and nation and of the issues at stake go some way towards explaining the distinctive patterns of territorial government in the four states, setting boundaries to what forms of plurinational recognition are acceptable. The differences can be portrayed in three dimensions: functional decentralization to the periphery; incorporation of peripheral influences in the centre; and symbolic recognition (Table 4.1). The dimensions by no means coincide. So, for example, the United Kingdom has until recently been very generous in recognizing the nationality of its constituent parts and its own status as a plurinational state, but reluctant to concede the substance of power. There is no constitutional recognition of the role of the nations in central government, even after devolution, but there is a well-established system for voicing their concerns at the centre, through the Secretaries of State for Scotland, Wales, and Northern Ireland. It has long been understood that this arrangement involves a series of trade-offs (Keating 1975) so that it is not surprising that, after the election of an autonomous Scottish Parliament, steps were taken to reduce the over-representation at Westminster, to abolish the role of Secretary of State, and to reduce Scotland's advantage in public spending (see below). With Canada the balance between symbol and substance has been the other way round, with a high degree of decentralization to Quebec under the evolving federal system but no willingness to contemplate multiple nationality. Instead Canada has chosen to incorporate the French language as an integral part of the Canadian identity, while detaching this from any specific reference to the territorial nation of Quebec. There is no constitutional mechanism to represent

Table 4.1. Recognition of plurinationalism or diversity

	Functional decentralization	Representation at centre	Symbolic recognition
UK	Partial. Highly asymmetrical. Different powers	Medium. Secretaries of state. Over-representation in Parliament (pre-devolution)	Strong. Name of state. Flag etc.
Spain	Universal. Largely symmetrical. Some differences in powers	Weak	Weak. Unitary Spanish nation
Belgium	Universal. Asymmetrical. Uniform powers	Strong. Consociational constitution of central government. Senate representing communities	Weak
Canada	Universal. Largely symmetrical. Differences in use of powers. Aboriginal governments	Medium. Regional ministers	Weak for Quebec. Stronger for aboriginal peoples. Official bilingualism only

Quebec in Canadian federal politics, but party practices have ensured a large Quebec contingent in the federal political elite. Belgium has both a high degree of functional decentralization and strong representation of the nationalities at the centre. On the other hand, it has not produced a plurinational synthesis in the symbolic representation of the state. Efforts to produce an ideology of 'Belgitude' based precisely on the country's status as a meeting place of Germanic and Latin cultures found little popular or official response (Fontaine 1998). Spain has progressively devolved powers to its autonomous communities but has sought to equalize their powers and gives little recognition to the plurinational principle in the state itself. Arrangements for representing peripheral interests at the centre are weak.

Until 1999 none of the states had conceded both a high degree of symbolic recognition to the constituent nationalities and a large amount of functional decentralization since, as we have seen, this has been considered explosive. Nor, until then, had any of them conceded a form of self-government to some parts of the state which was not available to all the others; this too was considered destabilizing. Now the United Kingdom has proceeded along both of these roads, constituting itself as one of the most explicitly plurinational states in the world. In doing so, it has apparently violated most of the rules laid down by constitutional scholars on the constitution of federal and complex states.[15]

What is Wrong with Asymmetrical Government?

Asymmetry is untidy and irrational to those whose frame of reference is the nation-state. They may also see it as an affront to the equality of citizenship rights, giving undue privileges to one part of the state or one group of citizens. Yet in complex states we do not start from an ideal social contract among individuals but from a union of parts or fragments, none of which is institutionally complete, but whose institutional coverage is also very different. So far as asymmetries reflect historic rights and traditions, then to suppress them would be to violate the acquired rights of citizens in those territories. To extend them to the whole state would equally violate historic practice and would impose on the rest of the state a system that evolved for the minorities. So to abolish the fiscal system of the Basque Country and Navarre or the system of Scottish law would be to violate the founding principles of the union state itself. Peacock and Crowther-Hunt (1973), in their minority report to the Royal Commission on the Constitution, were obsessed with symmetry to the point of recommending an identical system of

---

[15] In January 2001, however, there was a strange explosion over the apparently innocuous proposal to replace the confusing term 'Scottish Executive' with 'Scottish Government'. Westminster MPs from both main parties rushed in to insist that this was impossible in a unitary state, or was tantamount to separatism.

devolution for Scotland and the regions of England. This would have meant either suppressing the entire system of Scottish and criminal law, or setting up different systems for each English region, an implication that seems to have escaped them.

In defence of asymmetry it is argued that it reflects differing demands in various parts of the state. It is apparent, for example, that the demand for home rule in Scotland has been higher than in Wales and much higher than in England or its regions. If other parts of the state also want decentralization, this could in principle be extended to them. This has certainly been a factor in pushing devolution in Canada and Spain, where Quebec and the stateless nations have taken the lead and others have followed. If the rest of the state does not wish to decentralize, however, the question arises as to whether it can prevent the stateless nations going ahead. This is a critical issue where there is a majority nation so that a principled decision to retain matters at the state level may be a way of allowing the majority to enjoy untrammelled rule over the whole. This was certainly the way many Scots thought in the 1980s and 1990s, although it would be a simplification to portray the English majority as a homogeneous whole. Should the majority not wish to decentralize along with the minorities, there are many technical ways to allow them to proceed on matters together while allowing minorities to opt out. Canada has developed a formula to allow provinces to opt out of new federal spending programmes in matters of provincial jurisdiction, with compensation for the fact that their taxpayers are contributing, provided that they are pursuing programmes with similar ends. Provinces other than Quebec have decided not to exercise their option to set up their own income tax system or pension plans, leaving these in federal hands. Following devolution for Scotland, Wales, and Northern Ireland, the most institutionally incomplete part of the United Kingdom is England, yet English voters have failed to demand a parliament of their own, being content to leave matters to Westminster. This reflects the knowledge that there is an English majority so that the creation of a separate parliament would bring little benefit for a lot of confusion. Such an agreed bargain among the component parts of a union hardly seems an affront to democracy. Even staunch opponents of asymmetry like Rubio Lloriente (1993) may concede that some Spanish autonomous communities might agree to accept lesser powers than the historic nationalities.

Many of the complaints about privilege and discrimination turn on financial matters to do with taxation and redistribution, and indeed when we turn to spending and taxation matters, we find many examples of inequality and asymmetry. None of the states has a system of fiscal equalization designed to provide equal levels of spending per head in all its constituent parts, or to allocate spending according to needs. Nor does any of them simply rely on the constituent parts to fund their own spending needs. Instead, there are differences both among the states and within them, with regard to both taxation and intergovernmental transfers. The most stark asymmetry is in Spain, where the Basque Country and Navarre, by virtue of their historic rights, collect nearly all taxes and pass on a share to Madrid for common services. They are free to determine their own rates of taxation, but the scope for variation is limited by an agreement within the *concierto económico* about the overall burden, and by European rules. There are continuous arguments about the amounts to be paid over, about state-wide solidarity, and about the ability of the Basque and Navarre governments to give favourable treatment to inward investors, but these are resolved in negotiation. Elsewhere autonomous communities can opt to take 30 per cent of personal income tax, which they can vary within limits. Catalonia, which pressed hard for this provision, is now demanding that it be given the Basque system, on the ground that it too is a historic nationality, although it has been incorporated within the Spanish fiscal system since 1714. Its motives are partly to do with recognition, but also stem from its status as a large net contributor to the Spanish budget. The distribution of state transfers, which make up most of the spending of the autonomous communities, is based on the historic costs of transferred services and pays rather little attention to needs or resources. As in other states, it is an accretion of historic practices and successive amendments rather than a unitary scheme based on clear principles.

In the United Kingdom devolved assemblies are financed almost entirely from state transfers. These are based on pre-devolution arrangements which are generally considered to have favoured the stateless nations as part of an elaborate strategy of accommodating them to the union (Midwinter *et al.* 1991; Heald *et al.* 1998). Scottish public spending has never been treated the same as that for other parts of the United Kingdom. From the late nineteenth century it was allocated by a formula based on population (the Goschen formula), although the relative fall in Scottish population levels led to steady increases in the per capita relativities. After the Second World War this formula was gradually eroded as secretaries of state, in favourable political circumstances, were able to negotiate with the Treasury on individual services whenever they could make a case. In the 1970s there was a return to a formula, the Barnett formula, which allocates changes in expenditure levels across the four parts of the United Kingdom on a population basis. This system was retained for the devolution settlement, although it contains no internal logic or consistency. Spending in the three minority nations is based neither on locally raised taxes, nor on population, nor on needs. The only devolved tax is in Scotland,[16] where the Parliament can vary the basic rate of

---

[16] The original draft of the Northern Ireland Bill incorporated the old Stormont provision for Northern Ireland taxes to be used to fund the Assembly, with an additional transfer from Westminster. Although Northern Ireland would not have had the power to change the tax rates, this raised fears about the province being left to fend for itself, and at the insistence of the Northern Ireland parties the entire provision was deleted except for the clause about the transfers, which thus remain the sole source of funding.

income tax by up to three points. In practice it cannot exercise this power without sparking off a controversy on the whole funding formula, including transfers from the centre which account for most of its budget. The Barnett formula, widely regarded in England as a system that benefits the minority nations, is in fact a mechanism for reducing their advantage over time as the historic base becomes a smaller part and the population-based element a larger part of their budgets. This 'Barnett squeeze' was repeatedly postponed under the Conservative governments of the 1980s and 1990s, aware of their precarious political position in Scotland and Wales and the sensitivity of politics in Northern Ireland. With the arrival of devolved government, there is less need to compensate with material benefits the lack of political recognition, and the formula has started to erode the advantages of the periphery.

Canadian provinces have identical competences in matters of taxation, but they are exercised differently, with Quebec choosing to run its own income tax and some provinces integrating their sales taxes with the federal goods and services tax. Federal support programmes tend to be formula-based and applicable state-wide, so that there is nothing like the UK system of determining each unit's transfers separately. While federal transfers have been cut sharply since the 1990s, Quebec is a net beneficiary and there would certainly be a political problem if it were to cease being so. On the other hand, Quebec nationalists complain that they do not benefit as much as Ontario from certain federal spending programmes, notably in research.

Belgium has a very complex system for allocating resources to regions and communities. Regions receive a share of locally raised income tax, which they can alter within narrow limits, with an equalization mechanism to benefit the poorer regions (in effect Wallonia). They are also assigned a range of 'regional taxes', but changes in the rates must be agreed with the centre. Communities receive a share of income tax but without powers to alter the rate, plus a share of value added tax. A complicated regime will bring these provisions in over time and provide for adjustments in line with increases in gross domestic product. This is a state-wide scheme, intended to maintain solidarity and equalization among the regions and communities, but Flanders has been pressing for more fiscal decentralization and, in particular, for the communitarization of the social security scheme, in order to reduce its transfer payments to Wallonia.

There is certainly a tension between the need to recognize the plurinationality of the state and the distinctiveness of its parts on the one hand, and the commitment to territorial equity on the other. While in an ideal world it might be possible to distribute resources equitably and then give the constituent parts of the state freedom in spending them, this is both politically and practically difficult. There is continual argument about figures and what to include, and the extent to which resources should be redistributed. More fundamentally, there is an argument about the obligations of the minority nations to contribute to state-wide solidarity, or their right to benefit from it.

This is inseparable from other issues pertaining to their position within the state, as we have seen in the case of Scotland, where favourable spending treatment was generally seen as a compensation for lack of autonomy. If in the context of globalization and, more particularly, European integration, the state is able to offer less economic protection and sustenance, then constituent nations and regions will look more to their own competitive advantage (Keating 1998*a*). In that case, they will be less inclined to contribute to fiscal equalization within their host states, an effect already visible in Flanders.

Another fear is that asymmetrical government may generate inequalities in citizen rights, both civil and social. There is a general fear about devolving matters of rights to small jurisdictions, often born of memories of the southern states of the United States, where it was only by asserting their rights as citizens of the wider state that black people gained their democratic rights and freedoms. Northern Ireland is cited as a society where asymmetrical devolution allowed violations of the human rights of the local minority, although whether this can be put down to minority nationalism is a moot question, since the statelet was set up precisely to frustrate Irish nationalism. There is also a lurking concern, more or less articulated, that stateless nations are likely to be less liberal and more committed to the promotion of collective group values than to individual rights. Both fears may be justified in specific cases, but they cannot be accepted as general propositions. There is no a priori reason to believe that large states are likely to be more liberal, or that symmetry will maintain human rights. After all, the UK Parliament did retain full sovereign authority over Northern Ireland between 1922 and 1972 but chose to ignore violations of rights there. It took the US Supreme Court a hundred years to respond to the violations of civil rights in the southern states. Once again, opponents of asymmetrical devolution here confuse state-wide uniformity with the upholding of universal values. States cannot be assumed to be the bearers of such values, and even where they are, the rights may come attached to a specific model of national identity.

This may not be a problem in nationally homogeneous states like the United States or Germany, but it will be in plurinational states. Civil rights are indeed vital to a liberal and democratic polity, but if they are tied to a specific conception of nationality, they lose their universal applicability. This is the crux of the problem with the Canadian Charter of Rights in Quebec. It is not that the Québécois are any less committed to rights than people in the rest of Canada; indeed Quebec's own charter bears a remarkable similarity to the Canadian one. It is that the Canadian charter has been used as an instrument of Canadian nation-building on the Trudeau model, which assumes a unitary national identity and denies the plurinationality of the state (Laforest 1992). In the process of aboriginal self-government, the issue of charter rights has been approached slightly differently. While it is clear that the basic charter provisions will apply to native governments (and indeed the organizations representing aboriginal women have insisted on this), there is more scope for interpretation and for respect for indigenous traditions under Section 25, which provides that it shall not be construed so as to erode aboriginal or treaty rights, or rights assured under the Royal Proclamation of 1763. There is a similar problem with proposals for Northern Ireland postulated on a new form of British civic nationalism in which Catholics would be guaranteed all manner of rights on condition that they accept the legitimacy of the UK state. While the civil rights campaigners of the 1960s, following those in the United States, initially claimed the rights due to them as British citizens, this was more of a tactical move than an aspiration to assimilate with their co-citizens on the mainland. It may therefore be better in these cases to take the issue of rights out of the nation-state context, an issue discussed in the next chapter. The European Court of Human Rights, while serving to spread a common rights understanding, has also been sensitive to local conditions and the need to engage in a dialogue with national political traditions. This gives us a more realistic as well as sensitive insight into the issues involved here. It is not a matter of states insisting on basic liberal rights against illiberal stateless national movements, but rather differences, often subtle, in the interpretation and application of liberal rights.

A particularly sensitive rights issue in Canada, Spain, and Belgium concerns language laws and usage. In the stateless nations the view is generally taken that maintaining and developing the language is a public good which may properly be regulated by public policy, but the regime varies considerably. In English Canada and in the Castilian-speaking parts of Spain it is seen as a matter of individual rights and choice. This is not really, as it is sometimes cast, a conflict between collective rights and individual rights, but more about the conditions in which individuals will be able to exercise their rights. If a minority culture or language is in the process of disappearing, then it is futile to proclaim that individuals have the free choice of whether or not to use it. Given the weight of the majority state languages, a 'free market' is likely to lead to the extinction of the minority languages or, at least, their consignment to the private or family sphere.

In Belgium there is a strict unilingualism in Flanders and Wallonia, with bilingualism in Brussels. The language frontier is fixed for all time, and individuals are expected to assimilate accordingly. This is a policy of territorial and individual monolinguism, and there are no all-Belgian language rights. In Canada there is bilingualism in the federal public service, but all the provinces except New Brunswick are unilingual, with varying provision for linguistic minorities. There is thus effective territorial bilingualism but individuals tend to be monolingual, living and working within their own language communities. The English-speaking minority in Quebec is the largest and best provided for, being protected in the Canadian constitution and, in recent years, by consensus between the Quebec political parties themselves. Bill 101, passed by the Parti Québécois government in the 1970s, sought to promote the use of French and, more controversially, restrict the use of

English. Court challenges under the constitution and later the Charter of Rights struck down parts of it concerning the right to education in English[17] and the freedom to display commercial signs in languages other than French—in the latter case the law was held also to violate Quebec's own charter. Premier Robert Bourassa then came up with a compromise allowing English signs inside stores but not outside, using the 'nothwithstanding clause' allowing governments to opt out of parts of the charter. When the clause came up for renewal, the sign law was simply dropped, leaving a delicate truce on the issue. It remains true that language is a matter for public policy to a greater extent than in the other provinces, but this is because the language situation is different.

In Spain, Castilian is, under the constitution, the official language of the whole state and citizens have the right and duty to know it, while the minority languages are official only within their respective autonomous communities. Catalonia, the Basque Country, and Galicia have programmes to extend and deepen the use of their local languages. There is thus effective territorial and individual bilingualism. There are no restrictions on the use of Castilian but there have been court challenges to linguistic normalization laws seeking to promote the minority languages in education and recruitment to the public administration. By and large the laws have stood up to these challenges. In the United Kingdom the most important language issue arises in Wales, where Welsh language services have been extended considerably over the years in the face of fears that the language faces decline in competition with English. As in the Spanish minority nations, the entire population speaks the state language so that the pressure is in effect designed to increase bilingualism.

So, with great variations in practice, there is a certain commitment to territorial bilingualism in much of Canada including Quebec, but individuals remain largely monolingual. Problems arise where individuals find themselves in a local minority. In Belgium, by contrast, there is both territorial and, increasingly, individual monolingualism. In Spain there is territorial bilingualism both officially, because of the entrenchment of Castilian in the constitution, and *de facto*, because of the absence of monolingual speakers of the minority languages. Despite the fact that the language laws have mainly been left intact, the subject is one of extreme sensitivity, and even moderate Quebec and Catalan nationalists consistently demand that issues of language rights and usage should be settled within the stateless nation, with no recourse to state-wide jurisdiction. This would certainly not be acceptable to minorities within the stateless nations. To portray the issue purely as one of individual rights, however, is surely misleading as it concerns the existence

---

[17] The original law restricted English language education rights to people who had been educated or whose parents had been educated in English in Quebec. The courts extended this to include education in English elsewhere in Canada (but not abroad).

and development of whole communities and of policies that must be applied to territorial units. The Belgian solution is a draconian one and has the effect of dissolving the national deliberative community into two solitudes, so undermining the plurinational state itself. On the other hand, aiming for multilingualism across the national territory is utopian and, in the case of Spain, a sheer impossibility given the number of languages. There seems no reasonable alternative in these cases to linguistic toleration, but with the predominance of the local language in the public sphere, an inherently asymmetrical solution.

One of the most vexed questions in asymmetrical devolution concerns the rights of members of the state parliament from the stateless nations. This issue, over which Gladstone confessed to have spent sleepless nights during the elaboration of his Irish Home Rule Bills, resurfaced in Britain in the 1970s in the form of the 'West Lothian Question'. Tam Dalyell, MP for West Lothian and indefatigable opponent of devolution, kept on asking why he, as a Scottish MP, should be allowed to vote on a range of matters in England while neither he nor English MPs would be able to vote on them as they affected his own constituency. The issue arose in Spain under the Second Republic and has been posed in Canada as an objection to Quebec's gaining competences not available to other provinces. The basic problem is that, if MPs from the minority nation are allowed to vote on matters that in their own nations are devolved, the majority may have forced on them policies for which they have not voted. So England could vote for a Conservative majority but have a Labour government imposed by Scottish and Welsh MPs. In the 1990s successive Spanish minority governments were sustained by the Catalan and Basque nationalist parties, enabling them to push through policies for the rest of Spain on matters like taxes or education which did not affect their own autonomous communities. Quebec's federal MPs vote on the Canada Pension Plan and the income tax bands on which nine of the provinces base their own tax schedules, although these votes do not apply in Quebec itself.

Gladstone's initial answer to the problem was to exclude the Irish MPs from the UK Parliament. This would have solved one injustice by creating another, since the imperial Parliament would still have dealt with matters concerning Ireland. Unionists also complained that excluding Irish MPs would amount to Irish independence, and indeed such a settlement would probably have evolved into a dominion status like that of Canada or Australia. Gladstone's final bill kept the Irish MPs but reduced their numbers from 103 to forty-two, so making it much less likely that they would hold the balance of power.[18] The 1998 Scotland Act similarly makes provision for reducing the number of Scottish MPs but only to bring it into line with England on a population basis. This may limit the scope of the problem, but

[18] At this point the unionists also changed tack and attacked the retention of the Irish MPs.

it is not eliminated as long as a single Scottish or Northern Irish MP is able to vote on legislation affecting only England and Wales. Another solution, incorporated in Gladstone's 1893 bill and adopted by the Conservative Party after Scottish devolution in 1998, would allow MPs from devolved nations to vote on UK matters but not on those affecting only the non-devolved parts of the state. The usual objection to this is that it would make parliamentary government impossible, depending, as this does, on consistent, stable, and disciplined majorities. This is a curiously conservative argument for constitutional reformers to deploy since one of the central aims of reform, including devolution, is to challenge the rule of untrammelled majority government. If governments without an English majority were forced to seek a wider basis of parliamentary support for their measures, this would merely bring them into line with the more inclusive systems in Scotland and Wales where the administrations cannot count on single-party majorities.[19]

In any case, the existing electoral systems in the United Kingdom and Canada produce stable majorities only by seriously distorting the electoral choice both on a partisan and a territorial basis. For example, the majority Liberal government elected in Canada in 1997 found 101 of its 155 seats in Ontario but saw no problem in governing the whole country. If we are really concerned with inequities in representation, this rather than the presence of the stateless nations is the big issue. With proportional representation, governments would normally have to seek wider bases of support, forge coalitions, or accept that their legislation might be amended in Parliament. Belgium, which does not have a tradition of majoritarian government, has adopted an 'in and out' system for the Flemish Parliament, which includes members from Brussels when it is dealing with community matters but not for regional matters that are the competence of the Brussels regional council. This has forced the parties to adopt slightly different coalition formulas at the federal and regional levels. A stronger objection to the 'in and out' system is that it is not always clear under asymmetrical devolution just what matters only affect the rest of the country. Under the Barnett formula, the functional allocations for funding in England determine the amounts of transfers to Scotland, Wales, and Northern Ireland, making them a legitimate concern for MPs from the periphery. In Spain the central government has withdrawn entirely from very few areas, so that the framework for policies in matters like education or health is often decided centrally, with varying degrees of freedom to alter the details at the periphery. These, however, are largely technical matters, which could be resolved with a clearer allocation of competences and a more transparent system of financing.

The significance of the West Lothian Question also depends on the party system. Where the MPs from the peripheral nations have belonged to the

---

[19] I have never understood, for example, why preventing Scottish MPs from voting on the abolition of fox-hunting in England and Wales should upset the constitution.

state-wide parties, as has generally been the case in Britain (not Northern Ireland) and, until the 1990s, Canada, then the distortion arises from the different balance between these parties in various parts of the state. The net effect of this is likely to be slight. As it happens, Quebec was a power base both for the Trudeau Liberals and for the succeeding Mulroney Conservatives and has provided the Canadian prime minister almost continuously since 1968, and this has caused some resentment elsewhere but has also served to integrate Quebec into the federation. Scotland has been dominated by the Labour Party since the late 1950s but only in the brief parliaments of 1950–1 and February–October 1974 did they impose a government on England.

Where the minority nations have their own party systems, larger problems arise since the party balance in centre and periphery is likely to be radically different. In Belgium there are no state-wide parties, which means that every coalition government has to take into account both ideological and community–regional balance. There was more of a problem with the Irish MPs in the late nineteenth and early twentieth centuries, since they could often prevent either party from winning a majority and could not easily coalesce with either. From 1993 until 2000 the Bloc Québécois dominated Quebec's representation in the Canadian House of Commons. None of the seventeen Northern Ireland MPs is from a state-wide party, and there is a significant nationalist presence in the Westminster representation from Scotland and Wales. Catalonia, the Basque Country, and Galicia similarly elect nationalist MPs to the central Parliament. The role that these MPs play then becomes critical. Scottish National Party MPs make a rule of not voting on English and Welsh legislation, imposing the 'in and out' rule on themselves. The Catalan nationalists of Convergència i Unió, following a long tradition, are committed to participating in the government of the state with the aim of transforming it into a plurinational federation. The Basque Nationalist Party has been more particularistic, but in 1996 signed an agreement to support the incoming conservative Spanish government. The Flemish Volksunie participates in federal coalitions, while pressing for a loosening of the federal state. So, given a willingness to accept the legitimacy of plurinational representation, there is no reason in principle why nationalist parties cannot govern in the state or should be considered outside the coalition game. On the other hand, this would have to be accompanied by a recognition that in matters controlled by the central government and parliament in the non-devolved parts of the state, the governing coalition should include a majority in those parts. All this, however, would require an adaptation on the part of both the state-wide parties and the minority parties to the idea of plurinational politics. Such an adaptation is, as we have seen in the previous chapter, only gradually occurring.

Asymmetrical government is thus more common and less problematic than is often assumed. There are indeed serious issues posed of representation and of distribution, but most of these arise also in symmetrical systems. As so often, established anomalies seem to be easier to live with than new ones, whatever the relative scale of the two. We are dealing here with distinct conceptions of the state, as a community of individuals, or as a community of communities each of which contains its own historic traditions, current demands, and conceptions of authority and legitimacy. A strictly Cartesian logic applied to the plurinational state can itself create problems where they need not exist, as in the fierce arguments over symbols and the definition of nationality which the more pragmatic British tradition has largely managed to avoid. Other asymmetries are more substantive but also admit of no geometrical solution, since they represent the coexistence of different, if not incommensurate, principles of political authority. The question is not whether we can extinguish these, but whether we can live with them. This requires that all matter of adopt the appropriate conceptual frame. Changing the frame of reference from the nation-state to the plurinational state or the historically informed concept of the union state opens new perspectives, although it does not itself provide an alternative, universally applicable model of the state. It is also a matter of political practice, as we have seen, that different forms of asymmetry are seen as problematic in different contexts. More radically, placing the issue in the context of the transformation of the state itself provides further avenues for addressing the issue of plurinational accommodation.

5

Beyond Sovereignty: Nations in the European Commonwealth

State Transformations

To equate the nation with the state is, as we have seen in earlier chapters, both a conceptual and a historical error, the product of a partial and teleological view of history, strongly influenced by dominant state traditions. Indeed we might argue that it is specifically the French and German state traditions that, in their very different ways, have insisted on this confluence of state and nation. For the French, the logical conclusion is the unitary, Jacobin state without any room for intermediate authority; Germans have a more federalist tradition, but one that also finds it difficult to cope with differentiation and plurinationality. In recent decades the state has come under increasing pressure even as it has assumed new responsibilities. Challenges have appeared to its functional capacity, its ability to mould and sustain identity, and its institutional structures. These have served to demystify the state and undermine its old monopolies, and provide a cue for in the new historiographies, which have traced other, competing state traditions lost since the rise of the monolithic nation-state (Chapter 2).

A powerful agent in the changing relationship between function and territory is economic restructuring. National economies are challenged by globalization and, nearer home, the construction of a single European market. At the same time, there is a growing acceptance that economic change responds to very local factors, and many scholars have seen the emergence of local systems of production as a key factor in the new economy. Changes in the sphere of social policy have been less dramatic. Welfare states tend still to be national in scope, but there are some trends to decentralization and a search for new forms of local solidarity. It may be that in the future the stateless nations, regions, or cities may come to embody the social solidarity hitherto carried by the nation-state. Culture has also increasingly escaped the framework of the nation-state. Global culture may be little more than an extension of United States influence but, like the English language, is must nonetheless be seen as a universal product. Migration, in response to economic globalization, has created new multicultural societies. The state remains the main framework for citizenship and for the rights that stem from it, but here too there are signs of change. A start has been made on detaching human rights from states and citizenship and placing them on a genuinely global basis, although enforcement is highly problematic. Citizens are able to operate with multiple identities, spanning the state and the stateless nation and, in some cases, extending also to Europe. Finally, the state is experiencing institutional change, challenged from above by European integration, from below by regional affirmation, and laterally by the advance of the market and of civil society. There is still no consensus on the political import of these changes. Some see them as eroding the state, while others insist that they merely represent a strategy on the part of states to consolidate their authority by pooling certain tasks and offloading other tasks to subordinate bodies. Indeed in some ways the state has been expanding its scope, particularly in social regulation, but at the same time losing much of its autonomy.

More specifically, these changes together serve to break up the old model of the nation-state (itself perhaps more of an ideal-type than a reality), which contained the following elements within a defined space:

- a set of functional systems, such as a 'national economy' and 'national welfare state';
- a national culture and identity;
- a corresponding national population, or *demos*, defined by common identity, a range of shared values, and mutual trust and interaction;
- a set of governing institutions;
- a claim to internal and external sovereignty.

For many scholars, this disaggregation heralds the 'end of territory' (Badie 1995) as social and political life dissolves into networks based on functional logic or on shared cultural identities. Some have even announced the 'end of democracy' (Guéhenno 1993). Certainly, it was the coincidence in space of these elements that provided for the possibility of national democracy, and their fragmentation is one factor causing the democratic deficit. Functional systems are fragmenting, with decision-making disappearing into networks. Cultures are becoming complex and multiple. The *demos*, if it can be identified, no longer corresponds to the functional systems which democracy is there to control; and power seems to have escaped the control of democratic and accountable institutions. Yet the 'end of territory' and 'end of democracy' theses are as premature as the 'end of history' announced with such fanfares in the 1990s (Fukuyama 1992).

Countering the tendencies to fragmentation are powerful forces for reterritorialization both of functional systems and of the political order. Economic change may respond to a global logic, but there is a large literature now to the effect that the response is less a matter of deterritorialization than of reterritorialization in the form of new, spatially specific systems of production (Balme 1996; Keating 1998a: Scott 1998; Storper 1997; Castells 1997). Similarly, the weakening of the territorial nation-state as a framework for representative and deliberative democracy is one factor in the rise of new nationalist movements below and beyond the state, some with a profound democratizing potential, others more populist or xenophobic in orientation. A combination of functional restructuring and political change has fostered new nationalisms whose whole essence is based on the need to maintain internal social and cultural cohesion while projecting themselves in the new global economy (Keating 1996a, 2001a). Globalization and the new transnational order in general have thus favoured the rise of new nationalisms, but at the same time they provide new means for accommodating them (Keating and McGarry 2001).

For some stateless nationalists, the new dispensation allows them to proceed to statehood without the economic or security risks which this might have posed in past epochs. Global and regional free trade regimes guarantee market access and take care of many of the externalities of independence, while the Pax Americana allows them to free-ride on a hegemonic security regime. This, as noted earlier (Chapter 3), is the position of a section of Quebec nationalism. Yet in so far as the emerging transnational order is market-driven, it has a strong neo-liberal bias; indeed most of the objections to globalization hinge on the argument that it serves the interest of capital at the expense of social and cultural considerations. Nationalism, on the other hand, is about confronting the market with political and cultural priorities and about establishing public spaces beyond the market-place. Just as regionalism and minority nationalism cannot, *pace* Ohmae (1995), be reduced to a functional logic of market competition, but must be understood also as a response to cultural and political factors, so transnationalism has a cultural and political dimension. This implies a new form of territorial order above as well as below the state.

There are signs here and there of such an order emerging, in the United Nations, or in the increased attention to social issues and matters of 'governance' in the work of bodies like the World Bank and the International Monetary Fund. Environmental and labour matters were incorporated into the North American Free Trade Agreement, albeit in the form of rather weak side agreements. There is an inter-American Convention on Human Rights. It is only in Europe, however, that an effort is being made to establish a comprehensive transnational regime explicitly committed to political as well as economic integration. There is a huge literature on the political implications of European integration, although much of it has yet to move beyond the debate between intergovernmentalists and neo-functionalists that has been going on for over forty years. In politics there is a continuing debate between those who want to restrict Europe to a common market and those who dream of creating a federal state. Since this debate has largely exhausted itself, I propose to pass it by and to postulate a Europe that is a *sui generis* political order, neither a state nor a mere alliance of states, but not without some antecedents in history. To capture this emerging order Neil MacCormick's (1999*a*) expression 'European Commonwealth' seems particularly felicitous.

The Uses of Europe

Europe has become a densely organized economic, social, and political space, encompassing a variety of transnational regimes which overlap in many places but are not quite coterminous. At the centre is the European Union (EU), based on economic integration but with officially declared, if contested, political aims. The Western European Union (WEU) is a defence organization linked both to the EU and to the North Atlantic Treaty Organization (NATO); it does not, however, include all members of either. Ireland, Austria, and Sweden are in the EU but not NATO or the WEU. Norway is in NATO but neither the EU nor the WEU, while Denmark is in NATO and the EU but not the WEU. The Organization for Security and Cooperation in Europe (OSCE) includes the countries of Europe, the United States and Canada, and the former Soviet republics, and is charged with security issues, including nationality questions, in the former Soviet and satellite states. The Council of Europe includes all European countries and many former Soviet republics and has an interest in democratization, minorities issues, and human rights. Its European Convention on the Protection of Human Rights and Fundamental Freedoms is upheld by the European Court of Human Rights, whose decisions have direct force in many member states; and it has generated a series of initiatives on human rights, cultures, and democratization.

This emerging European space provides a new context for the articulation and pursuit of nationalist demands. One dimension of this is symbolic but nonetheless of critical importance. In a Europe where there is no majority, all nations are in a sense 'minorities', allowing those who are minorities within their own states to project their concerns as part of a wider issue. As European institutions expand to take in more small nations and cultures, it will look more pluralistic and diverse, and the recognition of the smaller nations, whether these be states or not, will come onto the agenda. As noted earlier, the European theme is increasingly used to frame nationalist demands in the United Kingdom, Spain, and Belgium and, in the process, nationalism is itself tamed and modernized. The Europe of the Peoples may be no more than a slogan, but it represents an important discursive turn for nationalists, showing that other ways of realizing nationhood can at least be imagined. It also allows stateless nationalists to turn the tables on their own state elites, by demonstrating their greater international commitment, and, as nationalists are prepared to wait for the evolution of Europe, it converts the absolute issue of self-determination into a series of arguments about steps within a broader process. Symbols like the common practice of flying stateless national flags alongside the state and European flags indicate the linkage of nationality into the wider European order, as do the rapidly developing alliances among minorities across the continent.

There is a debate on whether or not Europe constitutes a cultural space (Puntscher Riekmann 1997) or should do so. This is often a question of definition and how restrictive a culture needs to be in order to exist as a discrete entity. Nor is it reasonable to say that Europe does not exist culturally because the boundaries are ill defined. It shares this characteristic with every social system or aggregate. There is certainly a European culture, but it is not monolithic and one feature of Europe is its very cultural diversity. As I shall be arguing repeatedly in various spheres, Europe should not be judged on the template of the nation-state, and attempts to promote a European culture could be positively harmful. Yet the existence of a European cultural space does allow minority cultures to project themselves as part of this and of a European tradition, rather than being seen as minor branches of state cultures. In many cases, these minority cultures have affinities with other European cultures which they do not share with their state counterparts and can gain fuller expression within a European framework.

Legal Pluralism

A crucial effect of the new European order is the way in which it throws into question the whole state-centred doctrine of sovereignty and opens up the possibility of new and pluralistic normative orders. This too is rejected by statists and intergovernmentalists who argue that the EU is an inter-state alliance built precisely on the principles of state sovereignty. States, in this view, cannot by definition alienate their own sovereignty, just as British parliaments cannot bind their successors. The argument is really tautological since the conclusion is embodied in the premiss. It is empirically weak, since new states are created constantly through decolonization and secession, while federations are created through consolidation, with sovereignty reconfigured accordingly. Although the Canadian constitution was repatriated by act of the British Parliament as recently as 1982, nobody seriously claims that the United Kingdom could even theoretically reassert its authority in Canada. The rigorously intergovernmental view of Europe is also historically ill informed, ignoring the experience of overlapping territorial and functional legal orders in history, and taking the ideological claims of the state at face value—this is particularly ironic for a group of scholars who like to call themselves 'realists'. Of course the radical alternative, that Europe is a new, independent legal order, is equally unfounded (Walker 1998*a*) since that too would substitute an ideal for the reality.

Yet between these two extremes there is the view that there exists a corpus of European law with its own foundations and principles, and its own path of development (Shaw 2000). It is not self-contained, but penetrates and shapes state law, being in turn penetrated and influenced by it. There is certainly a conflict of principle as yet unresolved. The European Court of Justice has held that European law is independent of, and superior to, state laws in its area of application, while national courts have clung to the doctrine that European law is merely the product of delegated authority (MacCormick 1999*a*). We have met this sort of argument before (Chapter 2) between those who hold that Scots law, the Basque *fueros*, or Catalan and Quebec civil law are founded in their respective state constitutions and those who claim that they represent original law. Again, a more plausible solution is to see them as founded in original law but having to accommodate to state constitutions. So whether we are looking from the supra-state or the sub-state level, it does seem that there are other sources of law than the constitution of the state. With at least three levels for these sources, we have the possibility of pluralistic legal orders. This gives a new meaning to the idea of constitutionalism. Instead of the unitary constitution (whether written or, as in the United Kingdom, embodied in parliamentary sovereignty) being the source of all norms, there are multiple sites of constitutional authority. The relaxation of the condition that the state be the source of all legal authority has opened up myriad new possibilities for plurinational politics and new forms of democracy (Jáuregui 2000).

It is no surprise that among the scholars most open to this possibility have been Scottish lawyers, accustomed to Scots and British law coexisting with a certain ambivalence over the ultimate source of authority. It has long been clear that there are distinct Scottish and English interpretations of parliamentary sovereignty and ultimate authority. In a famous case in 1953 Lord Justice Cooper in the Court of Session even ruled that the principle of parliamentary sovereignty did not apply in Scotland (Mitchell 1996; MacCormick 2000).[1] A similar ambiguity exists over Catalan civil law, which lacked its own legislative body from 1714 until 1980, apart from the brief period of the Second Republic. Although the Franco regime had abolished the reforms of the Second Republic, it was prepared to update the Catalan civil code on the curious grounds that this had been made in 'Spain' whereas the Spanish civil code was an import from France. Since the 1980s the Catalan parliament has assumed the task of modernizing the civil code, despite a central government challenge to the effect that it only has the

---

[1] The case was brought by John MacCormick, father of Neil MacCormick, law professor and MEP, who is one of the leading figures in the debate on legal pluralism. It concerned the question of whether the Queen should be known as Elizabeth II in Scotland, when neither Scotland nor the United Kingdom had had an Elizabeth I.

power to alter the code of 1961, not the corpus of indigenous Catalan law itself (Oranich 1997). There is even more confusion over the status of the historic rights of the Basque provinces. As we have seen, these were not recognized in the 1978 Spanish Constitution, which was itself considered to be the fount of Basque autonomy, but, under pressure, it was agreed to include them in an annexe, the First Additional Disposition. Two interpretations have resulted. Some believe that the historic rights are thus subject to the constitution; others believe that if this were the case the clause would be redundant and that the rights are original. The Spanish Constitutional Court at first tended to the first reading, but later admitted that the second was possible (Lasagabaster and Lazcano 1999). Basque and Navarrese foral law has been adopted and updated by the new or (in Navarre) newly democratized institutions, which have, like Catalonia, sought to preserve the integrity of their own systems of law, rather than merely filling in gaps left by the Spanish legislature and civil code. This type of legal ambiguity takes us beyond sovereignty altogether, at least in its usual formulations (MacCormick 1999*a*; Jáuregui 1999). If purists still insist that sovereignty cannot by definition by shared or divided, then MacCormick's formulation of 'normative orders' will do as well. So far, it must be said, courts have not interpreted these forms of original law as trumping state law or constitutions, but, with the development of autonomous governments in the United Kingdom and Spain, we may see a new jurisprudence gradually emerging in which autonomous legislatures, entrenched by referendum and drawing on distinct legal traditions and precedents, are conceded original rights. Just as European law developed, contrary to expectations, as an autonomous system, so might the law on devolution. A similar argument could be made for the accommodation of aboriginal law traditions in Canada.

This might seem like a recipe for anarchy or constitutional deadlock, but it need not necessarily be so. A certain restraint is provided by the threat that non-cooperation will bring the whole system down, a threat that has been compared to the military doctrine of mutual assured destruction in the cold war (Weiler 1999). Equally important is that the various normative orders develop within a shared community of values. For some, this implies the need for an overarching European sovereign, in the form of a state, whether federal or unitary. There is a sociological basis for this argument, that any legal order must be underpinned by a unitary political community; and a normative one, that such an order must, in accordance with democratic theory, be underpinned by a European nation, or *demos*. This was, in essence, the view of the German Constitutional Court in the *Brunner* case, when it refused to allow that the EU was an independent source of law. We will return to the democratic aspect of this shortly. The sociological argument is to the effect that Europe cannot function as a political order because, unlike the nation-state, it does not rest on the nationality principle and shared identity. Some conclude that Europe must therefore be refounded as a federation on American lines, with a founding moment, a constitution, and a people (Weale 1995). Anthony Smith (1995, 1999) takes this even further, arguing that Europe cannot forge a common political community since it lacks a core *ethnie*, or common ethnosymbolic base; and that such historical myths as it possesses are politically unacceptable or unsuitable. So European integration and other such projects must represent either 'heroic, if doomed, attempts to supersede the nation [or] new, emergent types of national community' (Smith 1995: 143). Both, in Smith's view, are futile. Yet this is surely to misunderstand the nature of the European project, which is and must remain rooted both in states and in the nations and regions that compose them (Jáuregui, 1997). It also rests on a contentious view of the European states themselves as the expression of ethnic cores, and a reliance on state-nationalist historiography which ignores the plurinational trajectories of so many states.

In any case, Europe is not a state, federal or otherwise, and the analogy is fundamentally misleading. The legal pluralism on which it rests implies neither the existence of a single fount of authority (in a constitution, a parliament, or a unitary *demos*), within which authority can be devolved, nor a series of independent, sealed legal orders. Rather it implies a series of linked normative orders, intercommunicating with each other (Bankowski and Christodoulidis 2000). This concept bears obvious affinities to the idea of plurinationality, in which national identities are shared and overlap in complex ways, as well as to cultural pluralism and communicative democracy in which cultures are neither assimilated to a single norm, nor exist in isolation (Tully 1995). The result has sometimes been described as post-national constitutionalism (Shaw 2000), but this is an unfortunate term since it conflates the nation with the state; post-statist or post-sovereign constitutionalism would be better terms. There is no uniform overall design, nor fixed end point, but rather a deliberative order in which constitutionalism is a part of 'normal' politics (Bellamy 2001). There do need to be common values here, and the limits to Europe may be defined by these values; the question as to whether Islamic states could be admitted to the EU has been carefully avoided in principle if not in practice. Yet these values do not need to be rooted in ethnocultural homogeneity (Carter and Scott 2000) and may well be universal in application. The countries of the EU, for example, have agreed on the abolition of capital punishment and have not only written this into their charter of rights, but have also undertaken to promote it globally. Capital punishment is also outlawed under the Council of Europe conventions, although this is an altogether thinner normative order and the ban has not always been accepted outside the EU and its candidate states. Universal health care and welfare provision are also a shared European value which, like capital punishment, demarcates it sharply from the United States, although there is no single European health or welfare regime but a variety of systems. A common European identity will not be based on cultural and political homogeneity. Indeed, given its very origins in the effort to overcome nationalist particularism, that would be a perverse outcome (Weiler 1999). It will be founded, rather, on shared interests and institutional cooperation. Habermas's (1998) concept of 'constitutional patriotism' might serve here, whatever its weakness as a basis for national identity (Chapter 1). Some people have criticized this as too thin a basis for political order (Weiler 1999[2]), yet it is precisely such 'weak ties' (Grannoveter 1973) that allow common purpose to be combined with flexibility and innovation.

Similarly, although there is no European *demos* on national lines, there is a form of European identity, invoked and used by those who need it. There is a class of Europeans, whose pilgrimages through European space evoke those of Anderson's (1983) nation-builders, who he sees as constructing communities of communication. Again, this is not for most people a strong identity, does not monopolize identity, and may not even be the most important of an individual's multiple identities, but then neither, for most of history, were state identities. If European identity is not something for which people die (Smith 1995), this is surely to be welcomed rather than seen as a problem; being prepared to make sacrifices to maintain human values is another matter. To argue, as do so many, that Europe is divided by religion or values, or to point to its history of wars (Smith 1995, 1999), is beside the point unless we also take into account common values or the political commitment to overcome this history.[3] The whole point of the exercise is to achieve unity in diversity. Communities of identity, like legal systems, can coexist and interpenetrate without domination, as we have seen in the case of those stateless nationalist movements who are so keen to work within the broader European space. Democratizing the European order, from this perspective, requires not the construction of a homogeneous community, but a form of democratic dialogue in which parties must invoke arguments that would be valid for the other side, so leading to integrative compromises (Bellamy and Castiglione 2000).

There is a legal European citizenship, founded in the Maastricht Treaty, but appropriately it is not like a state citizenship with its general rights. Rather it consists of a bundle of entitlements, including free movement around the EU and the right to vote in European and municipal elections in any of the states where one is resident. When linked to civil and social entitlements arising from state citizenship and residence in a region or stateless nation, this gives rise to a complex and multiple regime of citizenship, again challenging the old monolithic state regime. It would perhaps be

[2] Weiler's argument is unclear since he criticizes the idea of a European nationalism and at one point he seems to imply that a constitutional identity is what Europe needs, but then agrees with Anthony Smith that this is not enough (Weiler 1999: 344–6).
[3] Critical moments in which nation-states decided to set aside a past of civil conflict and forge a new union are not so uncommon in history as to make the European project implausible. One could cite, for example, the Swiss federation of 1848 (Steinberg 1976).

redundant to note once again that criticisms of European citizenship for not being state-like are beside the point. This form of complex and unbundled citizenship not only allows a European order to exist alongside nation-states; it also allows us to bring the stateless nationalities in as part of the same complex order. It is notable that few of the scholars who complain about Europe's lack of something analogous to a national identity seem to come from these stateless nations, where people are more accustomed to multiple forms of belonging.

Europe as a Rights Regime

In the previous chapter I argued that human rights were increasingly divorced from national citizenship, opening more possibilities for asymmetry within states and for constitutional creativity. Again Europe provides the most advanced case. Common European values have been articulated through human rights regimes, notably the European Convention for the Protection of Human Rights working through the European Court of Human Rights in Strasbourg. The convention detaches individual rights from citizenship and nationality and provides a mechanism for their realization. It does not aspire to universal jurisdiction but is confined to Europe. This regime, which, like other European institutions, is less than a state but more than an intergovernmental compact, works with national systems of law, allowing a margin of appreciation, rather than seeking to overturn national laws or substitute its own. This permits a dialogue among legal systems, as well as giving some flexibility in the application of human rights principles in different contexts. The European framework also enables rights discourse to be freed from nationalist or nationalizing rhetoric. Thus Europe has largely escaped the problems experienced in Canada, where the Charter of Rights was promoted in the early 1980s as a measure of Canadian nation-building and has consequently been widely rejected in Quebec. Human rights are not explicitly protected in the treaties of the EU, but, under pressure from states who have wanted to place their rights guarantees above EU law, the EU's European Court of Justice has recognized the need to incorporate both national and the European charters of rights in its jurisprudence (Moravcsik 1995). The EU itself has not become a signatory to the European Convention, but in 2000 began to develop its own charter of rights, adopted at the Nice Summit but not in a binding form.

The incorporation of the European Convention directly into the law of Scotland and Northern Ireland as a result of the devolution settlements of the late 1990s shows the value of denationalizing rights. Any purely British charter would have been unacceptable, especially to the minority community in Northern Ireland, as an expression of nation-building. The European Convention is more neutral in this sense, without being completely unfounded in a value community. Of course, the British government maintains the pretence that it is merely delegating power to the Northern Ireland Assembly and Scottish Parliament on the one hand, and to the European Court of Human Rights on the other. Yet there is now a direct interaction between European jurisprudence and the legal systems in the devolved territories. Parliament, anxious to maintain its theoretical supremacy, has allowed laws in devolved areas to be struck down by the courts where they violate the convention but not its own laws, which include all the laws of England and, for primary legislation, Wales. Here the courts can only ask Parliament to intervene. There is thus the possibility of the same law being open to legal challenge in some parts of the United Kingdom and not in others.

It is easy to dismiss the European rights regime as of no account because it does not displace states or operate like the United States Supreme Court in imposing a European legal order against national law. Again, this betrays a misunderstanding both of Europe and of the way in which legal regimes operate. European human rights law works not by overturning national legal regimes, but by a process of mutual penetration and learning, through jurisprudence. There will always be gaps and even contradictions between the regimes, and European norms will enter national systems in different ways; as we have seen, they can even enter the United Kingdom in different ways in England and Wales, in Scotland, and in Northern Ireland. Some have criticized the idea of a European rights regime on the ground that there are no common understandings of rights among Europe's various cultures (Bellamy 1995). It is true that, at the margins, there are differences, and it is easy to cite examples, and, as in the United States, rights issues can easily dissolve into pure politics. But this is not a reason to abandon the idea of rights altogether, any more than it is a reason to despair of the possibility of common European policies on other matters. Europe does have a rather broad understanding of common rights, some of which it shares with the United States and others, such as opposition to capital punishment, which it does not (Weiler 1999). The critical issue is to frame rights in such a way as to be generally universal but defined flexibly enough to fit into the legal idiom and culture of distinct nations. This is, broadly, the line which the European Court of Human Rights has sought to follow, in contradistinction to the centralizing tendencies of the United States Supreme Court in its more activist phases.

Of course, an individual rights regime does not address the issue of collective identity and the need to protect and develop people's own cultures and traditions. It is mistake to believe, with Siedentop (2000), that the cause of stateless nationalism is simply the failure to integrate individuals into the state culture, and that this can be 'remedied' by guaranteeing individual rights. It may be that the proximate cause of the Northern Ireland Troubles in the late 1960s was the failure to accord Irish Catholics the full rights of British citizens, but it is stretching matters to suggest that extending such rights would have made the Catholic community into loyal British subjects, as Siedentop suggests.[4] Transnational rights regimes are important for our purpose in divorcing individual rights from state citizenship and the state-nationalist implications of this. Guarantees of collective rights are another matter.

Legal protection for the collective rights of minorities in Europe is less well developed, but there is a broad consensus that this matter can only properly be tackled at a pan-European level. After the First World War, the minorities question in central and eastern Europe was addressed through a series of bilateral and multilateral treaties, mostly on the same template but without creating any pan-European system of minority rights (Capotorti 1991). Britain and France, struggling with rebellion in Ireland and the reincorporation of Alsace-Lorraine, were completely unwilling to allow the system of minority guarantees in the territories of the former central empires to be extended to their own minorities. This attitude has reappeared since the 1990s, hampering moves towards a genuine European regime of minority rights. Following the Second World War, the emphasis moved to individual rights, as enshrined in the European Convention for the Protection of Human Rights (ECHR), with some bilateral treaty arrangements, for example in the Tyrol or Trieste and Istria. Some cases concerning language rights in Belgium were brought under the ECHR, but the Court generally upheld the right of the state to impose territorial unilingualism (Hillgruber and Jestaedt 1994). During the 1960s Germany and Austria sought broader protection for ethnic minorities, but this made little headway (Fenet 1995). The issue came back on the agenda with the end of the cold war, and since then there has developed a complex net of charters, institutions, and guarantees under the auspices of the Council of Europe, the OSCE, and the EU. While these are separate organizations and the resulting provisions vary greatly in their legal scope and enforcement, they do form an interlinked system, with mutual penetration and influence, and a growing tendency for judgments under one to cross-reference the others (Fenet 1995).

The OSCE has been drawn into the question since the Helsinki Accords of 1975 as an inescapable part of its concern with human rights, and because of its intimate connection with matters of security. Gradually it has incorporated the idea of minority rights as opposed to mere individual rights but has been reluctant to be drawn too deeply into broader issues of self-determination. In 1992, following its failure to prevent the conflict in Yugoslavia, the OSCE appointed a High Commissioner for National Minorities whose task is to intervene in situations of potential conflict and seek negotiated solutions. His brief limits him to situations where security is threatened and, in practice but not officially, he has been confined to the countries of central and eastern Europe and the former Soviet Union.

---

[4] It is also difficult to see how they could have become unhyphenated British citizens when each part of the United Kingdom perceives its Britishness differently.

The Council of Europe's first real foray into the issue was the Charter on Regional and Minority Languages, adopted at the inspiration of its Conference of Local and Regional Authorities. First suggested in 1981, this was finally adopted in 1992 with reservations from several states including France and the United Kingdom, who would have preferred a very general declaration. There is no mechanism for enforcement except a three-yearly report to the Council of Ministers; otherwise the charter depends on changing norms and ways of thinking. This did not prevent the charter from becoming embroiled in a controversy in France where Jacobin elements of the left and right conspired to prevent the constitutional amendment which, according to the Constitutional Court ratification would have required.

The end of the cold war and incorporation of central and eastern European countries forced the Council of Europe to return to the minorities question in the 1990s with the Framework Convention for the Protection of National Minorities, adopted in 1995. This was specifically designed as a 'framework' to be adopted in appropriate form by signatory states but without direct application. It does not define minorities or recognize them as collectivities, but rather addresses itself to the rights of individuals belonging to them. Membership of a minority is determined by a mixture of self-designation and objective criteria. Matters covered include the use of language, education, the media, public administration, commercial signs, and cross-border contacts. Despite its focus on individual rights, the convention stands out among the European instruments for its intention to protect and preserve the minority communities themselves, so going beyond the mere prohibition of discrimination. Signatory states themselves were allowed to designate their own minorities before ratification, further weakening the convention's application. So Estonia included only its own citizens in the convention's scope, allowing it to refuse to recognize Russians who had not met its strict citizenship requirements; Russia's own reservation was aimed specifically at denying this. Luxembourg, worried about the rights of immigrants and their descendants, confined its protection to minorities who had been present for 'several generations' and then declared that, on this criterion, there were no minorities in Luxembourg. Other states, however, took the matter more seriously and many national minorities were expressly singled out for protection.

The EU has also moved slowly to recognize national minorities. Indeed many of the internal market policies can be seen as a threat to minority cultures and languages. Flemish nationalists, while in favour of Europe in general, have complained about the threat to their language and culture in the single market and an institutional structure dominated by English and French (Laible 2001). Restrictions on outsiders buying property in fragile traditional communities have been disallowed, except in Denmark, where a treaty opt-out was negotiated. Requirements to label products in a minority language are illegal under provisions confining regulation to an official community language comprehensible to the customers; since Spanish is comprehensible to Catalans and Basques, any additional requirement is considered an obstacle to the free movement of goods. Ethnic quotas in employment for Germans and Italians in South Tyrol have also come under threat. Gradually, however, the EU has incorporated some measures for minority protection. The Maastricht Treaty had a clause in favour of cultural and regional diversity and this was used by the European Parliament and Commission to fund various measures, including the Bureau of Less Widely Spoken Languages in Dublin (Fenet 1995). The Parliament and the Committee of the Regions have also pressed for wider recognition of culture and language in the operation of regional policies. Catalan was the subject of a special resolution of the Parliament in 1990, and the Catalan government has made a great deal of political mileage out of this since. The EU has intervened more effectively in candidate countries, as has the Council of Europe, making treatment of minorities a condition for membership.

So there is a great deal of European activity on minority rights, but no single, binding regime; mechanisms remain focused on the states (Roter 1997). Priority is given to individual rights, although there is more attention on the collective means by which these rights are exercised in matters like educational provision or public services. Broader political issues are avoided. No European regime recognizes a right of self-determination for minorities,[5] although the Council of Europe insists on the need for local self-government, and there is always explicit recognition of the integrity of states and their borders. There is a persistent bias towards seeing central and eastern Europe as the seat of the problem, rather than taking a broader pan-European perspective, and west European states including France, Spain, and the United Kingdom have jealously guarded their own rights to deal with their minorities in their own way. Enforcement mechanisms are still weak and dependent on political negotiation rather than legal application. Much of this is no doubt inevitable. Defining a national minority or ethnic group is scientifically impossible, politically fraught, and ethically dubious, since it reifies the group and prevents evolution and change. Giving legal rights to groups as opposed to individuals would create an immediate conflict with European norms of individual liberty and free choice, and would also tend to freeze groups in time. Challenging state borders in the name of group rights would be profoundly destabilizing and counter-productive, as states would then see group rights as a threat to their very existence. So it may be more fruitful to construct a series of pan-European regimes incorporating political principles and norms and encouraging their mutual penetration. The bias to central and eastern Europe is less easy to justify since it perpetuates an old stereotype and works against the construction of a common European space of values.

[5] The European Court of Human Rights refused to entertain a complaint from the Sudeten Germans against the German–Czech treaty of 1973 (Hillgruber and Jestaedt 1994). I have argued (Ch. 1) that self-determination must be seen as a political principle rather than a justiciable right.

Democratizing Europe

Europe is thus emerging as a complex system of regulation and norms but definitely not as a state. This is precisely the point of the exercise, to transcend statehood, despite the repeated attempts to convert it into some sort of state by giving it a constitution or defined catalogue of competences. Were it to become a state, or even to aspire to being one, then it would provoke a reaction from both state and stateless nationalists, who would resent it as a new form of domination. It would also rigidify its institutions and ways of working, depriving it of the flexibility that has proved its strength. A European state or federation would have to follow a specific model, as we see from the different visions of what is might look like coming from French and German enthusiasts. Constitutionalization would also impose a rigid framework on an evolving political order and encourage the juridification of politics and the constitutionalization of political and social cleavages, as has happened in Canada.

This is not to say that we must just muddle on. Complexity and the proliferation of levels of decision-making do reduce democracy as power seeps from elected institutions into networks. If multilevel governance means anything, it is surely a highly undemocratic order in which organizational elites and those with the skills, time, and resources to operate in complex sectoral and territorial networks have immense advantages over their fellow citizens. When combined with the New Public Management and its tendency to reduce citizens to market consumers, this raises serious problems for deliberative democracy. For some people, the answer to the democratic deficit is to build systems analogous to parliamentary democracy at the European level, merging the various European regimes, strengthening the European Parliament, and having a European government accountable to it. There is no doubt a great deal that could be done at the European level to strengthen democracy, but the analogy to the nation-state again lets us down. The assumption is usually made that in Europe, as in the classic nation-state, functional systems, political representation, democratic mobilization and accountability can all be contained within the same territorial framework. This is a highly dubious proposition, relying on a particular model of the state. If Europe is to be democratized, it must be done in new ways, corresponding to the new forms of political authority.

Democratic and accountable government is a complex matter, but there would seem to be two basic requirements. The first is the existence of deliberative spaces for the formation of a democratic will. I am assuming here, against the Public Choice school, that citizens' democratic preferences are not the mere sum of individual desires, which could be left to the market or to referendums, but result from deliberation and exchange.[6] It is these

---

[6] Bellamy and Castiglione (2000) draw a distinction between liberalism, which takes choices as given, and republicanism, which is predicated on dialogue and debate.

deliberative spaces that need to correspond to a sense of common or shared identity, or to a *demos*, if not an exclusive one. The second requirement is a system of accountability corresponding to the areas of decision-making in the emerging functional systems. In a complex system with functional and territorial divisions these can no longer always be done by the same institutions.

For example, the European Parliament is probably as good as most national parliaments (admittedly not a difficult test) in scrutinizing executive institutions and holding them to account (the fall of the Santer Commission is exemplary). It does not, on the other hand, sustain a pan-European deliberative community or help form a pan-European democratic will. It probably never will, and possibly never should. We may therefore need to delink these activities. Accountability and scrutiny may take a variety of forms—audit, legal control, parliamentary investigation, adversary politics—and work at various levels. Deliberative democracy and will formation can similarly occur at various levels. In some cases, the state remains the main focus. This is clearly so in Denmark, Portugal, and Ireland, and is still largely true in the larger states of France and Germany. In Belgium, on the other hand, deliberation is increasingly confined to the two main linguistic communities. In the multinational states of Spain and the United Kingdom there are deliberative communities within the nations of Catalonia, the Basque Country, Scotland, and Wales, as well as at the state level. Northern Ireland presents further complexity, caught as it is between a UK community with which its links are weakening, an all-Irish community, and an Ulster or Northern Irish community. This last has hitherto been divided into two segments but might find some common interests, especially in economic matters and Europe, as a result of the peace process and the new institutional framework. There is a persistent prejudice against recognizing national communities other than states or as the building blocks of democracy. Siedentop (2000: 175) insists that 'few such [European historic] regions have any civic tradition, any tradition of democracy or citizenship in working order'.[7] I would like to argue that there are sites of democratic initiative and deliberation.

Elsewhere, the pressures for participation and democratization have favoured deliberative communities at the city level. This is notably the case in France, where decentralization has strengthened the local level as a political arena, and in Italy, where the crisis of the central state has coincided with a revalorization of the local level. In other cases again, the deliberative community might be a large region, beyond a city but without the characteristics of a stateless nation. In the limiting cases, democratic will and identity may be located at a very small scale, as in the small communes of many countries, which are too small to correspond to any functional system. Reforms of local and regional government in the past have often fallen into

---

[7] Even more contentiously, Siedentop compares European regions unfavourably with the original American colonies, without mentioning slavery or the disfranchisement of women.

the technocratic fallacy of trying to align all systems of decision-making and representation with functionally defined units (the British were particularly prone to this in their frequent reorganizations). This theme has re-emerged now in the debate about the need for large regions to compete in Europe, or the insistence on the need for a regional level of government across the entire EU, whatever the local conditions.

Deliberative democracy may therefore be located at various levels, and stateless nations, far from being a problem for Europe, may serves as exemplars of such communities. Yet to create a democratic commonwealth, these communities must be linked and not isolated. This intercommunicative aspect of democracy is essential (Tully 1995), with ideas and practices flowing from one to another and a continuing debate on the common good articulated at various levels. Pillarized societies are ill equipped to do this, as critics of consociational democracy have often pointed out. The relationship between English and French Canada has often been described as one of two solitudes, a tendency that may increase with the reassertion of nationalism on both sides. Belgium is in the process of falling into the same problem, as intercommunication between the two communities declines; it is fortunate in this case that both communities are part of a broader European communicative order. Northern Ireland is a deeply divided society, but there is now a conscious policy of building links across the communities, to the Republic, to the United Kingdom, and to Europe. There is a historic fear in Scotland of parochialism, and this has placed a barrier in the path of home rule; it is greatly lessened in the European context. Similarly, the traditional isolation of much of Basque society is being overcome by linking it to other European communities.[8] In this vision, the democratization of Europe would come not through strengthening summit-level institutions on the assumption that they correspond to a unitary demos, but through a whole system of parliamentarism, linking Europe, states, and sub-state levels (Ferry 1997).

Stateless Nations in the European Commonwealth

Europe not only sustains a new context for the symbolic recognition of stateless nations and for legal pluralism. It also provides new opportunities for their institutional differentiation and for their projection as actors in the new political order. One way in which it does this is by permitting greater asymmetry within states. Its unified market regime allows a loosening of single market rules within states themselves, and a greater diversity of development policies and institutions. EU competition rules are often stricter than

---

[8] This argument must not be confused with the old liberal hope that, as individuals get to know each other, differences will disappear. I am arguing that differences can be valuable, as can the existence of distinct deliberative communities. What is important is that they not be closed and that there exist strong and, if necessary, formalized mechanisms for intercommunication.

those of the states themselves and have created trouble for the German *Länder* with their state banks, stakes in firms, and subsidies to investment. Basque rules discriminating in favour of local investors have been challenged by the European Commission, with the curious conclusion that the Basque government can discriminate against citizens from the rest of Spain but not other Europeans. In a similar case, it appeared that Scotland could impose differential university fees on students from other parts of the United Kingdom but not from elsewhere within the EU. Such European rules have often caused resentment within the regions and accusations of EU-level centralization, but they show how the unifying regulation of the nation-state is giving way to a European system of regulation in which regions and stateless nations are operating in European markets. An analogous situation exists with regard to the human rights regime, which is increasingly detached from states, so allowing institutional and legislative asymmetry within states, notably in the United Kingdom.

European market integration also provides new opportunities for autonomy and self-government, although one constrained by the needs of economic competition. In modern conditions, territorial self-government is more than a matter of constitutional, legal autonomy. It requires a policy capacity, and the ability to operate through complex networks, at local, state, and European level, and crossing the boundaries between the public and the private sector. Economic competitiveness is a critical, although not the only, element of this. As we have seen earlier (Chapter 3), stateless nationalists have generally abandoned dreams of self-sufficiency or economic autarky, and embraced global and regional free trade as an integral part of their policy prospectus. They have bought into the new models of economic development, which put the emphasis on the region as a production unit in competition with others, on endogenous growth, and on the mobilization of productive capacities through partnerships, associations, and research and development. These new models of economic development are still rather controversial, especially in their neo-mercantilist versions, which present regions as engaged in a competition for absolute advantage in European and global markets (Lovering 1999; Keating 2000*a*). Politically, however, they have obvious advantages for stateless nation-builders since they replace the old paradigm in which the region was engaged in a relationship of mutual dependency with the state with one in which the region becomes a more or less autonomous agent within the broader market. It is not surprising, then, to find Catalonia, Flanders, or the Basque Country presenting economic competitiveness in Europe as a centrepiece of the national project. In Scotland, where the nationalists' main focus is still on statehood within an intergovernmental Europe, this emphasis has so far been much less marked.

Self-government in modern conditions also requires social cohesion, both as a contribution to economic competitiveness and sustaining the necessary synergies, and for its own sake as part of the national project. A third part of this project is sustaining a living and vibrant culture in the face of market and social pressures from outside. These objectives can and often do clash. Market integration may be socially disintegrative, as disparities open up between those groups, localities, and sectors that can compete and those that cannot. Local cultures may fall victim to larger ones, or to the global domination of English language and especially American products. While it is possible to use minority languages in the school system, as has been done successfully in Catalonia, the Basque Country, and Wales, it is much more difficult to get them accepted as working languages in the economy, where the state languages, or English, prevail (Keating 2000*a*). On the other hand, nationalists see the local culture as a means of sustaining cohesion and the capacity for collective action necessary to face market competition, transcending the conflict of objectives through a conscious nation-building strategy.

Stateless nations also have opportunities to become more direct protagonists in Europe since, while the EU is fundamentally an organization of states, it is also a complex multilevel system of decision-making with multiple points of access. Territorial actors of various types have become active in this process, giving rise to a substantial literature on the Europe of the Regions (Jones and Keating 1995; Hooghe 1996; Keating and Hooghe 1996; Bullman 1994; Jeffery 2000; Petschen 1993). Stateless nationalists have entered into this game enthusiastically, while insisting on their special status as more than mere regions and without renouncing longer-term ambitions. The EU itself took significant steps to incorporate the regions as a third level of the European polity in the 1990s, but these soon reached their limits as states reasserted their powers and as the very heterogeneity of territorial interests prevented a uniform solution. Since then, individual regions or alliances of regions have sought to exercise influence wherever available giving rise to a wide variety of strategies.

Institutional recognition was first given to the regional level in the Treaty on European Union (Maastricht Treaty), which established a Committee of the Regions representing sub-state entities of all types. This has kept the issue of regionalism alive and provided some input into the deliberations of the European Commission and the Council of Ministers but has proved a disappointment to many stateless nationalists because of its weak status and the variety of its membership. By including representatives of municipalities alongside the leaders of Catalonia, Flanders, or the large German *Länder*, it has diluted the regionalist dynamic and undermined the status of the large players. These have consequently demanded a separate institution, representing regions only, or even just regions with legislative powers. This would bring in the Spanish stateless nations, along with Flanders and Scotland. While this would still not create a category of nations as opposed to regions, it would have the advantage of giving them powerful allies. The European Commission has also recognized regional associations for consultative purposes, giving them another channel of access.

A second mechanism for institutional representation is the provision in the Treaty on European Union whereby in systems where regions have governments with a ministerial structure, these can represent the state in the Council of Ministers. The exercise of this power is at the discretion of states, and the regions must represent a state position and not their own particular interests. Provision has been regularized in Germany and Belgium, with legal provisions for dividing European business between matters of state, regional and shared competence, and for representing the state according- ingly. In Germany, regional issues are handled through the Bundesrat, which agrees, by majority vote if necessary, on a common line for the *Länder* and assigns one of the *Länder* to speak for them all. Belgium, in consequence of the more conflictual nature of intergovernmental relations, requires unanim- ity among the affected governments, which may include the federal govern- ment, the regions, and the language communities, depending on the issue. If no agreement is reached, the Belgian delegation in the council must abstain. UK devolution legislation provides for the participation of Scottish, Welsh, and Northern Ireland ministers in the council, alongside those of the state. There are non-statutory concordats to regulate relations and the procedure for agreeing the line to pursue, but the UK government has the last word. In fact, the UK system is really a carry-over from the pre-devolution practice whereby ministers of the Scottish and Welsh offices could participate in European business as part of a unified UK delegation. In the event of the devolved Scottish and Welsh governments being controlled by parties other than that ruling at Westminster, the system would come under extreme tension and there might have to be more formalized rules. Northern Ireland raises different questions again, with the possibility of cooperation between its government and that of the Republic of Ireland on European matters of common interest. There have been strong demands from the minority na- tionalities of Spain for the application of this rule, but so far the Spanish state has resisted, preferring to negotiate with the devolved governments within the framework of Spanish politics. There was a bilateral committee with the Basque Country to discuss European matters, but it fell victim to the polar- ization of Basque politics.

The EU has also incorporated regional interests through the Structural Funds, which, since 1988 have been dispersed on the basis of partnership programmes in which regional interests must be present. The quality of these partnerships has varied greatly (Hooghe 1996) and the substantive impact of the funds has been questionable, given the complicated national rules whereby states manage to keep the moneys for themselves or subordinate them to national priorities. Politically, however, the funds have played a vital role in raising the profile of regional policies and linking regional assertion with European integration. Regional leaders, including those from stateless nations, have made much of their ability to extract funds from the EU, often giving a misleading impression that they have been able to bypass the state and deal directly with Brussels. By the late 1990s, however, this movement had peaked. The Commission was increasingly concerned with the administrative and political burden of administering funds, and aware of its limited ability to engage in detailed spatial planning. States were asserting more control over the designation of eligible areas and the terms of partnership, while everyone was aware that the EU could not afford to extend to the candidate countries of central and eastern Europe the same generous aid that had been given to Spain, Portugal, and Greece.

Cross-border collaboration has developed to cover all the borders within the EU and with the candidate countries, facilitated by the institutional structures and resources from Europe. The EU's INTERREG programme does not transfer a lot of money, but unlike most other Structural Fund programmes, it comes directly under the Commission and its funding can, at the margin, give an incentive to work in partnership. It also provides political incentives, allowing politicians to present themselves as good Europeans or as outward-looking and progressive. The absence of any such mechanism in North America goes a long way towards explaining the difficulties in sustaining cross-border cooperation there. The Council of Europe also sustains cross-border cooperation, through its Madrid Convention of 1980, which provides a legal framework, and its Convention on Minorities, which deals with the issue of minorities straddling state borders. Experience here, too, is mixed. Many cross-border operations remain at the level of intentions or symbolism, and the willingness to cooperate is often frustrated by the pressures of inter-regional competition. In others, however, they have served to bring together cultural regions or stateless nations divided by state borders. A critical element in the success of these ventures is precisely that they should not challenge state borders, and they only really work where border issues are settled. In this way, it is possible to work around the border, to penetrate it peacefully; where borders are contested, then almost any proposal for collaboration can be seen by state elites as a threat to the border itself. More generally, stateless nations have been active in 'paradiplomacy' (Aldecoa and Keating 1998), projecting themselves in transnational networks without trying to rival the high diplomacy of the nation-state.

One might be sceptical about each of these institutional devices and policy programmes; they have certainly not created a coherent 'third level' of government within the EU. Yet they have created a new political space, or a multiplicity of spaces, for sub-state actors. Indeed the fact that there is not a single institutional framework for them all might be seen as the essence of the movement, allowing multiple strategies of working in Europe for the very varied interests involved. Within these new spaces, stateless nations have mounted lobbies and opened offices in Brussels and have forged a multitude of trans-state alliances. These can serve to pursue issues in multiple forums, within different states, through the Commission, and via the European Parliament.

Euro-Strategies

Stateless nations have availed themselves of these opportunities in diverse ways.[9] Catalonia has been extremely active in external relations, revalorizing its history as a medieval trading nation embedded in Spanish, European, and Mediterranean networks. Its nation-building project places a strong emphasis on language and culture and the projection of the Catalan language abroad (Cardus *et al.* 1991). There is an active paradiplomatic effort, based in civil society as much as the autonomous government, and relying on public–private partnerships of various sorts to maintain a presence across Europe and the world more widely. Representation in Brussels is assured by the Patronat Català Pro Europa, a public–private partnership founded in advance of Spain's accession to the European Community. Catalonia has preferred to work with the Spanish government rather than against it, seeking to influence the Spanish position within the EU as well as playing in its own pan-European networks. It long hesitated to call for representation of the autonomous communities in the Council of Ministers, ostensibly on the ground that this would require a constitutional amendment, although an important factor appears to have been a concern that Catalonia would be reduced to one of seventeen autonomous communities rather than an interlocutor of the state. Since the late 1990s, however, the Catalan government has supported the incorporation of the autonomous communities into the European process on the same lines as in Germany or perhaps Belgium. Catalonia has also been very active in the Europe of the Regions movement, in the Committee of the Regions, and in the Assembly of European Regions, pressing constantly for a recognition of the regional level and a particular place for strong and cultural regions within it.

The Basque nationalists have a long history of Europeanism (Ugalde 1998) going back to the Civil War era, but since the transition to democracy in Spain have been less active than the Catalans. The Basque government under the leadership of the Basque Nationalist Party has over time placed more emphasis on Europe, but with a more particularlist strategy than the Catalans. Their presence in Brussels is a government office, not a partnership as in the Catalan case, and had to be delayed some years while the Constitutional Court considered the legality of so overtly political a representation. Proposals in the early 1990s envisaged a direct Basque presence in European institutions, although it was not quite clear how this would work according to the Spanish constitution or the European treaties. Basque nationalists were even more reluctant than the Catalans to share a regional representation with the other autonomous communities. With the Declaration of

---

[9] The following discussion is brief, as I have discussed paradiplomacy and regional strategies in Europe at length elsewhere (Jones and Keating 1995; Keating and Hooghe 1996; Keating 1998*a, b*, 2000*c*).

Barcelona (BNG–PNV–CiU 1998) and subsequent Declarations of Vittoria and Santiago de Compostela, however, they have come round to the idea of using the Maastricht provisions for regional representation, but with special consideration for the historic nationalities. The Basques have also been active in the Committee of the Regions, the Assembly of European Regions, and other pan-European bodies, and have made efforts to mobilize the Basque diaspora, especially in North and South America. From the 1990s they have sought to influence opinion-makers in other European countries, combating the unfavourable image given to the Basque Country by political violence.

Flanders was particularly active in paradiplomacy under the former Christian Democrat-led government, with its nation-building programme. Like Catalonia, it used the theme of regional development and its trading history as a motif for external projection, while taking steps to protect its language and culture. Belgian regions and communities have full external competences corresponding to their internal competences, and this has led to a large presence abroad, promoting the image of Flanders in general and its merits as an investment location in particular. Regions and communities regularly speak for Belgium in the Council of Ministers, and, while they must promote a Belgian line, they do use the opportunity to press their own concerns. The unanimity rule means that they cannot take a purely selfish line, but it also encourages bargains and trade-offs whereby the communities and the regions can get their own particular concerns onto the agenda. At one time Flanders's protagonism in Europe was so pronounced as to provoke the suggestion that it was trying to promote itself from a 'third (regional) level' actor to the 'second (state-like) level' (Kerremans and Beyers 1996). Another initiative of the government was the Foundation Europe of the Cultures (1996), an alliance among politicians, social actors, and others in 'cultural regions'. These were essentially historic nations, but the list was chosen to include both states and stateless territories, carefully blurring the distinction. The theme of the Foundation is the importance of culture and identity for economic development in the modern era, and the need for an institutional recognition of cultural regions in the European institutional design.

Scotland and Wales have never been controlled by nationalist or quasi-nationalist parties and so the question of carving out their own space in Europe has not arisen. The Scottish National Party (SNP) is in any case committed to statehood within the EU as its minimum demand, and has given little thought to solutions short of this. The Labour Party's strategy is to tie Scotland tightly into the UK line in Europe. Yet the Scottish presence abroad and especially in Europe has gradually expanded as the Foreign Office has become more relaxed about paradiplomacy in fields such as culture, inward investment, and tourist promotion. It is likely that future Scottish governments whether led by Labour or the SNP will have to explore further the scope for a Scottish presence and influence in Europe. In Wales, where the nationalists have explicitly renounced separatism, there is similarly a search for opportunities within the new European order. The very complexity and asymmetry of the UK system allows for various patterns of alliance, while the Northern Ireland peace process, with its involvement of the Irish Republic in cross-border institutions and the British-Irish Council, creates a potential for still more.

There is thus not one single place for stateless nations in the European commonwealth and no single strategy for projecting nationality and self-government. Rather there is a multiplicity of opportunities and strategies, involving not only different actors but different types of actor in each case. Stateless nations can work with their states, they can play the Europe of the Regions game, or they can lobby on their own. They can ally on some issues with the German *Länder*, as in the emerging alliance of regions with legislative powers. They can make common cause with small states, as in the Europe of the Cultures concept. They can argue for special recognition within their own states, or join with other regions in pressing for regional joint representation in the Council of Ministers. While Europe remains so fluid, without a clear end point in sight, it makes obvious sense to keep all options open. As Europe develops, these opportunities are likely to expand, and regions and stateless nations will gain influence in new policy fields. States may be forced to accommodate this, developing a more 'plurinational diplomacy' (Aldecoa 1998), in which different instruments are used and different interests are represented depending on the issue at stake. Traditional diplomacy is predicated on the existence of a single 'national interest', defined by the state and underpinned by the idea that in matters of external relations the integrity and very existence of the state is constantly at stake. With the state itself demystified and sovereignty unpacked in the ways suggested so far, this doctrine is increasingly untenable. The principle may be expanded beyond the EU. There seems to be no reason in principle why, for example, the UK government should monopolize British representation at Unesco when there is no UK department for education nor for culture. A similar case can be made for Quebec. Of course, it is always possible that some cataclysmic crisis will destroy the current regime of global and European integration just as the Concert of Europe and the first era of globalization at the end of nineteenth century collapsed; but if current trends continue, there is an ever-expanding array of opportunities for nations to express themselves other than as states.

The Limits to Europeanization

Europe thus provides multiple opportunities for accommodating minority national demands. These do not, however, constitute a single or consistent regime, and many of them were designed with other purposes in mind.

Europe does not resolve the issue of self-determination, and indeed it is difficult to envisage what a general European norm on the right of self-determination would look like. We would be back with the old questions of who has the right, what the boundaries of self-determining units should be, and under what circumstances the right could be exercised. These are fundamentally political issues, and what matters is to establish the right political frameworks in which they can be addressed. Europe helps here in lowering the stakes in independent statehood and introducing the idea of shared sovereignty and pluralism, so helping forms of accommodation short of secession. It also makes it likely that secessions, should they occur, will be peaceful and preserve common market structures and systems of rights.

There are, of course, disadvantages in placing too much stress on rights in the political realm. As Canadian experience shows, political issues rapidly become converted into rights issues, which then become absolutes and can be obstacles to flexibility in public policy and the allocation of resources. Individuals who can make rights-based claims on public resources will win out over those who cannot make such claims. Politics will increasingly be taken into the courts, and lawyers will proliferate. Yet it seems that the juridicization of politics is the inevitable consequence of the increasing complexity of government, the existence of multiple levels of authority, and the decline in citizen deference. The answer is not to exclude law from the regulation of social conflicts, but to make the law and the legal profession itself more sensitive to cultural differences and to the political context in which it operates.

Nor is Europe a panacea for the problems raised by the coexistence of different levels of authority or of cultural pluralism. European market integration has at times been seen as a threat to minority cultures. The growing interventionism of the European Commission in the 1990s provoked reactions from regional governments which had previously been regarded as something of an ally. This led, in 2000, to the constitution of a group of regions with legislative powers seeking to incorporate provisions for subsidiarity and a measure of flexibility in implementation into future treaty revisions.

Another problem in systems of normative pluralism and multiple-level government is the threat to the territorial equity and the redistributive capacity of government. The nation-state has been a powerful agent for interterritorial resource transfers, partly through explicit programmes of redistribution, but mainly through the automatic fiscal stabilizers provided by state-level taxation and spending programmes. The EU has sought to compensate for the adverse affects of market integration through the Structural Funds, aimed at helping declining or underdeveloped regions to reinsert themselves into the single market. These, however, are small in scale compared with the effects of state programmes, and there is no political will to introduce into the EU a system of full fiscal federalism along United States or

Canadian lines. As the state framework weakens, there are signs of increasing competition among regions for inward investment, markets, and technology (Keating 1998*a*), with the risk of a 'race to the bottom' or 'social dumping' as regions subordinate social, cultural, and environmental concerns to growth, although this is limited in Europe, as compared to the United States, by EU norms and a shared commitment to welfare. Territorial redistribution through the Structural Funds has been justified as a trade-off among states (Hooghe and Keating 1994) in which the advanced regions get access to wider markets and the poorer ones get help. It has not been underpinned, at least to the same extent, by a wider ethic of pan-European solidarity. Without such an ethic, the policy might become more difficult to sustain and will certainly be impossible to expand. Since the stateless nations of Europe include both poorer regions (like Wales) and wealthier ones (like Flanders) as well as many which are in between, there is no automatic relationship between accommodating minorities and redistributing resources progressively. The European project has served to reshape the nationality question, taking it at least partly beyond the state framework and calling into question the old sovereignty doctrines. Stateless nationality movements have invested a great deal in this, especially where they can call on historic traditions of diffused authority and negotiated order (Chapter 3). Yet Europe does not provide a complete external support system permitting nations to spin right out of the orbit of member states. Plurinational democracy requires a rethinking of all three levels and the relationships among them.

6

Plurinational Democracy

It is clear that in order to understand the complexities of nationality and political order in the modern world we need to get beyond the old models of statehood based on a uniform order, whether federal or unitary. The concept of the multinational state gets closer to capturing reality but is still not quite satisfactory. It suggests the existence of discrete nations brought together in a union, federation, or confederation while retaining their distinct identities. This describes some cases well, but in the cases examined here, which may be more typical, the very concept and meaning of 'nation' varies from one to another. Nationality may be confined to cultural matters or the private sphere, or it may be more politicized. Individuals may have multiple national identities, themselves more politicized in some places and at some times than at others. Identities may overlap and may correspond more or less to territorial spaces, as noted in Chapter 1, to generate a variety of territorially integrated, dispersed, or interlinked nationality claims, as charted in Chapter 3. Nationality is too complex a concept to capture in a single definition or fix in a single moment; indeed the possibility for a nation to represent itself in its own way is part of the essence of self-determination and thus of justice and stability (Tully 1999). Some of the nations that have affirmed or are affirming their existence are territorially integrated and nested within overarching states; probably the clearest case is Scotland. Others are more contested, with different groups feeling different loyalties to the stateless nation, to the state, or to a nation included in another state. Hence the term 'plurinationalism' better captures the more fluid and pluralistic nature of this social reality, which presents more complex issues of recognition in some cases than in others. It is important to emphasize that we are not dealing here merely with cultural pluralism, or with claims to special policy concessions, but with nationality claims, with all that this implies. This includes a territorial basis, however much this may be contested. It is indeed an 'architectonic illusion' (Brubaker 1998) to believe that identity claims can be satisfied by redrawing lines on maps, yet political authority and functional capacity remain rooted in a territorial order, and territorial institutions remain the most inclusive and most effective mechanisms for a democratic order.

There are those who see the answer in asserting the rights of the sovereign state and in seeking a clarity reminiscent of the old state order. The Canadian federal government's Plan B, as exemplified by its Clarity Bill of 1999, makes it clear that the only self-determination option open to Quebec is secession to become a separate state with no institutional links whatever to Canada. This would have to take place following a 'clear' majority on a 'clear' referendum question. The argument of this book has been that there are no longer clear questions where matters of sovereignty are concerned and that, in divided societies, there are no clear majorities. Indeed the Clarity Bill itself concedes the latter point while further muddying the issue by suggesting that, even after a clear majority decision in Quebec, the minority might be allowed to opt back into Canada. The response of the Spanish state to the Basque question has been no more imaginative, refusing even to broach the question of self-determination on the grounds that this would violate the constitutionally guaranteed unity of the state. Of course, the Canadian and Spanish governments can reasonably protest that they are a great deal more accommodating than a French Jacobin like Jean-Pierre Chevènement, who resigned as Minister of the Interior in 1999 over the issue of home rule for Corsica. After all, Quebec and the Basque Country do enjoy a substantial measure of self-government within their own constitutions. The states have now, however, recognized the symbolic dimension of nationality and self-determination, the idea that these stateless nations possess a constituent power of their own, whether or not this entails the right of separation.

Of course, many of the stateless nationalists suffer from the same illusion, that there can be a defining moment in which the issue will be resolved. The Parti Québécois has staged referendums in 1980 and 1995, albeit on very ambiguous questions, without resolving the issue, and propose a third in due course, giving rise to gibes about the 'referendum-neverendum' or the strategy of pestering the people with the same question until eventually they answer yes. The Scottish National Party propose a referendum on independence should they win office, and the evidence suggests that the response might be the same as in Quebec, that the nationalists could win an election and even be re-elected but fail to convince the people on independence. Again the prospect is for endless revisiting of the independence question since, with one of the principal parties being a nationalist one, people are deprived of the chance to change the government or vote against Scottish Labour or the Quebec Liberals without precipitating another referendum. More fundamentally, nation-statehood, with its implications that there is one national identity and one solution for the nationality question, would still raise the objection that in some cases it would create more national minorities within the seceding states. It would also violate the new understanding of nationality itself as plural, felt and expressed differently by different sectors of the population.

Nor can we resolve the problem by deterritorializing nationality, making it no more than a personal attribute. Terrritory is still central to nationality and to the resolution of nationality claims, because of its symbolic importance, because control of space is still critical to self-government in practice, and because the territorial criterion is still among the most inclusive forms of defining a people. Territorial spaces are important sites of sovereignty (or post-sovereign authority) in the new world of dispersed and diffused sovereignty. Yet, while territory may be central to the nationalist project, a territory can be shared by more than one nation, in both a symbolic and a substantive way. So the Royal Commission on Aboriginal Peoples was right to emphasize the critical importance of territorial self-government, while not denying the importance of the issue of aboriginal recognition and culture in mixed urban areas. Even in such cases as the Canadian aboriginal peoples or the Basques, who are only partly concentrated in self-governing territories, these territories can provide a base for the development of their culture and reference point for identity. On the other hand, to align territory and identity through partitioning historic or institutional territories or by population transfers in pursuit of an illusory ethnic homogeneity would be impractical, if not logically impossible given the problems of identifying individuals. It would also be ethically indefensible. Instead, recognition is a matter of continued compromise and negotiation, taking different forms according to circumstance. So recognition of Quebec's national identity implies a respect for its territorial integrity but does not imply either that Quebec should become an independent state, or that only those whose primary loyalty is to Quebec have a place there (McClure 2000).[1]

This is not to deny that an independent Quebec or Scotland would be viable or represent a legitimate democratic choice for their respective peoples. It is merely to question the wisdom of pursuing the vision and to point to the fact that, after independence, the nations in all their complexity would still have to live with each other. The Northern Ireland Peace Agreement is exemplary here, which is why it has been followed with such interest in other parts of the world. It provides both symbolic and substantive recognition of the nationality claims of both communities, and allows both states to maintain a degree of influence and trusteeship of the territory. At the same time, it is open-ended, allowing the people to determine their future freely over time. Of course, there are special circumstances, notably the reluctance of either claimant state to assume full responsibility for the region, but another conditioning factor is undoubtedly the changing nature of state sovereignty and a recognition that the stakes have changed (McGarry 2001). Progress on aboriginal self-government in Canada has been painfully slow, but this is another instance in which a state has recognized the need for a radically different way of dealing with nationality issues.

We need, indeed, to rethink the idea of the state itself, and move towards a more plurinational conception, focused both on territory and on political identities (Pacheco 1998). We also need to rethink the concept of sovereignty.

---

[1] Michel Seymour (1999, ch. 8) recognizes that respect for diversity means that each nation must choose its own meaning of nationality, a point with which I wholly agree. I do, however, take issue with his application of the principle to Quebec (ch. 9) in which he labels every group and insists that Anglo-Quebeckers must identify themselves with the Quebec nation or leave the territory.

I have used the term 'post-sovereignty' not to indicate a world without any principles of authority and legitimacy, but to indicate that sovereignty in its traditional sense, in which it is identified exclusively with the independent state, is no more. Rather there are multiple sites of 'sovereign', in the sense of original, authority. States have, not surprisingly, been reluctant to accept this idea, but in Europe it is becoming a reality of the transnational system. Even within states there have been sporadic and ad hoc concessions to the principle of diffused sovereignty, even while states have refused to accept the general principle. Canadian governments have accepted an inherent right of aboriginal self-government and, following the Supreme Court ruling, that Quebec would have the right, under certain conditions, to secede. The United Kingdom has explicitly provided for the people of Northern Ireland to leave the state and join the Republic of Ireland, and UK governments and political parties have made repeated statements to the effect that Scotland could leave if it so chose, from John Major's statement that no nation could be kept in a union against its will, through the Labour Party's acceptance (albeit in opposition) that sovereignty lay with the Scottish people, to statements that a UK government could not stop a Scottish independence referendum. Spanish governments insist on the unity of the nation and deny the right of self-determination to its constituent parts, but have recognized the Basque *fueros* in one form or another. The issue of self-determination is less pressing in Belgium, but there is little effort to deny that Flanders could become independent if its people so wished. None of this amounts to a coherent doctrine of post-sovereignty, or to original sovereignty of the component parts of plurinational states, but it does represent a fraying of the old doctrines of statehood.

We cannot capture this plurinational state in a definitive constitutional settlement (Tully 2000). Liberal democracy has often been predicated on the idea of a founding moment in which a governing contract was sealed, whether this be the fictive moments of Lockean theory or a real event like the American Constitutional Convention. There are many who still believe that only such an event can legitimize the constitutional order in Europe or in Canada, or who want to resolve all the constitutional issues of the United Kingdom in one comprehensive settlement. Such reasoning is linked to an urge to define and nail down the principle of sovereignty and the distribution of power. Yet the search for sovereignty is more like the physicists' quest for the ultimate particle, a search that will never end. More sophisticated political theorists, like their counterparts in the physical sciences, know that the whole search is based on a misleading reification, for the question is really an epistemological one, of what we mean by sovereignty (or by matter). Knowledge is advanced not by finding the definitive answer, but by repeated rounds of questioning and exploration. So a better way of proceeding is to see constitutionalism as a dialogue or conversation, linking the various deliberative spaces, and allowing for mutual influence and learning (Tully

1995; Chambers 1996; Shaw 2000); but with universal principles incorporated into the various national and other experiences (Habermas 1992). This is thus a form of political practice, but one rooted in liberal and democratic principles. Such a practice can no longer be rooted merely within states, but is part of an emerging transnational order, most fully developed in Europe.

There is a literature on the growing complexity of government and the interpenetration of functional and territorial systems, but too often it is framed by the tenets of organizational theory, which is incapable of addressing normative issues, or merely reduces the whole to a pluralist game. This is the problem with the much-used term 'multilevel governance' which provides us with very little guidance through the complexity and no normative principles such as those that traditionally frame discussions of the state or the institutions of parliamentary democracy. Nor do we really know in discussions of multilevel governance just what the unit of analysis is or indeed at what level the analysis is being conducted. Similar problems beset public choice approaches, which reduce everything to bargaining among individuals, abstracting from the very claims to communities which are the central concern of this work (e.g. Frey and Eichenberger 1999). The stateless nation as a unit of analysis is, of course, elusive and changing, as I have shown, and its definition is essentially bound up with a set of normative claims. Yet it at least allows us to address questions of identity, of legitimacy, and of democracy.

It also provides some structuring principles for the emerging order, founded in historic experience, political practice, institutions, and identities. This is necessary to avoid complete indeterminacy, since I am not developing a postmodernist argument to the effect that all identities are the basis for political order, nor the purely individualist idea underlying public choice theories of political order, in which the individual is the only unit of analysis. The nation-state is itself a structuring principle of political order and, as I argued in the introductory chapter, rests to a larger degree on tradition and on nationality than many of its defenders would admit. The argument here is that it does not have a monopoly either of these legitimizing features, or of democratic and liberal foundations. The basis for political structure in the plurinational state will differ from one to another, given the different constructions and meanings of nationality, but there are common elements. Territory is an important structuring element, as a basis for power and authority, as a forum for democratic deliberation, and as a framework for public policy. History remains important as a source of legitimacy, values, and rights, provided that we do not regard history as lying purely in the past, but see it as a continuing process. As noted earlier, history does not give us a blueprint for political order, but does point to ways of thinking about political order beyond the state. Historical rights, for their part, are valuable not so much in their literal content, but as helping to define the owners of elements of sovereignty. In many cases, this is expressed in the form of institutions of self-government. Finally, there is identity, the fact that citizens do feel part of communities below or beyond the state, whether these stretch back far into the past or are of more recent vintage. The lack of correspondence between the various categories and definitions of nationhood does not mean that the idea itself is meaningless but points to a more open and pluralistic form of politics. Similarly, we should not assume that individuals have monolithic national identities which are exclusive and unchangeable. The evidence suggests that they are much more flexible than this, and that exclusive identities are mobilized only at times of threat, crisis, or political polarization.

This is not, to repeat again, an argument for ethnocracy or 'ethnic politics'. Ethnicity is both broader and narrower than nationalism and is no more to be linked to minority than to majority nationalism. Yet if stateless nationalism is not to identified with ethnicity, it can still in some cases represent ethnic politics, as is evident in many parts of the world. Generally speaking, the stateless nationalist movements in the four countries analysed here have de-ethnicized, even in those cases where ethnic particularism featured in their origins. Debates in Quebec and the Basque Country constantly remind us of the differences between a narrow ethnic and a broader, civic conception of the nation. While the issues of ethnic versus civic nationalism and separatism versus more moderate solutions are conceptually separate, they are in practice connected. Mobilizing a population to support full separation, with all the costs and sacrifices that this entails, is a great deal easier if emotions can be engaged or if the community can be presented as being threatened by the dominant Other. Since few stateless nations are ethnically homogeneous, this risks dividing the local society itself, hence the polarizing effects of separatist politics. Conversely, while the ethnic minorities within the stateless nation might accept moderate exercises in self-determination and differentiation, they are unlikely to buy into policies that cut them off from their fellow nationals in other parts of the state. This indicates a territorially inclusive form of nationality, but with respect for internal minorities.

The case of the aboriginal peoples in Canada is rather different, and there have been criticisms of self-government predicated on ethnic particularism here (Gibson 2000). It is true that measures like the Nisga'a treaty violate the preference that nations be based on territory rather than ethnic descent, but as a practical matter it is very difficult to see how aboriginal self-government can avoid this, given the fragility of aboriginal communities and their low capacity to assimilate incomers. A more persistent theme in the objections to aboriginal self-government, that it creates a distinct class of Canadian citizens (however defined), is predicated not just on civil equality but on the idea that this civil equality should be grounded in a homogeneous Canadian nationality. If the argument were based on a pure commitment to universal values, then Canada itself would not have citizenship restrictions and immigration laws. In fact, what is being proposed in Canada is neither the creation of separate ethnic states, nor racial segregation on South African lines, but rather a recognition of original rights with a high degree of interpenetration of aboriginal and other Canadian legal and political orders. The key test is whether such arrangements, in seeking to include nations, exclude others with legitimate claims; it is difficult to argue this against the Nisga'a treaty, the focus of much of this debate; on the contrary, it is designed to accommodate group rights with the minimum violation to the rights of the individual.

A post-sovereign conception of authority, by lowering the stakes in nationalist politics and favouring the diffusion of authority across multiple levels, eases the plight both of minority nations within states and of minorities within the minorities. In a complex, multiple level system of government, few citizens will find themselves in a permanent minority in every forum. So it is not surprising that Anglo-Quebeckers were among the strongest supporters of the Meech Lake Accord but have been almost unanimous in their opposition to the independence of Quebec. Incomers into Catalonia and the Basque Country from the rest of Spain show high levels of support for self-government and a high rate of assimilation into the local identity, but very low levels of support for independence. In Northern Ireland, either absolute solution, assimilation into the United Kingdom or unification with the Republic of Ireland, would increase polarization.

The most extreme form of polarization is caused by violence, which forces people to take sides and raises the political stakes. The high cost entailed by political violence in turn allows its exponents to insist on extreme ends as the only recompense. This is the grim logic of political violence, as practised in Northern Ireland and the Basque Country, too often dismissed as mindless. As a contribution to resolving the national question, of course, it is entirely negative, quite apart from the moral objections. After thirty years of violence Irish Republicans accepted in 1998 a settlement which they had refused in 1973. In the meantime, the society had been further polarized, the Catholic community which they purported to represent had suffered brutally, and the prospects for Irish unity had only receded. Similarly, in the Basque Country ETA terrorism is intended to force the nationalist community into line behind the most extreme option, thereby forcing a social polarization which, in contrast with Northern Ireland, previously existed only in a mild form. In the process it has made the satisfaction of Basque demands for recognition more remote.

So how can we recognize difference while deepening and strengthening democracy? It is clear that the formula of *demos* = *ethnos* = state, underlying much of the thinking about the democratic nation-state, will no longer work, if it ever did. If democracy is to be strengthened, it must be located where the *demos* is, not where theorists would like it to be. Once again, the argument here is based on political practice and how to democratize it, not on Platonic reasoning. There are, as we have seen, new political spaces beyond the state, whether above, below, or alongside, and these are the loci of new democratizing pressures. Miller (1995) may be right that democratic trust and practice are best founded on nationality. Universal democracy without a limited institutional base is as yet beyond practical politics, and may not be desirable in so far as it implies cultural uniformity. The Habermasian alternative, of constitutional patriotism in which democratic spaces and institutions are demarcated but not underpinned by nationality claims, may indeed be too thin a basis for democratic deliberation, practice, and competition. Yet Miller's formulation perhaps assumes too easily that we know what the nation is or that governments should seek to foster a common identity based on the state. This would be to do violence to the very principles underpinning the plurinational state, in which nationality is recognized but is multiple, complex, and overlapping. I have argued that we can take nationality as one of the building blocks of democracy, but we must recognize that, sociologically, nationality is a construction, something that is made and remade over time. Some nations, like Catalonia or Scotland, have deep historic roots, while others, like Flanders, are of more recent vintage. Some, like the Basque Country or the First Nations of Canada, have a national core, with rather indeterminate edges. Some are rooted in historic institutions, while others are focused on common culture and language, and in some cases (like the Basque Country) these criteria give different territorial dimensions to the community. To freeze these at any point of time is in contradiction to the evolving nature of national identities, and would do violence to the open politics that I am advocating. Similarly, to reorganize the state in the form of sealed communities, as is the tendency in Belgium, is to confine democratic deliberation and freeze communicative orders at a time of change and evolution. It risks divorcing deliberative communities from the evolving functional order, so repeating the problems of the nation-state. Most seriously perhaps, it neglects the intercommunicative aspects of democracy and a liberal order stressed notably by Tully (1995). So this is not an argument for ethnocracy or 'ethnic nationalism' with identity claims trumping all others, but it is equally important to avoid the other extreme, of reducing all social interaction to individualism as defined and mediated by the market (Touraine 1992, 1997; Keating 2001a). The complexity of the cases demands a variety of institutional responses, albeit informed by the same principles. For territorially integrated nationalities, federalism, confederalism, or sovereignty-association may be appropriate. In divided societies there is a need for the recognition of distinct nationality claims over the same territory, while some nationality claims span more than one state, although they very often take different forms on either side of the border. In these cases there is a need for further unpacking of sovereignty.

This would be an open politics but not, to repeat, a recipe for constitutional anarchy. Fears that, if we allow a degree of self-determination for the constituent nationalities of a state, then everyone will join in the game, inventing spurious nationality claims from nothing, are sustained neither by theoretical logic, nor by empirical evidence. On the contrary, one might argue that the tendency to respond with concessions of competences rather than bold forms of recognition is more destabilizing since it weakens the state while not satisfying the nationalities, leading to further concessions (Herrero de Miñon 1996). Still less does recognizing plurinationalism entail condoning the excesses of nationalism in the Balkans and elsewhere; quite the contrary. It does, however, invite us to place the stateless nation on the same moral plane as the consolidated nation-state, rather than assuming that the latter represents some culturally neutral proxy for cosmopolitan enlightenment.[2]

What are the prospects for such a constitutional politics? Some will say that the whole idea is utopian because people are so attached to the nation-state as the primary point of political reference. Others urge that we cannot wait for the political world to catch up with the philosophers. The survey evidence presented in Chapter 3 would indicate that, at least in the four plurinational states considered here, there is already a debate on the conditions of post-sovereign political order. Indeed the mass public seem more open to new ways of thinking about the political order than most politicians or political scientists. Others insist that, in the world as it is, 'realism' (itself a remarkable intellectual abstraction) will prevail, with states pursuing their self-interest. Yet even 'realists' have been forced to admit that the state is itself an abstract concept, referring to complex systems of power relations, and that to attribute interests to it is at best an interpretative short cut.

There is a danger, on the other hand, of falling into a postmodernist trap and denying the validity of any universal values or principles of order. This is far from my purpose, at a normative level; and it would be politically unrealistic for two reasons. Firstly, most of what I have been discussing is predicated on the existence of a system of internal and international security. Secondly, I recognize the need for a level of 'metaconstitutionalism' (Walker 1998*a*), some way of working through issues of normative authority, on the basis of shared values but without the old legal hierarchies. Here the European example is important. We are seeing the emergence in Europe of a complex new order that is ever more difficult to squeeze into the procrustean form of the nation-state. This new order is based neither on traditional inter-state diplomacy nor on self-renunciation on the part of states, but on new roles and relationships, embedded in a series of founding principles. Cynicism about Europe is common but both unfounded and dangerous. There is an extraordinary commitment to a common European defence and security system, the main item in contention being the extent to which this will be nested within the broader North Atlantic Alliance. Complaints about Europe being a matter only for elites seem often to be based on nationalistically biased accounts of the formation of nation-states as

---

[2] Nairn (1997: 181) comments, in reply to accusations that thinkers from the peripheral nations are biased and narrow, that this 'nearly always emanates from some metropolitan thought-world within which the thinker assumes his or her privileged and instinctive access to the universal'.

the spontaneous product of the masses and therefore somehow more demo-cratically grounded than Europe. For most people most of the time what matters is consent to the rules under which they are governed, not active mobilization. If they choose to be more active politically at levels closer to their everyday experience and frame of reference (which usually means below the nation-state), this does not in itself represent a rejection of the wider transnational order.

Nor should we underestimate Europe as a value system. It is easy to respond that the Balkan killing grounds are an integral part of the European experience, as indeed they are, but Europe as a contemporary political idea is linked to democracy, liberalism, and prosperity. This Europe, as shorthand for an emerging normative order, may also provide new ways to manage a plurinational space. It would be equally wrong, on the other hand, to invest too much in Europe. In these pages I have repeatedly noted the danger of reifying Europe or making it into some kind of federal super-state. Europe is an essentially contested project (Bankowski and Christodoulidis 2000) and this contestation is not a transitional phase to a new, integrated state, but its essence. It is a place where, within a common value set and through evolving institutions, the question of state and nation can continually be debated, in the search for positive-sum outcomes.

Canada does not have such an external support system to help manage its internal diversity. Yet it is itself a constitutional project with some parallels to the European one. It is not a nation-state in the classical European or the American sense, with a unified identity and powerful mechanisms for cultural integration, but nor is it a mere congeries of territories brought together for convenience. It is a plurinational state in which the principal parts, Quebec, the Rest of Canada, and the native peoples have different ways of being national, but which does share a set of common values and procedural assumptions. It was a fundamental misconception (McRoberts 1997) to try and forge a European or US-type of nation out of this; but it is equally misconceived to believe that breaking it up into its component parts would provide a more definitive solution.

The most utopian post-sovereigntist position envisages the nation-state disappearing altogether in favour of a Europe or a transnational order in general, based on the 'peoples'. This is an unrealistic scenario, for a number of reasons. States are powerful sets of institutions, in which important social, economic, political, and indeed military forces have invested a great deal of capital, and are not going to fade away simply because they are becoming functionally redundant. There are still many political movements and leaders engaging in a very traditional form of sovereignty discourse. In any case, it is a primordialist illusion to think that if we removed the artificial framework of the state, the world would fall into ready-made national units. As we have seen, there are some territorially integrated stateless nations which could take their place in such a new order, but more commonly there are mixed nationalities, and there are state majorities which identify with the whole state rather than one of its parts and who would therefore have nowhere to go. Nor would the disappearance of the nation-state be a pure good from the normative point of view. States still form the basis for the emerging global security system and for the various proposals for a European security order, and indeed it is the very strength of this assumption that allows security issues to be neglected in so many of the discussions on accommodating nationalism in Western states. States also underpin much of the structure of domestic and international law, however much they have had to concede their monopoly in this field (Jáuregui 2000). Respect for state borders has been a key factor in the plethora of cross-border initiatives allowing new forms of cooperation on economic, environmental, and cultural issues.

We do, however, need a new form of state, and since this cannot by definition take the form of a universal blueprint, it can best be realized as a new form of statecraft, which is why this book has emphasized political practice. There are signs of such a practice emerging, in a new understanding of the past, in a reinterpretation of constitutional practice and possibilities, and in an appreciation of the new opportunities presented in the transnational order. Theorizing in this case seems to be following the events. Tully (2000) stresses the positive aspects of the Canadian Supreme Court decision on Quebec secession contained in the court's reasoning, rather than the delphic conclusions which I have mentioned. Stressing the court's recognition of the need to reconcile unity in diversity, Tully concludes that such an interpretation, while not current, is attainable. The emerging practice of aboriginal self-government shows how politics can bridge issues that theory finds difficulty in encompassing. The United Kingdom presents another case in which twentieth-century conceptions of statehood seem to be giving way to ideas that are both older and newer. It may be that Tom Nairn (2000) is right and that devolution represents no more than the death throes of 'Ukania', comparable to the terminal decline of the Austro-Hungarian Empire from the late nineteenth century. But I argued in an early chapter that the dissolution of the Austro-Hungarian system into nation-states was by no means historically inevitable and, in the event, proved a historic mistake. It may be that the United Kingdom will go the same way, but this is to assume either that the politicians bungle matters (not an impossible scenario) or that nation-statehood is somehow the natural state of mankind rather than a historically contingent political form. In Northern Ireland the United Kingdom has suspended most of the rules of state sovereignty, and, if this should be considered too much a special case, there is the example of Scotland, more indisputably part of the metropolitan homeland. In successive moves the main UK parties have declared that Scotland can become independent if it wants, have conceded the sovereignty of the Scottish people (at least Labour did this in opposition), and have established a national Parliament for Scotland without counterparts elsewhere in the state. The

Scottish Constitututional Convention, while it is in danger of being myth-ologized, did represent an original way of redesigning the constitution from the bottom up, and the referendums on home rule in Scotland, Wales, and Northern Ireland gave implicit sanction to the idea that the constitution was not the sole property of the Westminster Parliament. Of course, much of this represents the art of muddling through rather than a grand plan, but, if we are to be honest, this is true of most of the great constitutional reforms of history. Perhaps the biggest obstacle to the further evolution of the United Kingdom is successive governments' dithering about Europe and whether, or how far, to be part of the European project. If the state should indeed sunder, Europe may be the issue that provokes it.

Belgium has evolved, in the course of thirty years, from a unitary state to a decentralized federation in which the constituent units have a rather high level of competence in external matters. There is much to criticize in the Belgian federal system, notably its complexity, the way in which the reform has worked to the advantage of existing elites, and the tendency of the two linguistic communities to drift into two solitudes. Public opinion has often been denied a voice with the result that the pro-Belgian perspective has often been silent. Yet the transition has been managed without violence and with a recognition of the changing nature of the state. Europe has been crucial here, in providing an external support system for the state, in requiring cooper-ation across the communities, and in ensuring that, should a break occur, it will be peaceful and democratic. Spain, too, has undertaken a transition, in this case from a centralized dictatorship to a decentralized and federalizing state with recognition of the constituent nationalities (Moreno 1997). Central political elites have yet to make the imaginative leap to conceiving of Spain as a plurinational state, but the practicalities of having to manage a plurina-tional party system have led successive socialist and conservative govern-ments to make concessions to the nationalities. The political violence in the Basque Country is a highly negative factor here, creating all manner of resistances in Madrid and in public opinion.

The book has tried to present, not a blueprint for constitutional reform, but an evolving political practice, in which issues of plurinationality can be worked out through politics. They do not have to be treated as absolutes, as non-negotiable items or matters to be settled once and for all, but as part of a continual process of adjustment. There is no shortage of ingenious devices involving federalism, second chambers, charters of rights, and intergovern-mental relations. What is missing is a philosophy to bind them together and give them a democratic rationale. The study has been largely informed by four states, which are far from resolving their own constitutional problems and cannot be generalized in any simple or literal way. Yet the general principles, of respect for difference, of suspending belief in old doctrines of sovereignty, and of putting the state in proper perspective, may help in managing nationality conflicts in places where they are much more difficult.

REFERENCES

ACTON, LORD (1972), 'Nationality', in Gertrude Himmelfarb (ed.), *Essays on Freedom and Power* (Gloucester, Mass.: Peter Smith).

AGNEW, JOHN, and STUART CORBRIDGE (1995), *Mastering Space: Hegemony, Territory and International Political Economy* (London: Routledge).

ALBAREDA I SALVADÓ, JOAQUIM, and PERE GIFRE I RIBES (1999), *Historia de la Catalunya moderna* (Barcelona: Edicions de la Universitat Oberta de Catalunya).

ALDECOA LUZARRAGA, FRANCISCO (1998), 'Towards Plurinational Diplomacy in the Context of the Deepening and Widening of the European Union (1985–2005)', in Francesco Aldecoa and Michael Keating (eds.), *Paradiplomacy: The International Relations of Sub-State Governments* (London: Frank Cass).

—— and MICHAEL KEATING (eds.) (1998), *Paradiplomacy: The International Relations of Sub-State Governments* (London: Frank Cass).

ANDERSON, BENEDICT (1983), *Imagined Communities: Reflections on the Origins and Spread of Nationalism* (London: Verso).

ANDRÉS ORIZO, FRANCESCO, and ALEJANDRO SÁNCHEZ FERNÁNDEZ (1991), *El sistema de valors dels catalans: Catalunya dins l'enquesta europea de valors dels anys 90* (Barcelona: Institut Català d'Estudis Mediterranis).

ANGUS REID, *The Reid Report* (Winnipeg), various years; cited by number.

ARTOLA, MIGUEL (1999*a*), *La monarquía de España* (Madrid: Alianza).

—— (1999*b*), 'La monarquía de España', *Claves de la Razón Práctica*, 89 (Jan. 1999), 23–31.

AUGHEY, ARTHUR (1991), 'Unionism and Self-Determination', in P. Roche and B. Barren (eds.), *The Northern Ireland Question: Myth and Reality* (Aldershot: Gower).

—— PAUL HAINSWORTH, and MARTIN J. TRIMBLE (1989), *Northern Ireland in the European Community. An Economic and Political Analysis* (Belfast: Policy Research Institute).

BADIE, BERTRAND (1995), *La Fin des territoires: Essai sur le désordre international et sur l'utilité sociale du respect* (Paris: Fayard).

BALFOUR, ARTHUR (1912), *Aspects of Home Rule* (London: Routledge).

BALME, RICHARD (1996), 'Pourquoi le gouvernement change-t-il d'échelle', in Richard Balme (ed.), *Les Politiques du néo-régionalisme* (Paris: Economica).

BALTHAZAR, LOUIS (1992), 'L'émancipation internationale d'un état fédéré (1960–1990)', in François Rocher (ed.), *Bilan québécois du fédéralisme canadien* (Montreal: vlb).

BANKOWSKI, ZENON, and EMILIOS CHRISTODOULIDIS (2000), 'The European Union as an Essentially Contested Project', in Zenon Bankowski and Andrew Scott (eds.), *The European Union and its Order: The Legal Theory of European Integration* (Oxford: Blackwell).

BARBER, SARAH (1995), 'Scotland and Ireland under the Commonwealth: A Question of Loyalty', in Steven G. Ellis and Sarah Barber (eds.), *Conquest and Union: Fashioning a British State, 1485–1725* (London: Longman).

BARTLETT, ROBERT (1993), *The Making of Europe: Conquest, Colonization and Cultural Change 950–1350* (London: BCA).

BASHAI, LINDA (1998), 'Secession and the Problems of Liberal Theory', in Percy Lehning (ed.), *Theories of Secession* (London: Routledge).

BATTLE, CARME (1988), *L'expansió Baixmedeval*, vol. iii of *Història de Catalunya* (Barcelona: Edicions 62).

BEAUCHEMIN, JACQUES (1997), 'Conservatisme et traditionalisme dans le Québec duplessiste: aux origines d'une confusion conceptuelle', in Alain-G. Gagnon and Michel Sara-Bournet (eds.), *Duplessis. Entre la Grande Noirceur et la société libérale* (Montreal: Québec Amérique).

BEINER, RONALD S. (1998), 'National Self-Determination: Some Cautionary Remarks concerning the Practice of Rights', in Margaret Moore (ed.), *National Self-Determination and Secession* (Oxford: Oxford University Press).

BELLAMY, RICHARD (1995), 'The Constitution of Europe: Rights or Democracy?', in Richard Bellamy, Victorio Bufacchi, and Dario Castiglione (eds.), *Democracy and Constitutional Culture in the Union of Europe* (London: Lothian Foundation).

——(2001), 'The "Right to have Rights": Citizenship Practice and the Political Constitution of the European Union', in Richard Bellamy and Alex Warleigh (eds.), *Citizenship and Governance in the European Union* (London: Pinter).

——and DARIO CASTIGLIONE (2000), 'Democracy, Sovereignty and the Constitution of the Europe Union: The Republican Alternative to Liberalism', in Zenon Bankowski and Andrew Scott (eds.), *The European Union and its Order: The Legal Theory of European Integration* (Oxford: Blackwell).

BERAN, HARRY (1998), 'A Democratic Theory of Political Self-Determination in the New World Order', in Percy Lehning (ed.), *Theories of Secession* (London: Routledge).

BERIAIN, JOSETXO (1999), 'Del reino de Jaungoikoa el politeísmo moderno', in Josetxo Beriain and Roger Fernández Ubieta (eds.), *La cuestión vasca: Claves de un conflicto cultural y político* (Barcelona: Proyecto).

BERNIER, GÉRALD, and DANIEL SALÉE (2001), 'Les Patriotes, la question nationale et les rébellions de 1837–1838 au Bas-Canada', in Michael Sarra-Bournet (ed.), *Les Nationalismes au Québec du XIX au XXI siècle* (Quebec: Presses de l'Université Laval).

BEYERS, JAN, and BART KERREMANS, (2000), 'Diverging Images of Consensus: Belgium and its Views on European Integration', paper presented at the Seminar on National Identity and European Integration, University of Leuven, 26–7, May 2000.

BILLIET, JAAK (1999), 'Les Opinions politiques des Flamands', *La Révue Générale*, 5: 9–17.

——R. DOUTRELEPONT, and M. VANDEKEERE (2000), 'Types van sociale identiteiten in België: Convergenties en divergenties', in K. Dobbelaere, M. Elchardus, J. Kerkhofs, L. Voyé, and B. Bawin-Legros (eds.), *De verloren zekerheid: De Belgen en hun waarden, overtuigingen, houdingen* (Tielt: Lannoo).

BILLIG, MICHAEL (1995), *Banal Nationalism* (London: Sage).

BIORCIO, ROBERTO (1997), *La Padania promessa* (Milan: Il Saggiatore).

BLAIS, ANDRÉ, and RICHARD NADEAU (1992), 'To be or not to be Sovereigntist: Quebeckers' Perennial Dilemma', *Canadian Public Policy*, 18/1: 89–103.

BLANCO VALDÉS, ROBERTO L. (1997), 'Nacionalides históricas y regiones sín historia: Algunas reflexiones sobre la cuestión de los nacionalismos en el estado de las autonomías', *Parlamento y Constitución*, 1: 33–75.

BNG (1997), *Programa de governo, autonómicas '97* (Santiago de Compostela: BNG).

BNG–PNV–CiU (1998), *Declaración de Barcelona* (no place: no publisher).

BODIN, JEAN (1992), *On Sovereignty: Four Chapters from 'The Six Books of the Commonwealth'* (Cambridge: Cambridge University Press).

BOUCHARD, GÉRARD (1999), 'L'Histoire comparée des collectivités neuves: une autre perspective pour les études québécoises', *Grandes Conférences Desjardins*, 4 (Montreal: McGill University).

——(2000), 'Construire la nation québécoise: manifeste pour une coalition nationale', in Michel Venne (ed.), *Penser la nation québécoise* (Montreal: Québec Amérique).

BRASSINNE, JACQUES (1994), *La Belgique fédérale* (Brussels: CRISP).

BRAUDEL, FERNAND (1986), *L'Identité de la France* (Paris: Arthaud-Flammarion).

BREEN, RICHARD (1996), 'Who Wants a United Ireland? Constitutional Preferences among Catholics and Protestants', in *Social Attitudes in Northern Ireland: 5th Report* (Belfast: Appletree).

BRETON, RAYMOND (1993), *Why Meech Lake Failed: Lessons for Canadian Constitution Making* (Montreal: C. D. Howe Institute).

BROCKLISS, LAURENCE, and DAVID EASTWOOD (eds.) (1997), *A Union of Multiple Identities: The British Isles, c.1750–1850* (Manchester: Manchester University Press).

BROWN, ALICE, DAVID MCCRONE, and LINDSAY PATERSON (1996), *Politics and Society in Scotland* (London: Macmillan).

——————and PAULA SURRIDGE (1999), *The Scottish Electorate: The 1997 General Election and Beyond* (London: Macmillan).

——JOHN CURTICE, KERSTIN HINDS, DAVID MCCRONE, and LINDSAY PATERSON (2001), *New Scotland, New Politics?* (Edinburgh: Polygon).

BROWN, DAVID (1999), 'Are there Good and Bad Nationalisms?', *Nations and Nationalism*, 5/2: 281–302.

BRUBAKER, ROGERS (1998), 'Myths and Misconceptions in the Study of Nationalism', in John A. Hall (ed.), *The State and the Nation: Ernest Gellner and the Theory of Nationalism* (Cambridge: Cambridge University Press).

BUCHANAN, ALLEN (1991), *Secession: The Morality of Political Divorce from Fort Sumter to Lithuania and Quebec* (Boulder, Colo.: Westview Press).

BULLMAN, UDO (ed.) (1994), *Die Politik der dritten Ebene. Regionen im Europa der Union* (Baden-Baden: Nomos).

BUTTERWELD, HERBERT (1968), *The Whig Interpretation of History* (first pub. London: Bell, 1931; Harmondsworth: Penguin).

CAIRNS, ALAN C. (2000), *Citizens Plus: Aboriginal Peoples and the Canadian State* (Vancouver: University of British Columbia Press).

CAMILLERI, J., and J. FALK (1992), *The End of Sovereignty? The Politics of a Shrinking and Fragmenting World* (Aldershot: Edward Elgar).

CANADA (1996), Royal Commission on Aboriginal Peoples, *Report of the Royal Commission on Aboriginal Peoples* (Ottawa: Minister of Supply and Services).

——(1997), Department of Indian Affairs and Northern Development, *Aboriginal Self-Government*, www.inac.qc.ca

CANTIN, SERGE (2000), 'Pour sortir de la survivance', in Michel Venne (ed.), *Penser la nation québécoise* (Montreal: Québec Amérique).

CAPOTORTI, FRANCESCO (1991), *Study on the Rights of Persons Belonging to Ethnic, Religious and Linguistic Minorities* (New York: United Nations).

CARDUS, S., J. BERRIO, L. BONET, E. SAPERAS, J. GIFREU, and I. MARI (1991), *La política cultural Europea: Una aproximación desde Cataluña al problema de las identidades culturales* (Madrid: Fundación Encuentro).

CARENS, JOSEPH (2000), *Culture, Citizenship and Community: A Contextual Exploration of Justice as Evenhandedness* (Oxford: Oxford University Press).

CARTER, CATRIONA, and ANDREW SCOTT (2000), 'Legitimacy and Governance beyond the Nation State: Conceptualizing Governance in the European Union', in Zenon Bankowski and Andrew Scott (eds.), *The European Union and its Order: The Legal Theory of European Integration* (Oxford: Blackwell).

CASTELAO, ALFONSO (1992), *Sempre en Galiza*, critical edn. (Santiago de Compostela: Parlamento de Galicia and Universidade de Santiago de Compostela).

CASTELLS, MANUEL (1997), *The Information Age: Economy, Society and Culture, vol. i: The Power of Identity* (Oxford: Blackwell).

CDC (Convergència Democràtica de Catalunya) (1997), *Por un nuevo horizonte para Cataluña* (Barcelona: CDC).

CENTER FOR WORLD INDIGENOUS STUDIES (1999), *Universal Declaration of the Indigenous Aboriginal Nations of Canada*, www.cwis.org

CHAMBERS, SIMONE (1996), 'Contract or Conversation? Theoretical Lessons from the Canadian Constitutional Crisis', *Politics and Society*, 26/1: 143–72.

CHAUVEL, L. (1995), 'Valeurs régionales et nationales en Europe', *Futuribles*, 200: 167–201.

CLARK, GEORGE (1971), *English History: A Survey* (Oxford: Clarendon Press).

CLOUTIER, E., J. H. GUAY, and D. LATOUCHE (1992), *Le Virage: L'évolution de l'opinion publique au Québec depuis 1960, ou comment le Québec est devenu souverainiste* (Montreal: Québec Amérique).

COCHRANE, FEARGAL (1997), *Unionist Politics and the Politics of Unionism since the Anglo-Irish Agreement* (Cork: University of Cork Press).

COLLEY, LINDA (1992), *Britons: Forging the Nation 1707–1837* (London: Pimlico).

COLLINGE, MICHEL (1987), 'Le sentiment d'appartenance: une identité fluctuante', *Cahiers du CACEF*, 130: 7–23.

COLOMER, JOSEP (1986), *Cataluña como cuestión de estado: la idea de nación en el pensamiento político catalán (1939–1979)* (Madrid: Tecnos).

CONGRÈS DE CULTURA CATALANA (2000), *Països Catalans segle XXI: identitat, societat i cultura* (Lleida: El Jonc).

CONNOR, WALKER (1978), 'A Nation is a Nation is a State, is an Ethnic Group, is a...', *Ethnic and Racial Studies*, 1/4: 379–400.

CONVERSI, DANIELE (1997), *The Basques, the Catalans and Spain. Alternative Routes to Nationalist Mobilisation* (London: Hurst).

COOK, RAMSAY (1995), *Canada, Québec and the Uses of Nationalism* (Toronto: McClelland & Stewart).

COULOMBE, PIERRE (1992), 'The End of Canadian Dualism?', *Canadian Parliamentary Review* (Winter 1992–3), 7–10.

Council for Canadian Unity (1998), *Portraits of Canada, 1998* (Ottawa: Council for Canadian Unity).

COURCHENE, THOMAS (1995), *Celebrating Flexibility: An Interpretative Essay on the Evolution of Canadian Federalism*, C. D. Howe Institute, Benefactors' Lecture, 1995 (Montreal: C. D. Howe Institute).

COWAN, EDWARD (1998), 'Identity, Freedom and the Declaration of Arbroath', in Dauvit Broun, R. J. Finlay, and Michael Lynch (eds.), *Image and Identity: The Making and Remaking of Scotland through the Ages* (Edinburgh: John Donald).

CREVELD, MARTIN (1999), *The Rise and Decline of the State* (Cambridge: Cambridge University Press).

CSA (Campaign for a Scottish Assembly) (1988), 'A Claim of Right for Scotland', in O. Dudley Edwards (ed.), *A Claim of Right for Scotland* (Edinburgh: Polygon).

CURTICE, JOHN, and ANTHONY HEATH (2000), 'Is the English Lion about to Roar? National Identity after Devolution', in Roger Jowell *et al.* (eds), *British Social Attitudes Survey: The 17th Report* (London: Sage).

DAHRENDORF, RALPH (1995), 'Preserving Prosperity', *New Statesmen and Society*, 13/29 (Dec.), 36–40.

——(2000), 'La sconfitta della vecchia democrazia', *La Repubblica*, 12 Jan.

DALYELL, TAM (1977), *Devolution: The End of Britain?* (London: Jonathan Cape).

DAVIDSON, NEIL (2000), *The Origins of Scottish Nationhood* (London: Polity).

DAVIES, D. HYWEL (1983), *The Welsh Nationalist Party, 1925–1945: A Call to Nationhood* (Cardiff: University of Wales Press).

DAVIES, NORMAN (1997), *Europe: A History* (London: Pimlico).

——(1999), *The Isles: A History* (London: Macmillan).

DE BLAS GUERRERO, ANDRÉS (1978), 'El problema nacional–regional español en los programas del PSOE y PCE', *Revista de Estudios Políticos*, 4: 155–70.

——(1989), *Sobre el nacionalismo español*, Cuadernos y Debates, 15 (Madrid: Centro de Estudios Constitucionales).

——(1991), *Tradición republicana y nacionalismo español* (Madrid: Tecnos).

——(1994), *Nacionalismos y naciones en Europa* (Madrid: Alianza).

DE LA GRANJA SAINZ, JOSÉ LUIS (1995), *El nacionalismo vasco: un siglo de historia* (Madrid: Tecnos).

DEPREZ, KAS, and LOUIS VOS (1998), 'Introduction', in Kas Depres and Louis Vos (eds.), *Nationalism in Belgium: Shifting Identities, 1780–1995* (London: Macmillan).

DERRIENEC, JEAN-PIERRE (1995), *Nationalisme et démocratie: Réflections sur les illusions des indépendantistes québécois* (Quebec: Boreal).

DEUTSCH, KARL (1966), *Nationalism and Social Communication: An Inquiry into the Foundations of Nationality* (Cambridge, Mass.: MIT Press).

DEVINE, T. M. (1999), *A History of the Scottish Nation* (Harmondsworth: Penguin).

DE WACHTER, WILFRED (1996), 'La Belgique d'aujourd'hui comme societé politique', in A. Dieckhoff (ed.), *Belgique: La force de désunion* (Paris: Éditions Complexe).

DE WINTER, LIEVEN, and ANDRÉ-PAUL FROGNIER (1997), 'L'évolution des identités politiques territoriales en Belgique durant la période 1975–1995', in Serge Jaumain (ed.), *La réforme de l'Etat . . . et après?* (Brussels: Presses de l'Université de Bruxelles).

——and JAAK BILLIET (1998), 'Y a-t-il encore des Belges? Vingt ans d'enquêtes sur les identités politiques territoriales', in Marco Martinello and Marc Swyngedouw (eds.), *Où va la Belgique?* (Paris: L'Harmattan).

DE WITTE, HANS, and GEORGI VERBEECK (2000), 'Belgium: Diversity in Unity', in Louk Hagendoorn, György Csepeli, Henk Dekker, and Russell Farnon (eds.),

European Nations and Nationalism: Theoretical and Historical Perspectives (London: Ashgate).

DICEY, ALBERT VENN (1886), *England's Case against Irish Home Rule* (reissued 1973; Richmond: Richmond Publishing).

—— (1912), *A Leap in the Dark: A Criticism of 'The Principles of Home Rule as Illustrated by the Bill of 1893'*, 3rd edn. (London: John Murray).

—— and ROBERT RAIT (1920), *Thoughts on the Union between England and Scotland* (London: Macmillan).

DICKINSON, H. T., and MICHAEL LYNCH (2000), 'Introduction', in H. T. Dickinson and Michael Lynch, *The Challenge to Westminster: Sovereignty, Devolution and Independence* (East Linton: Tuckwell).

DIECKHOFF, ALAIN (2000), *La Nation dans tous ses états* (Paris: Flammarion).

DION, STÉPHANE (1991), 'Le Nationalisme dans la convergence culturelle: le Québec contemporain et le paradoxe de Tocqueville', in R. Hudon and R. Pelletier (eds.), *L'Engagement intellectuel: mélanges en l'honneur de Léon Dion* (Sainte-Foy: Presses de l'Université de Laval).

DOUTRELPONT, RENÉ, JAAK BILLIET, and MICHEL VANDEKEERE (2000), 'Profils identitaires en Belgique', in Bernadette Bawin-Legros, Liliane Voyé, Karel Dobbelaere, and Mark Elchardus (eds.), *Belges toujours: fidelité, stabilité, tolérance. Les valeurs de Belges en l'an 2000* (Brussels: De Boeck Universitaire).

DOYLE, JOHN (1999), 'Governance and Citizenship in Contested States: The Northern Ireland Peace Agreement as Internationalised Governance', *Irish Studies in International Affairs*, 10: 201–19.

DUCHACHEK, IVO (1970), *Comparative Federalism: The Territorial Dimension of Politics* (New York: Holt, Rinehart, Winston).

DUMONT, FERNAND (1997), *Raisons Communes*, 2nd edn. (Montreal: Boréal).

DURAND, CLAIRE (2001), 'Mythes et réalités', *Le Devoir* (6 Mar.).

ELAZAR, DANIEL (1993), 'International Comparative Federalism', *Political Science and Politics*, 26/2: 1990–5.

—— (1996), 'From Statism to Federalism—A Paradigm Shift', *International Political Science Review*, 17/4: 417–29.

ELLIOT, J. H. (1992), 'A Europe of Composite Monarchies', *Past and Present*, 137: 48–71.

ELLIS, STEVEN G. (1995), 'The Concept of British History', in Steven G. Ellis and Sarah Barber (eds.), *Conquest and Union: Fashioning a British State, 1485–1725* (London: Longman).

ELLIS, STEVEN G., and SARAH BARBER (1995), *Conquest and Union: Fashioning a British State, 1485–1725* (London: Longman).

ERK, CAN, and ALAIN-G. GAGNON (2000), 'Constitutional Ambiguity and Federal Trust', *Regional and Federal Studies*, 10/1: 92–111.

ERSKINE MAY, THOMAS (1906), *The Constitutional History of England since the Accession of George the Third, 1760–1860*, 3 vols. (London: Longmans, Green).

ESTADÉ, ANTONI, and MONTSERRAT TRESERRA (1990), *Catalunya Independent? Anàlisi d'una enquesta sobre la identitat nacional i la voluntat d'independència dels catalans* (Barcelona: Fundació Jaume Bofill).

EVANS, GEOFFREY, and MARY DUFFY (1997), 'Beyond the Sectarian Divide: The Social Bases and Political Consequences of Nationalist and Unionist Party Competition in Northern Ireland', *British Journal of Political Science*, 27: 47–81.

——and BRENDAN O'LEARY (1997), 'Frameworked Futures: Intransigence and Flexibility in the Northern Ireland Elections of May 30 1996', *Irish Political Studies*, 12: 23–47.

FEILING, KEITH (1959), *A History of England: From the Coming of the English to 1918* (London: Macmillan).

FENET, ALAIN (1995), 'L'Europe et les minorités', in Alain Fenet (ed.), *Le Droit et les minorités* (Brussels: Bruylant).

FERGUSON, WILLIAM (1977), *Scotland's Relations with England: A Survey to 1707* (Edinburgh: John Donald).

——(1998), *The Identity of the Scottish Nation: An Historic Quest* (Edinburgh: Edinburgh University Press).

FERRETTI, ANDRÉE, and GASTON MIRON (1992), 'Introduction', in Andrée Ferretti and Gaston Miron, *Les Grandes Textes indépendantistes: écrits, discours et manifestes québécois, 1774–1992* (Montreal: Editions de l'Hexagone).

FERRY, JEAN-MARC (1997), 'Quel patriotisme au-delà des nationalismes? Réflexion sur les fondements motivationnnels d'une citoyenneté européenne', in Pierre Birnbaum (ed.), *Sociologie des nationalismes* (Paris: Presses Universitaires de France).

FINLAY, RICHARD (1992), ' "For or Against?" Scottish Nationalists and the British Empire, 1919–39', *Scottish Historical Review*, 71/1.2: 184–206.

——(1997), *A Partnership for Good? Scottish Politics and the Union since 1880* (Edinburgh: John Donald).

——(1998), 'Caledonia or North Britain? Scottish Identity in the Eighteenth Century', in Dauvit Broun, R. J. Finlay, and Michael Lynch (eds.), *Image and Identity: The Making and Remaking of Scotland through the Ages* (Edinburgh: John Donald).

FLORA, PETER (ed.) (1999), *State Formation, Nation-Building and Mass Politics in Europe: The Theory of Stein Rokkan* (Oxford: Oxford University Press).

FONTAINE, JOSÉ (1998), 'Four Definitions of Culture in Francophone Belgium', in Kas Deprez and Louis Vos (eds.), *Nationalism in Belgium: Shifting Identities, 1780–1995* (London: Macmillan).

FOSSAS, ENRIC (1999a), 'Constitucionalisme i diversitat cultural', in Ferran Requejo (ed.), *Pluralisme nacional i legitimat democràtica* (Barcelona: Prova).

——(1999b), *Asymmetry and Plurinationality in Spain*, Working Paper no. 167 (Barcelona: Institut de Ciènces Polítiques i Socials, Universitat Autónoma de Barcelona).

FOSTER, ROY (ed.) (1989), *Oxford Illustrated History of Ireland* (Oxford: Oxford University Press).

——(1998), 'Storylines: Narratives and Nationality in Nineteenth Century Ireland', in Geoffrey Cubitt (ed.), *Imagining Nations* (Manchester: Manchester University Press).

FOUNDATION EUROPE OF THE CULTURES (1996), *Towards a Europe of the Cultures: Target 2002* (Brussels: Foundation Europe of the Cultures).

FOX, INMAN (1997), *La invención de España. Nacionalismo liberal e identidad nacional* (Madrid: Cátedra).

FRANK, T. M. (1968), 'Why Federations Fail', in T. M. Frank (ed.), *Why Federations Fail. An Inquiry into the Requisites for Successful Federalism* (New York: New York University Press).

FRANKLIN, JULIAN (1992), 'Introduction', to Jean Bodin, *On Sovereignty: Four Chapters from 'The Six Books of the Commonwealth'* (Cambridge: Cambridge University Press).

FREEMAN, MICHAEL (1999), 'The Right to National Self-Determination: Ethical Problems and Practical Solutions', in Desmond M. Clarke and Charles Jones (ed.), *The Rights of Nations: Nations and Nationalism in a Changing World* (Cork: Cork University Press).

FREY, BRUNO S., and REINER EICHENBERGER (1999), *The New Democratic Federalism for Europe. Functional, Overlapping and Competing Jurisdictions* (Cheltenham: Edward Elgar).

FUKUYAMA, FRANCIS (1992), *The End of History and the Last Man* (New York: Free Press).

FUSI, JUAN PABLO (2000), *España. La evolución de la identidad nacional* (Madrid: Temas de Hoy).

GAGNON, ALAIN-G., and CHARLES GIBBS (1999), 'The Normative Basis of Asymmetrical Federalism', in Robert Agranoff (ed.), *Accommodating Diversity: Asymmetry in Federal States* (Baden-Baden: Nomos).

——and MICHEL SARA-BOURNET (1997), 'Introduction', in Alain-G. Gagnon and Michel Sara-Bournet (eds.), *Duplessis. Entre la Grande Noirceur et la société libérale* (Montreal: Québec Amérique).

GARCÍA FERRANDO, MANUEL, EDUARDO LÓPEZ-ARANGUREN, and MIGUEL BELTRÁN (1994), *La conciencia nacional y regional en la España de las autonomías* (Madrid: Centro de Investigaciones Sociológicas).

GARMENDIA, VINCENTE (1985), 'Carlism and Basque Nationalism', in William A. Douglas (ed.), *Basque Politics. A Case Study in Ethnic Nationalism.* Basque Studies Program Occasional Paper 2 (Reno: University of Nevada).

GELLNER, ERNEST (1983), *Nations and Nationalism* (Oxford: Blackwell).

GIBSON, GORDON (2000), *A Principled Analysis of the Nisga'a Treaty*, Public Policy Sources no. 27 (Vancouver: Fraser Institute).

GIERKE, OTTO (1900), *Political Theories of the Middle Age* (Cambridge: Cambridge University Press).

GILLESPIE, RICHARD (2000), 'Profile: Political Polarization in the Basque Country', *Regional and Federal Studies*, 10/1: 112–24.

GINER, SALVADOR, LLUÍS FLAQUER, JORDI BUSQUET, and NÚRIA BULTÀ (1996), *La cultura catalana: El sagrat i el profà* (Barcelona: Edicions 62).

GLADSTONE, WILLIAM EWART (1886), speech presenting Government of Ireland Bill, *Hansard*, ccciv, pp. 1036–9.

GÓMEZ URANGA, MIKEL, IÑAKI LASAGABASTER, FRANCISCO LETAMENDÍA, and RAMÓN ZALLO (eds.) (1999), *Propuestas para un nuevo escenario. Democracia, cultura y cohesión social en Euskal Herria* (Bilbao: Fundación Manu Robles-Arangiz).

GONZÁLEZ, FELIPE (1982), speech in Parliament, *Congreso de los Diputados, 1 Legislatura, Diario de Sesiones*, 21 June.

GRANNOVETER, MARK (1973), 'The Strength of Weak Ties', *American Journal of Sociology*, 78: 1360–80.

GREEN, JOHN RICHARD (1896), *History of the English People* (London: Macmillan).

GUÉHENNO JEAN-MARIE (1993), *Fin de la démocratie* (Paris: Flammarion).

GUIBERNAU, MONTSERRAT (1999), *Nations without States* (Cambridge: Polity Press).

GURRUTXAGA ABAD, ANDER (1996), *Transformación del nacionalismo vasco* (San Sebastian: Haranburu).

—— (1999), 'Transformación y futuro del nacionalismo vasco', in Josetxo Beriain and Roger Fernández Ubieta (eds.), *La cuestión vasca: Claves de un conflicto cultural y político* (Barcelona: Proyecto).

HABERMAS, JÜRGEN (1992), 'The Limits of Neo-Historicism', in Peter Dews (ed.), *Autonomy and Solidarity: Interviews with Jürgen Habermas* (London: Verso).

—— (1998), 'Die postnationale Konstellation und die Zukunft der Demokratie', in *Die postnationale Konstellation. Politische Essays* (Frankfurt: Suhrkamp).

HALLIDAY, FRED (2000), 'The Perils of Community: Reason and Unreason in Nationalist Ideology', *Nations and Nationalism*, 6/2: 153–71.

HAWKES, DAVID C. (1999), *Indigenous Peoples: Self-Government and Intergovernmental Relations* (Ottawa: Forum of Federations).

HEALD, DAVID, NEIL GEAUGHAN, and COLIN ROBB (1998), 'Financial Arrangements for UK Devolution', in Howard Elcock and Michael Keating (eds.), *Remaking the Union: Devolution and British Politics in the 1990s* (London: Frank Cass).

HECHTER, MICHAEL (2000), *Containing Nationalism* (Oxford: Oxford University Press).

HERMANS, THEO, LOUIS VOS, and LODE WILS (1992), *The Flemish Movement: A Documentary History, 1789–1990* (London: Athlone Press).

HERNÁNDEZ, F., and F. MERCADÉ, (1981), *La ideología nacional catalana* (Barcelona: Anagrama).

HERNÁNDEZ LAFUENTE, ADOLFO (1980), *Autonomía e integración en la Segunda República* (Madrid: Encuentro).

HERRERO DE MIÑON, MIGUEL (1996), 'Nacionalismos y estado plurinacional en España', *Política Exterior*, 51 (May–June), 7–20.

—— (1997), 'Hacia el estado de la España Grande (Replica a Ramón Parada)', *Revista de Administración Pública*, 142: 103–10.

—— (1998a), *Derechos históricos y constitución* (Madrid: Tecnos).

—— (1998b), 'Estructura y función de los derechos históricos: Un problema y siete conclusiones', in Miguel Herrero de Miñon and Ernest Lluch (eds.), *Foralismo, derechos históricos y democracia* (Bilbao: Fundación BBV).

HERTZ, FREDERICK (1944), *Nationality in History and Politics* (London: Kegan, Paul, Trench & Turner).

HILLGRUBER, CHRISTIAN, and MATTHIAS JESTAEDT (1994), *The European Convention on Human Rights and the Protection of National Minorities* (Cologne: Verlag Wissenschaft und Politik).

HOBSBAWM, ERIC (1990), *Nations and Nationalism since 1780* (Cambridge: Cambridge University Press).

—— (1992), 'Nationalism: Whose Fault-Line is it Anyway?', *Anthropology Today* (Feb. 1992).

—— and TERENCE RANGER (eds.) (1983), *The Invention of Tradition* (Cambridge: Cambridge University Press).

HOFFMAN, JOHN (1998), *Sovereignty* (Buckingham: Open University Press).

HOOGHE, LIESBET (ed.) (1996), *Cohesion Policy and European Integration: Building Multi-Level Governance* (Oxford: Clarendon Press).

—— and MICHAEL KEATING (1994), 'The Politics of European Union Regional Policy', *Journal of European Public Policy*, 1/3: 53–79.

HORSMAN, MATHEW, and ANDREW MARSHALL (1994), *After the Nation-State: Citizens, Tribalism and the New World Disorder* (London: HarperCollins).

HUNTER, JAMES (1999), *The Last of the Free: A Millennial History of the Highlands and Islands* (Edinburgh: Mainstream).

ICPS (Institut de Ciènces Polítiques i Socials, Barcelona) (1998*a*), *Sondeig d'Opinió, 1998* (Barcelona: ICPS).

—— (1998*b*), *Sondeig d'Opinió: França, Bèlgica, Andalusia, Catalunya* (Barcelona: ICPS).

IVORY, GARETH (1999), 'Revisions in Nationalist Discourse among Irish Political Parties', *Irish Political Studies*, 14: 84–103.

JACKSON, ALVIN (1999), *Ireland, 1798–1998* (Oxford: Blackwell).

JÁUREGUI, GURUTZ (1996), *Entre la tragedia y la esperanza. Vasconia ante el nuevo milenio*, 2nd edn. (Barcelona: Ariel).

—— (1997), *Los nacionalismos minoritarios en la Unión Europea* (Barcelona: Ariel).

—— (1999), 'El estado, la soberanía y la constitución de la Unión Europea', *Revista Vasca de Administración Pública*, 53/2: 71–94.

—— (2000), *La democracia planetaria* (Oviedo: Nobel).

JAURISTI, JON (1998), *El linaje de Aitor. La invención de la tradición vasca*, 2nd edn. (Madrid: Taurus).

JEFFERY, CHARLIE (2000), 'Sub-National Mobilization and European Integration', *Journal of Common Market Studies*, 38/1: 1–24.

JELLINEK, GEORG (1981), *Fragmentos de Estado*, trans. of *Uber Staatsfragmente* by Miguel Herrero de Miñon (Madrid: Civitas).

JONES, BARRY (1985), 'Wales in the European Community', in Michael Keating and Barry Jones (eds.), *Regions in the European Community* (Oxford: Clarendon Press).

—— and MICHAEL KEATING (eds.) (1995), *The European Union and the Regions* (Oxford: Clarendon Press).

KANN, ROBERT A. (1977), *The Multinational Empire. Nationalism and National Reform in the Habsburg Monarchy, 1848–1918* (first pub. Cambridge: Cambridge University Press, 1950; New York: Octagon).

KEARNEY, HUGH (1995), *The British Isles. A History of Four Nations* (Cambridge: Cambridge University Press).

KEARNEY, RICHARD (1997), *Postnationalist Ireland. Politics, Culture, Philosophy* (London: Routledge).

KEAMEY, RICHARD (1998), *Post-Nationalist Ireland* (London: Routledge).

KEATING, MICHAEL (1975), 'The Role of the Scottish MP', Ph.D. thesis, Glasgow College of Technology and Council for National Academic Awards.

—— (1988), *State and Regional Nationalism. Territorial Politics and the European State* (London: Harvester Wheatsheaf).

—— (1992), 'Regional Autonomy in the Changing State Order: A Framework of Analysis', *Regional Politics and Policy*, 2/3: 45–61.

—— (1996*a*), *Nations against the State. The New Politics of Nationalism in Quebec, Catalonia and Scotland* (London: Macmillan).

—— (1996*b*), 'Scotland in the United Kingdom: A Dissolving Union?', *Nationalism and Ethnic Politics*, 2/2: 232–57.

—— (1997), 'Stateless Nation-Building: Quebec, Catalonia and Scotland in the Changing State System', *Nations and Nationalism*, 3/4: 689–717.

—— (1997), 'Les Régions constituent-elles un niveau de gouvernement en Europe?', in Patrick Le Galès and Christian Lesquesne (eds.), *Les Paradoxes des régions en Europe* (Paris: La Découverte).

——(1998*a*), *The New Regionalism in Western Europe. Territorial Restructuring and Political Change* (Aldershot: Edward Elgar).

——(1998*b*), 'Principes et problèmes du gouvernement asymétrique', *Politique et sociétés*, 17/3: 93–111.

——(1999), 'Asymmetrical Government: Multinational States in an Integrating Europe', *Publius: The Journal of Federalism*, 29/1: 71–86.

——(2000*a*), 'Reconsideración da rexión: Cultura, institucións e desenvolvemento económico en Cataluña e Galicia', *GRIAL*, 146, 38: 231–59.

——(2000*b*), 'So Many Nations, So Few States: Accommodating Minority Nationalism in the Global Era', in Alain-G. Gagnon and James Tully (eds.), Multinational Democracies (Cambridge: Cambridge University Press).

——(2000*c*), *Paradiplomacy and Regional Networking* (Ottawa: Forum of Federations).

——(2001*a*), *Nations against the State. The New Politics of Nationalism in Quebec, Catalonia and Scotland*, 2nd edn. (London: Macmillan).

——(2001*b*), 'Nations without States: The Accommodation of Nationalism in the New State Order', in Michael Keating and John McGarry (eds.), *Minority Nationalism and the Changing International Order* (Oxford: Oxford University Press).

——(2001*c*), 'Managing the Multinational State: The Constitutional Settlement in the United Kingdom', in Trevor Salmon and Michael Keating (eds.), *The Dynamics of Decentralization. Canadian Federalism and British Devolution* (Montreal: McGill-Queen's University Press).

——and DAVID BLEIMAN (1979), *Labour and Scottish Nationalism* (London: Macmillan).

——and LIESBET HOOGHE (1996), 'By-Passing the Nation State? Regions in the EU Policy Process', in Jeremy Richardson (ed.), *Policy Making in the European Union* (London: Routledge).

——and BARRY JONES (1995), 'Nations, Regions, and Europe: The United Kingdom Experience', in Barry Jones and Michael Keating (eds.), *The European Union and the Regions* (Oxford: Clarendon Press).

——and PETER LINDLEY (1981), 'Devolution: The Scotland and Wales Bills', *Public Administration Bulletin*, 37: 37–54.

——and JOHN MCGARRY (eds.) (2001), *Minority Nationalism in the Changing State Order* (Oxford: Oxford University Press).

——and NIGEL WATERS (1985), 'Scotland in the European Community', in Michael Keating and Barry Jones (eds.), *Regions in the European Community* (Oxford: Clarendon Press).

KERREMANS, BART (1997), 'The Flemish Identity: Nascent or Existent?', *Res Publica*, 39/2: 303–14.

——and JAN BEYERS (1996), 'The Belgian Sub-National Entities in the European Union: Second or Third Level Players?', *Regional and Federal Studies*, 6/2: 41–55.

KESTELOOT, CHANTAL (1993), 'Mouvement wallon et identité nationale', *Courier Hebdomadaire*, 1392 (Brussels: CRISP).

KEYDER, CAGLAR (1997), 'The Ottoman Empire', in Karen Barkly and Mark von Hagen (eds.), *After Empire: Multiethnic Societies and Nation-Building. The Soviet Union and the Russian, Ottoman and Habsburg Empires* (Boulder, Colo.: Westview Press).

KIDD, COLIN (1993), *Subverting Scotland's Past: Scottish Whig Historians and the Creation of an Anglo-British Identity, 1689–c.1830* (Cambridge: Cambridge University Press).

——(1999), *British Identities before Nationalism: Ethnicity and Nationhood within the Atlantic World, 1600–1800* (Cambridge: Cambridge University Press).

KOHN, HANS (1944), *The Idea of Nationalism: A Study in its Origins and Background* (New York: Macmillan).

KYMLICKA, W. (1995), *Multicultural Citizenship* (Oxford: Oxford University Press).

LAFOREST, GUY (1992), 'La Charte canadienne des droits et libertés au Québec: nationaliste, injuste et illégitime', in F. Rocher (ed.), *Bilan québécois du fédéralisme candien* (Montréal: vlb).

——(1995), *Trudeau and the End of a Canadian Dream* (Montreal: McGill-Queen's University Press).

——(1998), 'Standing in the Shoes of the Other: Partners in the Canadian Union', in Roger Gibbons and Guy Laforest (eds.), *Beyond the Impasse: Toward Reconciliation* (Montreal: Institute for Research on Public Policy).

LAIBLE, JANET (2001), 'Nationalism and a Critique of European Integration: Questions from the Flemish Parties', in Michael Keating and John McGarry (eds.), *Minority Nationalism and the Changing International Order* (Oxford: Oxford University Press).

LANGE, NIELS (2000), *Globalisierung und regionaler Nationalismus. Schottland und Québec im Zeitalter der Denationalisierung* (Baden-Baden: Nomos).

LANGLOIS, S. (1991a), 'Le Choc des deux sociétés globales', in Louis Balthazar, Guy Laforest, and Vincent Lemieux, *Le Québec et la restructuration du Canada, 1980–1992* (Saint-Laurent: Septentrion).

——(1991b), *Une société distincte à reconnaître et une identité collective à consolider*, Commission sur l'Avenir Politique et Constitutionel du Québec (Bélanger-Campeau Commission), Document de travail, no. 4 (Quebec: Commission).

LASAGABASTER HERRARTE, IÑAKI (1999), 'Cuestiones jurídicas en torno a la autodeterminación', in Iñaki Lasagabaster Herrarte *et al.*, *Soberanía politica y económica: El modelo vasco* (Bilbao: IPES).

——and IÑIGO LAZCANO BROTÓNS (1999), 'Derecho, política e historia en la autodeterminación de Euskal Herria', in Mikel Gómez Uranga, Iñaki Lasagabaster Herrarte, Francisco Letamendía, and Ramón Zallo (eds.), *Propuestas para un nuevo escenario: Democracia, cultura y cohesión social en Euskal Herria* (Bilbao: Fundación Manu Robles-Arangiz).

LASELVA, SAMUEL (1996), *The Moral Foundations of Canadian Federalism: Paradoxes, Achievements and Tragedies of Nationhood* (Montreal: McGill-Queen's University Press).

LATOUCHE, DANIEL (1991), *La Stratégie québécoise dans le nouvel ordre économique et politique internationale*, Commission sur l'Avenir Politique et Constitutionnel du Québec, Document de travail, no. 4 (Quebec: Commission).

LEHNING, PERCY B. (ed.) (1998), *Theories of Secession* (London: Routledge).

LÉTOURNEAU, JOCELYN (2000a), 'L'Avenir du Canada: Par rapport à quelle histoire?', *Canadian Historical Review*, 81/2: 230–59.

——(2000b), *Passer à l'avenir: Histoire, mémoire, identité dans le Québec d'aujourd'hui* (Montreal: Boréal).

LIPSET, SEYMOUR MARTIN, and STEIN ROKKAN (1967), *Party Systems and Voter Alignments* (New York: Free Press).

LLERA, FRANSISCO (1994), *Los Vascos y la política* (Bilbao: Servicio Editorial, Universidad del País Vasco).

LOBO, RICARD (1997), 'La devolución de la soberanía', in Xavier Bru de Sala *et al.*, *El modelo catalán: Un talante político* (Barcelona: Flor del Viento).

LOPEZ ARANGUREN, EDUARDO (1997), 'The Dimensions of National and Regional Consciousness', *REIS*, Eng. edn. 97: 37–73.

LORENZO ESPINOZA, JOSÉ MARÍA (1995), *Historia de Euskal Herria, iii: El nacimiento de una nación* (Tafalla, Navarre: Txalaparte).

LOVERING, JOHN (1999), 'Theory Led by Policy: The Inadequacies of the "New Regionalism" ', *International Journal of Urban and Regional Research*, 23: 379–90.

LYNCH, PETER (1996), *Minority Nationalism and European Integration* (Cardiff: University of Wales Press).

MACARTNEY, C. A. (1934), *National States and National Minorities* (New York: Russell & Russell).

—— (1969), *The Habsburg Empire, 1790–1918* (London: Weidenfeld & Nicolson).

MCCLURE, JOCELYN (2000), *Récits identitaires: Le Québec à l'épreuve du pluralisme* (Montreal: Québec Amérique).

MACCORMICK, NEIL (1995), 'Sovereignty, Democracy and Subsidiarity', in Richard Bellamy, Victorio Bufacchi, and Dario Castiglione (eds.), *Democracy and Constitutional Culture in the Union of Europe* (London: Lothian Foundation).

—— (1999*a*), *Questioning Sovereignty: Law, State and Nation in the European Commonwealth* (Oxford: Oxford University Press).

—— (1999*b*), 'Liberal Nationalism and Self-Determination', in Desmond M. Clarke and Charles Jones (ed.), *The Rights of Nations: Nations and Nationalism in a Changing World* (Cork: Cork University Press).

—— (2000), 'Is there a Scottish Path to Constitutional Independence?', *Parliamentary Affairs*, 53: 721–36.

MCCRONE, DAVID (1992), *Understanding Scotland: The Sociology of a Stateless Nation* (London: Routledge).

—— (1998), *The Sociology of Nationalism* (London: Routledge).

—— (1999), 'Review: History and National Identity', *Scottish Affairs*, 27: 97–101.

MCGARRY, JOHN (2001), 'Globalization, European Integration and the Northern Ireland Conflict', in Michael Keating and John McGarry (eds.), *Minority Nationalism and the Changing International Order* (Oxford: Oxford University Press).

MCKAY, IAN (2000), 'The Liberal Order Framework: A Prospectus for a Reconnaissance of Canadian History', *Canadian Historical Review*, 81/4: 621–45.

MCLEAN, IAIN (1995), 'Are Scotland and Wales Over-Represented?', *Political Quarterly*, 66/4: 250–68.

MCNAUGHT, KENNETH (1988), *The Penguin History of Canada* (London: Penguin).

MCROBERTS, KENNETH (1995), 'In Search of Canada "Beyond Quebec" ', in Kenneth McRoberts (ed.), *Beyond Quebec: Taking Stock of English Canada* (Montreal: McGill-Queen's University Press).

—— (1997), *Misconceiving Canada: The Struggle for National Unity* (Toronto: Oxford University Press).

McRoberts, Kenneth (2001), *Catalonia: Nation Building without a State* (Toronto: Oxford University Press).

Maddens, B., R. Berteen, and J. Billiet (1994), *O dierbaar Belgïe: Het natiebewustzin van Vlamingen en Walen* (Leuven: ISPO/Sol); cited in Hans de Witte and Georgi Verbeeck, 'Belgium: Diversity in Unity', in Louk Hagendoorn, Gijörgy Csepeli, Henk Dekker, and Russell Farnen (eds.), *European Nations and Nationalism: Theoretical and Historical Perspectives* (London: Ashgate).

Maitland, Frederick William (1900), 'Translator's Introduction', in Otto Gierke, *Political Theories of the Middle Age* (Cambridge: Cambridge University Press).

——(1908), *The Constitutional History of England* (Cambridge: Cambridge University Press).

Máiz, Ramón (1999), 'Democràcia i federalisme en estats multinacionals', in Ferran Requejo (ed.), *Pluralisme nacional i legitimat democràtica* (Barcelona: Prova).

Major, John (1993), 'Forword by the Prime Minister', in Secretary of State for Scotland, *Scotland and the Union* (Edinburgh: HMSO).

Martin, Pierre (1995), 'When Nationalism Meets Continentalism: The Politics of Free Trade in Quebec', *Regional and Federal Studies*, 5/1: 1–27.

——(1997), 'The Politics of Free Trade in Quebec', in Michael Keating and John Loughlin (eds.), *The Political Economy of Regionalism* (London: Frank Cass).

Martníez Montoya, Josetxu (1999), *La construcción nacional de Euska Herria. Etnicidad, política y religion* (San Sebastián: Ttarttalo Argitaletxea).

Martiniello, Marco (1997), 'The Dilemma of Separation versus Union: The New Dynamics of Nationalist Politics in Belgium', in Hans-Rudolph Wicker (ed.), *Rethinking Nationalism and Ethnicity. The Struggle for Meaning and Order in Europe* (Oxford: Berg).

La Météo politique (1998) (Montreal: Centre René Lévesque, CROP, and Sondagem, février).

Midwinter, Arthur, Michael Keating, and James Mitchell (1991), *Politics and Public Policy in Scotland* (London: Macmillan).

Mill, John Stuart (1972), *On Liberty, Utilitarianism, and Considerations on Representative Government* (London: Dent).

Miller, David (1995), *On Nationality* (Oxford: Clarendon Press).

——(2000), *Citizenship and National Identity* (Cambridge: Polity Press).

Mills, Kurt (1998), *Human Rights in the Emerging Global Order: A New Sovereignty?* (London: Macmillan).

Mitchell, James (1996), *Strategies for Self-Government. The Campaigns for a Scottish Parliament* (Edinburgh: Polygon).

—— and Michael Cavanagh (2001), 'Context and Contingency: Constitutional Nationalists and Europe', in Michael Keating and John McGarry (eds.), *Minority Nationalism and the Changing International Order* (Oxford: Oxford University Press).

Monreal, Gregorio (1985), 'Annotations regarding Basque Traditional Political Thought', in William A. Douglas (ed.), *Basque Politics. A Case Study in Ethnic Nationalism*, Basque Studies Program Occasional Paper 2 (Reno: University of Nevada).

MOORE, MARGARET (1998*a*) (ed.), *National Self-Determination and Secession* (Oxford: Oxford University Press).

——(1998*b*), 'The Territorial Element of Self-Determination', in Margaret Moore (ed.), *National Self-Determination and Secession*, (Oxford: Oxford University Press).

MORAL, FÉLIX (1998), *Identidad regional y nacionalismo en el Estado de las autonomías*, Opiniones y Actitudes, 18 (Madrid: Centro de Investigaciones Sociológicas).

MORAVCSIK, ANDREW (1995), 'Explaining International Human Rights Regimes: Liberal Theory and Western Europe', *European Journal of International Relations*, 1/2: 157–89.

MORELLI, ANNE (1995), 'Introduction', in Anne Morelli (ed.), *Les grands mythes de l'histoire de Belgique, de Flandre et de Wallonie* (Brussels: Vie Ouvrière).

MORENO, EDUARDO, and FRANCISCO MARTÍ (1977), *Catalunya para españoles* (Barcelona: DORESA).

MORENO, LUÍS (1997), *La federalización de España. Poder político y territorio* (Madrid: Siglo Veintiuno).

MORGAN, KENNETH (1980), *Rebirth of a Nation. Wales, 1880–1980* (Oxford: Oxford University Press).

MORIN, CLAUDE (2001), 'La Souveraineté et le partenariat: portée pratique', *Le Devoir*, 7 Mar.

MORRILL, JOHN (1995), 'The Fashioning of Britain', in Steven G. Ellis and Sarah Barber (eds.), *Conquest and Union. Fashioning a British State, 1485–1725* (London: Longman).

MOTA CONSEJERO, FABIOLA (1998), *Cultura política y opinión pública en las comunidades autónomas. Un examen del sistema político autonómico en España 1984–1996*, Working Papers, no. 153 (Barcelona: Institut de Ciènces Polítiques i Socials, Universitat Autónoma de Barcelona).

MOXON-BROWNE, EDWARD (1983), *Nation, Class and Creed in Northern Ireland* (Aldershot: Gower).

——(1991), 'National Identity in Northern Ireland', in *Social Attitudes in Northern Ireland* (Belfast: Blackstaff).

MOYNAHAN, DANIEL P. (1993), *Pandaemonium. Ethnicity in International Politics* (Oxford: Oxford University Press).

NAIRN, TOM (1997), *Faces of Nationalism. Janus Revisited* (London: Verso).

——(2000), *After Britain. New Labour and the Return of Scotland* (London: Granta).

NIETO ARIZMENDIARRETA, EDUARDO (1999), 'Reflexiones sobre el concepto de derechos históricos', *Revista Vasca de Administración Pública*, 54: 139–78.

NILT (1998–9), *Northern Ireland Life and Times Survey* (Belfast: University of Ulster).

NOGUE I FONT, JOAN (1991), *Nacionalismo y territorio* (Lleida: Milenio).

NORMAN, WAYNE (1995), 'The Ideology of Shared Values: A Myopic Vision of Unity in the Multi-Nation State', in Joseph Carens (ed.), *Is Quebec Nationalism Just? Perspectives from Anglophone Canada* (Montreal: McGill-Queen's University Press).

——(1998), 'The Ethics of Secession as the Regulation of Secessionist Politics', in Margaret Moore (ed.), *National Self-Determination and Secession* (Oxford: Oxford University Press).

NÚÑEZ ASTRAIN, LUIS (1997), *The Basques: Their Struggle for Independence* (Cardiff: Welsh Academic Press).

NUÑEZ SEIXAS, XOSÉ M. (1993), *Historiographical Approaches to Nationalism in Spain* (Saarbrücken: Breitenbach).

——(1999), *Los nacionalismos en la España contemporánea (siglos XIX y XX)* (Barcelona: Hipòtesi).

OHMAE, KENICHI (1995), *The End of the Nation State. The Rise of Regional Economies* (New York: Free Press).

OLIVER, PETER (1999), 'Canada's Two Solitudes: Constitutional and International Law in Reference re Secession of Quebec', *International Journal on Minority and Group Rights*, 6/1–2: 65–95.

ONAINDIA, MARIO, *Guía par orientarse en el laberinto vasco* (Madrid: Temas de Hoy).

ONETO, G. (1997), *L'invenzione della Padania. La rinascita della communità più antica d'Europa* (Bergamo: Foedus).

ORANICH, MAGDA (1997), 'Un derecho proprio para una sociedad democrática', in Xavier de Bru de Sala *et al.*, *El modelo Catalán. Un talante político* (Barcelona: Flor del Viento).

ORTEGA Y GASSET, JOSÉ (1975), *España invertebrada. Bosquejo de algunos pensamientos históricos*, 17th edn. (Madrid: El Arquero).

OSIANDER, A. (1994), *The States System of Europe, 1640–1990. Peacemaking and the Conditions of International Stability* (Oxford: Clarendon Press).

PACHECO AMARAL, CARLOS EDUARDO (1998), *Do estado soberano ao estado das autonomias* (Porto: Afrontamento).

PALLACH, ANTONIA (2000), *La identitat catalana. El fet diferencial; assaig de definició* (Barcelona: Proa).

PARADA, J. RAMÓN (1996), 'España ¿Una or Trina?', *Revista de Administración Pública*, 141 (Sept.–Dec.), 7–23.

PARELLADA, MARTÍ, and GEMMA GARCIA (1997), 'La doble convergencia económica: con España y con Europa', in Xavier Bru de Sala *et al.*, *El modelo catalán. Un talante político* (Barcelona: Flor del Viento).

PATERSON, LINDSAY (1994), *The Autonomy of Modern Scotland* (Edinburgh: Edinburgh University Press).

PEACOCK, ALAN, and LORD CROWTHER-HUNT (1973), *Royal Commission on the Constitution*, vol. xi, Memorandum of Dissent, Cmnd. 5460–1.

PETSCHEN, SANTIAGO (1993), *La Europa de las regiones* (Barcelona: Generalitat de Catalunya).

PINARD, M. (1992), *The Quebec Independence Movement. A Dramatic Reemergence*, McGill Working Papers in Social Behaviour, 92–06 (Montreal: Department of Sociology, McGill University).

——ROBERT BERNIER, and VINCENT LEMIEUX (1997), *Un Combat inachevé* (Quebec: Presses de l'Université du Québec).

PIRENNE, HENRI (1929), *Histoire de Belgique* (Brussels: Maurice Lamertin).

PITTOCK, MURRAY (1999), *Celtic Identity and the British Image* (Manchester: Manchester University Press).

PLAMENATZ, JOHN (1968), *Consent, Freedom and Political Obligation* (Oxford: Oxford University Press).

PNV (Partido Nacionalista Vasco, Asemblea General) (1995), *Ponencias aprobadas en la Asemblea General celebrada los días 2 y 3 de diciembre de 1995* (no place: PNV).

POCOCK, J. G. A. (1975), 'British History: A Plea for a New Subject', *Journal of Modern History*, 47/4: 601–28.

PRAT DE LA RIBA, ENRIC (1998), *La nacionalitat catalana*, facs. edn. (Madrid: Biblioteca Nueva).

PUIG I SCOTONI, PAU (1998), *Pensar els camins a la sobirania* (Barcelona: Mediterrània).

PUNTSCHER RIEKMAN, SONJA (1997), 'The Myth of European Unity', in Geoffrey Hosking and George Schöpflin (eds.), *Myths and Nationhood* (London: Hurst).

RAXHON, PHILIPPE (1998), 'Henri Conscience and the French Revolution', in Kas Depres and Louis Vos (eds.), *Nationalism in Belgium. Shifting Identities, 1780–1995* (London: Macmillan).

RENAN, ERNEST (1992), *Qu'est-ce qu'une nation? et autres essais politiques* (Paris: Presses-Pocket).

REQUEJO, FERRAN (1996), 'Diferencias nacionales y federalismo asimétrico', *Claves de la Razón Práctica* (Jan.–Feb.). 24–37.

——(1998), *Reconeixement nacional, democràcia i federalisme. Alguns límits del model constitucional espanyol* (Barcelona: Fundació Ramon Trias Fargas).

——(1999a), 'Pluralisme polític i legitimat democràtica', in Ferran Requejo (ed.), *Pluralisme nacional i legitimat democràtica* (Barcelona: Prova).

——(1999b), 'La acomodación "federal" de la plurinacionalidad. Democracia liberal y federalismo plural en España', in Enric Fossas and Ferran Requejo (eds.), *Asimetría federal y estado plurinacional* (Madrid: Trotta).

——(1999c), 'Cultural Pluralism, Nationalism and Federalism: A Revision of Democratic Citizenship in Plurinational States', *European Journal of Political Research*, 35: 255–86.

RESNICK, PHILIP (1995), 'English Canada: The Nation that Dares not Speak its Name', in Kenneth McRoberts (ed.), *Beyond Quebec. Taking Stock of English Canada* (Montreal: McGill-Queen's University Press).

RILEY, P. W. J. (1978), *The Union of England and Scotland. A Study in Anglo-Scottish Politics of the Eighteenth Century* (Manchester: Manchester University Press).

RIQUER I PERMANYER, BORDE DE (2000), *Identitats contemporànies: Catalunya i Espanya* (Vic: Eumo).

ROBERTSON, JOHN (1995), 'The Union Debate in Scotland, 1698–1707', in John Robertson (ed.), *A Union for Empire. Political Thought and the Union of 1707* (Cambridge: Cambridge University Press).

ROEGIERS, JAN (1998), 'Belgian Liberties and Loyalty to the House of Austria', in Kas Depres and Louis Vos (eds.), *Nationalism in Belgium. Shifting Identities, 1780–1995* (London: Macmilllan).

ROKKAN, STEIN (1980), 'Territories, Centres and Peripheries: Toward a Geoethnic–Geoeconomic–Geopolitical Model of Differentiation within Western Europe', in Jean Gottman (ed.), *Centre and Periphery. Spatial Variations in Politics* (Beverly Hills, Calif.: Sage).

——and DEREK URWIN (1983), *Economy, Territory, Identity. Politics of West European Peripheries* (London: Sage).

ROMNEY, PAUL (1999*a*), 'Provincial Equality, Special Status and the Compact Theory of Canadian Confederation', *Canadian Journal of Political Science*, 32: 21–39.

—— (1999*b*), *Getting it Wrong. How Canadians Forgot their Past and Imperilled Confederation* (Toronto: University of Toronto Press).

ROSE, RICHARD (1971), *Governing without Consensus. An Irish Perspective* (London: Faber & Faber).

ROSSITER, DAVID, RONALD JOHNSTON, and CHARLES PATTIE (1997), 'New Boundaries, Old Inequalities: The Evolution and Partisan Impact of the Celtic Preference in British Redistricting', *Regional and Federal Studies*, 7/3: 49–65.

ROTER, PETRA (1997), 'Towards an International Regime relating to the Protection of National Minorities in Europe', in Mitja Zagar, Boris Jesih, and Romana Bester (eds.), *The Constitutional and Political Regulation of Ethnic Relations and Conflicts*, 2, (Ljubljana: Institute for Ethnic Studies).

RUBERT DE VENTÓS, XAVIER (1999), *De la identidad a la independencia: la nueva transición* (Barcelona: Anagrama).

RUBIO LLORIENTE, FRANCISCO (1993), *La forma del poder. Estudios sobre la Constitución* (Madrid: Centro de Estudios Constitucionales).

RYNARD, PAUL (2000), '"Welcome in, but Check your Rights at the Door": The James Bay and Nisga'a Agreements in Canada', *Canadian Journal of Political Science*, 33/2: 211–43.

SALES, NÙRIA (1989), *Els sigles de la decadència*, vol. iv of *Història de Catalunya* (Barcelona: Edicions 62).

SANGRADOR GARCÍA, JOSÉ LUIS (1996), *Identidades, actitudes y estereotipos en la España de las autonomías*, Opiniones y Actitudes, 10 (Madrid: Centro de Investigaciones Sociológicas).

SANTACOLOMA, J. *et al.* (1995), *Eusdadi en el proyecto Europa* (Madrid: Fundación Encuentro).

SCOTT, ALLEN (1998), *Regions and the World Economy* (Oxford: Oxford University Press).

SCOTT, PAUL H. (1992), *Andrew Fletcher and the Treaty of Union* (Edinburgh: John Donald).

SCOTTISH CONSTITUTIONAL CONVENTION (1988), *A Claim of Right for Scotland* (Edinburgh: Polygon).

SEROO, ONNO, *et al.* (2001), *Exercir l'autodeterminació: Perspectives per al poble català al segle XXI* (Lleida: Pagès).

SERRA DEL PINO, JORDI, and ANTONI VENTURA I RIBAL (1999), *Catalunya 2015: Opcions polítiques per al segle XXI* (Barcelona: Centre Català de Prospectiva).

SEYMOUR, MICHEL (1999), *La Nation en question* (Montreal: l'Hexagone).

—— (2000), 'The Virtues of Partnership', in Guy Lachapelle and John Trent (eds.), *Globalization, Governance and Identity* (Montreal: Presses de l'Université de Montréal).

—— JOCELYNE COUTURE, and KAI NEILSON (1998), 'Introduction: Questioning the Ethnic/Civic Dichotomy', in Jocelyne Couture, Kai Neilson, and Michel Seymour (eds.), *Rethinking Nationalism* (Calgary: University of Calgary Press).

SHAW, JO (2000), 'Process and Constitutional Discourse in the European Union', in Colin Harvey, John Morison, and Jo Shaw (eds.), *Voices, Spaces, and Processes in Constitutionalism* (Oxford: Blackwell).

SIEDENTOP, LARRY (2000), *Democracy in Europe* (London: Allen Lane).

SKED, ALAN (1989), *The Decline and Fall of the Habsburg Empire, 1815–1918* (London: Longman).

SMITH, ANTHONY (1971), *Theories of Nationalism* (London: Duckworth).

—— (1986), *The Ethnic Origins of Nations* (Oxford: Blackwell).

—— (1991), *National Identity* (London: Penguin).

—— (1995), *Nations and Nationalism in a Global Era* (Cambridge: Polity Press).

—— (1999), *Myths and Memories of the Nation* (Oxford: Oxford University Press).

SOLDEVILA, FERRAN (1995), *Sintesi d'historia de Catalunya* (Barcelona: Publicacions de l'Abadia de Montserrat).

SOLOZÁBAL, JUAN JOSÉ (2000), 'Derechos históricos, constitución y soberanía', *Claves de Razón Práctica*, 107: 36–40.

SORAUREN, MIKEL (1998), *Historia de Navarra, el estado Vasco* (Pamplona: Pamiela).

SPRUYT, H. (1994), *The Sovereign State and its Competitors* (Princeton: Princeton University Press).

STAPLETON, JULIA (1999), 'Resisting the Centre at the Extremes: "English" Liberalism in the Political Thought of Interwar Britain', *British Journal of Politics and International Relations*, 1/3: 270–92.

STEINBERG, JONATHAN (1976), *Why Switzerland?* (Cambridge: Cambridge University Press).

STENGERS, JEAN (1995), 'La Révolution de 1830', in Anne Morelli (ed.), *Les grands mythes de l'histoire de Belgique, de Flandre et de Wallonie* (Brussels: Vie Ouvrière).

STEPAN, ALFRED (1998), 'Modern Multinational Democracies: transcending a Gellneran Oxymoron', in John A. Hall (ed.), *The State and the Nation. Ernest Gellner and the Theory of Nationalism* (Cambridge: Cambridge University Press).

STORPER, MICHAEL (1995), 'The Resurgence of Regional Economies, Ten Years Later: The Region as a Nexus of Untraded Dependencies', *European Urban and Regional Studies*, 2/3: 191–221.

—— (1997), *The Regional World. Territorial Development in a Global Economy* (New York: Guildford).

STOURZH, GERALD (1991), 'Problems of Conflict Resolution in a Multi-Ethnic State: lessons from the Austrian Historical Experience', in Uri Ra'anan, Maria Mesner, Keith Ames, and Kate Martin (eds.), *State and Nation in Multi-Ethnic Societies. The Breakup of Multinational States* (Manchester: Manchester University Press).

STUBBS, WILLIAM (1897), *The Constitutional History of England* (New York: Barnes & Noble).

SUPREME COURT of CANADA (1998), *Reference re Secession of Quebec*, file 25506 (Ottawa: Supreme Court of Canada).

TAMIR, YAEL (1991), 'The Right to National Self-Determination', *Social Research*, 58/3: 565–90.

TARLETON, CHARLES (1965), 'Symmetry and Asymmetry as Elements of Federalism: A Theoretical Speculation', *Journal of Politics*, 27: 861–74.

TAYLOR, A. J. P. (1948), *The Habsburg Monarchy, 1809–1918* (London: Hamish Hamilton).

—— (1975), 'Comment on Pocock's "British History: A Plea for a New Subject"', *Journal of Modern History*, 47/4: 622.

TAYLOR, CHARLES (1993*a*), 'Why do Nations have to Become States?', in Charles Taylor, *Reconciling the Solitudes: Essays on Canadian Federalism and Nationalism* (Montreal: McGill-Queen's University Press).

—— (1993*b*), 'The Deep Challenge of Dualism', in Alain-G. Gagnon (ed.), *Quebec: State and Society*, 2nd edn. (Scarborough, Ont.: Nelson).

TILLY, CHARLES (1975), *The Formation of National States in Western Europe* (Princeton: Princeton University Press).

—— (1990), *Coercion, Capital and European States, AD 990–1990* (Oxford: Blackwell).

—— (1994), 'Entanglements of European Cities and States', in C. Tilly and W. P. Blockmans (eds.), *Cities and the Rise of States in Europe, AD 1000 to 1800* (Boulder, Colo.: Westview Press).

—— and BLOCKMANS, W. P. (eds.) (1994), *Cities and the Rise of States in Europe, AD 1000 to 1800* (Boulder, Colo.: Westview Press).

TOCQUEVILLE, ALEXIS DE (1986), *De la démocratie en Amérique* (Paris: editions Robert Laffont).

TOMANY, JOHN (1999), 'In Search of English Regionalism: The Case of the North East', *Scottish Affairs*, 28: 62–82.

TOURAINE, ALAIN (1992), *Critique de la modernité* (Paris: Fayard).

—— (1997), *Pourrons-nous vivre ensemble?* (Paris: Fayard).

TOWNSEND, CHARLES (2000), 'The Home Rule Campaign in Ireland', in H. T. Dickinson and Michael Lynch, *The Challenge to Westminster: Sovereignty, Devolution and Independence* (East Linton: Tuckwell).

TOYNBEE, ARNOLD (1908), *Lectures on the Industrial Revolution of the Eighteenth Century in England* (London: Longmans, Green).

TRAGER, F. N. (1968), 'On Federalism', in T. M. Frank (ed.), *Why Federations Fail: An Inquiry into the Requisites for Successful Federalism* (New York: New York University Press).

TREMBLAY COMMISSION (1973), *Report of the Royal Commission of Inquiry on Constitutional Problems*, ed. David Kwavnick (Toronto: McClelland & Stewart).

TREVELYAN, GEORGE MACAULAY (1926), *History of England* (London: Longmans, Green).

—— (1937), *British History in the Nineteenth Century and After (1782–1919)* (London: Longmans, Green).

TREVOR ROPER, HUGH (1983), 'The Invention of Tradition: The Highland Tradition of Scotland', in Eric Hobsbawm and Terence Ranger (eds.), *The Invention of Tradition* (Cambridge: Cambridge University Press).

TULLY, JAMES (1995), *Strange Multiplicity. Constitutionalism in an Age of Diversity* (Cambridge: Cambridge University Press).

—— (1999), 'Liberté et dévoilement dans les sociétés multinationales', *Globe. Révue Internationale d'Études Québécoises*, 2/2: 13–36.

—— (2000), 'The Unattained yet Attainable Democracy. Canada and Quebec Face the New Century', *Grandes Conférences Desjardins* (Montreal: McGill University).

TURNER, DALE (2001), 'Vision: Towards and Understanding of Aboriginal Sovereignty', in Ronald Beiner and Wayne Norman (eds.), *Canadian Political Philosophy* (Toronto: University of Toronto Press).

TUSELL, JAVIER (1999), *España. Un angustia nacional* (Madrid: Espasa Calpe).

TWINING, WILLIAM (1999), 'Globalization and Comparative Law', *Maastricht Journal of European and Comparative Law*, 6/3: 217–43.

UDC (Unió Democràtica de Catalunya) (1997), *La sobirania de Catalunya i l'estat plurinacional* (Sant Cugat: UDC).

UGALDE, ALEXANDER (1998), 'The International Relations of Basque Nationalism and the First Basque Autonomous Government', in Francesco Aldecoa and Michael Keating (eds.), *Paradiplomacy: The International Relations of Sub-State Governments* (London: Frank Cass).

VAN DER VALTT VAN PRAAGE, MICHAEL, and ONOO SEROO (eds.) (1998), *The Implementation of the Right to Self-Determination as a Contribution to Conflict Resolution* (Barcelona: Unesco Catalunya).

VICENS VIVES, JAIME (1970), *Approaches to the History of Spain*, 2nd edn. (Berkeley and Los Angeles: University of California Press).

WALKER, NEIL (1996), 'European Consitutionalism and European Integration', *Public Law* (Summer), 266–90.

——(1998a), 'Sovereignty and Differentiated Integration in the European Union', *European Law Journal*, 4/4: 355–88.

——(1998b), 'Constitutional Reform in a Cold Climate: Reflections on the White Paper and Referendum on Scotland's Parliament', in A. Tomkins (ed.), *Devolution and the British Constitution* (London: New Haven).

——(1999), 'Setting English Judges to Rights', *Oxford Journal of Legal Studies*, 19: 133–51.

——(2000), 'Beyond the Unitary Conception of the United Kingdom Constitution?', *Public Law* (Autumn), 384–404.

——(2001), *Late Sovereignty in the European Union*, European Forum Discussion Paper (Florence: European University Institute).

WALZER, MICHAEL (1999), 'The New Tribalism: Notes on a Difficult Problem', in Ronald Beiner (ed.), *Theorizing Nationalism* (Albany: State University of New York Press).

WANK, SOLOMAN (1997), 'The Habsburg Empire', in Karen Barkly and Mark von Hagen (eds.), *After Empire. Multiethnic Societies and Nation-Building. The Soviet Union and the Russian, Ottoman and Habsburg Empires* (Boulder, Colo.: Westview Press).

WATTS, RONALD (1996), 'Canada: Three Decades of Federal Crisis', *International Political Science Review*, 17/4: 353–72.

——(1999), 'The Canadian Experience with Asymmetrical Federalism', in Robert Agranoff (ed.), *Accommodating Diversity: Asymmetry in Federal States* (Baden-Baden: Nomos).

WEALE, ALBERT (1995), 'Democratic Legitimacy and the Constitution of Europe', in Richard Bellamy, Victorio Bufacchi, and Dario Castiglione (eds.), *Democracy and Constitutional Culture in the Union of Europe* (London: Lothian Foundation).

WEILER, JOSEPH (1999), *The Constitution of Europe* (Cambridge: Cambridge University Press).

WICKHAM STEED, HENRY (1914), *The Habsburg Monarchy* (London: Constable).

WILS, LODE (1992), 'Introduction: A Brief History of the Flemish Movement', in Theo Hermans, Louis Vos, and Lode Wils, *The Flemish Movement: A Documentary History, 1789–1990* (London: Athlone Press).

——(1996a), *Histoire des nations belges* (Ottignies: Quorum).

WILS, LODE (1996*b*), 'Mouvements linguistiques, nouvelles nations?', in Alain Dieck-khoff (ed.), *Belgique: la force de désunion* (Paris: Éditions Complexe).

WILSON, C. (1970), 'Note of Dissent', *Scotland's Government. Report of the Scottish Constitutional Committee* (Edinburgh: Scottish Constitutional Committee).

YOUNG, JOHN R. (1998), 'The Scottish Parliament and National Identity from the Union of the Crowns to the Union of the Parliaments, 1603–1707', in Dauvit Broun, R. J. Finlay, and Michael Lynch (eds.), *Image and Identity. The Making and Remaking of Scotland through the Ages* (Edinburgh: John Donald).

Opinion Poll Data

Opinion poll data has been cited from published sources, where appropriate. In other cases, it has been obtained directly from the polling firms or academic organizations that undertook the surveys. These are:

Europe
Eurobarometer

United Kingdom
ICM
MORI
Northern Ireland Life and Times Survey
Scottish Election Study

Spain
CIRES, Madrid
Euskobarómeter
Institut de Ciènces Polítiques i Socials, Barcelona

Belgium
1995 General Election Study, Belgium

Quebec
Angus Reid
Council for Canadian Unity
CROP
Ekos
Ipsos

INDEX